Explore th

MOSCOW
ST. PETERSBURG

Authors:
Angela Plöger, Abraham Reitblat, Henning Sietz,
Hans-Horst Skupy, Valeri Sourov,
Alexandre Tshitinski

*An Up-to-date travel guide with 148 color photos
and 16 maps*

**Second Revised Edition
1998**

Dear Reader,

Being up-to-date is the main goal of the Nelles series. To achieve it, we have a network of far-flung correspondents who keep us abreast of the latest developments in the travel scene, and our cartographers always make sure that maps and texts are adjusted to each other.

Each travel chapter ends with its own list of useful tips, accommodations, restaurants, tourist offices, sights. At the end of the book you will find practical information from A to Z. But the travel world is fast moving, and we cannot guarantee that all the contents are always valid. Should you come across a discrepancy, please write us at: Nelles Verlag GmbH, Schleissheimer Str. 371 b, D-80935 München, Germany, Tel: (089) 3571940, Fax: (089) 35719430.

LEGEND

✼ Place of Interest	Suzdal'	Place Mentioned in Text	▨	National Border
▨ Public or Significant Building	✈	International Airport	▬	Expressway
■ Hotel	✈	National Airport	▬	Principal Highway
▨ Shopping Center	M 8	Route number	—	Main Road
○ Market	Ⓜ	Metro	—	Other Road
✝ Church			—	Railway
			\27\	Distance in Kilometers

MOSCOW / ST. PETERSBURG
© Nelles Verlag GmbH, D-80935 München
All rights reserved

Second Revised Edition 1998
ISBN 3-88618-904-X
Printed in Slovenia

Publisher:	Günter Nelles	**Translation and editor,**	
Project Editors:	Hans-Horst Skupy	**English edition:**	Angus Mc Geoch
	Dr. Angela Plöger		
Editor-in-Chief:	Berthold Schwarz	**Cartography:**	Nelles Verlag GmbH,
Editorial:	H.-H. Skupy, H. Hartl		with kind permission of
	Dr. J.-Martina Schneider		Freytag & Berndt, Vienna
	K. Bärmann-Thümmel	**Lithos:**	Priegnitz, München
	Dr. Angela Plöger	**Printing:**	Gorenjski Tisk

- X03 -

TABLE OF CONTENTS

ST. PETERSBURG

FEATURES

LIST OF MAPS

Note: The names of streets and locations in the maps correspond to the official transcription of the Cyrillic alphabet (see p. 247).

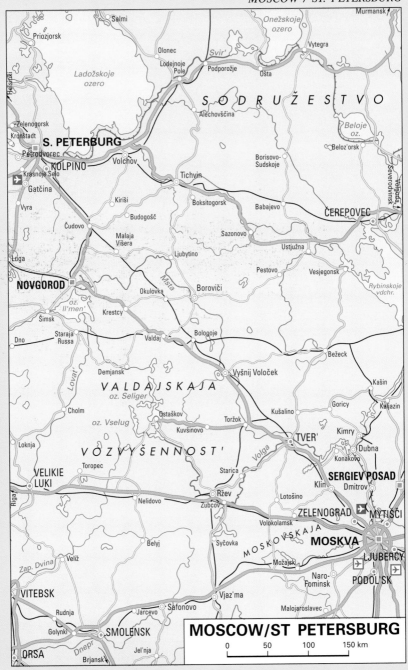

MOSCOW/ST PETERSBURG

0   50   100   150 km

RUSSIAN HISTORY
AND CULTURE

The accepted date for the founding of Moscow is 1147, since this is the year in which the name is first mentioned in a document, as the scene of a meeting between two princes, at a place which is today called Borovitsky Hill. One of them was the Prince of Novgorod, the other the Prince of Vladimir and Suzdal, named Yuri Dolgoruky (Yuri the Long-Armed), who some time later, in 1156, fortified the little settlement at the confluence of the Neglinka and Moskva rivers. It was strategically situated at the intersection of important trade routes: to Rostov and Vladimir, and from Novgorod to Ryazan; and Yuri built it up into a frontier fort guarded by wooden towers and palisades. From that time on, the peasants and craftsmen who lived in the area sought refuge in times of danger behind the walls of the Kremlin, which were then still built of wood. Thus Moscow became known as the cradle of the Russian nation. As Tolstoy put it: "Every Russian who looks toward Moscow, considers it to be his mother-city."

The Beginnings of Russia

Long before there was ever a people called the "Russians," at the time of the Greek historian Herodotus, tribes called the Scythians and later the Sarmatians roamed over the endless steppes of what is now Russia. Today we know little more about them than did Herodotus, or

Previous pages: Prayer helps many Russians to cope with daily life. Modern matryoshka dolls. Left: Czar Boris Godunov in a painting by J. Glazunov.

the Roman writer Pliny, who in the first century AD wrote fanciful tales about the legendary race of Hyperboreans, said to live in those parts. For even the Roman merchants and legionaries only penetrated a little way into southern Russia, and by the end of the third century their influence had petered out completely.

Between the years 200 and 375 AD the Goths migrated from Scandinavia and settled in the area between the river Vistula and the Crimea, before being driven out in the 4th century by the Huns, whose incursions caused the great westward migration of populations through Europe.

Amid the mingling of races which ensued, the Slavs emerged for the first time in the 6th and 7th centuries. They were divided up into numerous tribes, who occupied the densely forested region that stretches from Novgorod to the Black Sea – with a more or less open frontier to the vast steppe in the East. What we can be sure of is how and from what date the "East Slavs" became "Russians" – it was in the middle of the 9th century. At that time the huge tract of land lying between the Gulf of Finland and the Black Sea was a kind of corridor for trade and traffic from Scandinavia to Byzantium (Constantinople), which was then the capital of Christendom and of the western world. From the Baltic came Varangians – Swedish Vikings – merchant warriors who forced their way along the north-south waterways, in order to secure the – "Great Way" southeast to Byzantium and thus open up vast new markets. For this purpose they established strongholds and extracted tribute not only from the East Slavs but also from the Finno-Ugrian and Baltic tribes.

Probably the most significant leader of the Varangians was the legendary Rurik who founded Novgorod in 862 and Kiev in 879, around which the first "Russian" principalities grew up. The ethnic blending of the Varangians, East Slavs and Finno-Ugrian tribes produced a people

who called themselves "Rus," which is derived from "ruotsi," the Finnish name for the Swedes. However, the Varangians or Swedes only had a marginal influence on the language and social structure of the native East Slavs and acted more as a ruling elite. The true progenitor of the House of Rurik, which ruled until 1598, was Rurik's son Oleg (879-912) who was the first ruler to unite the Varangian principalities of Novgorod and Kiev, and thus create the state of Kiev Rus. Kiev itself became "mother of all Russian cities" at a time when the site of Moscow was still deserted marshland.

The Empire of Kiev

Oleg's son Igor (912-945) expanded the territory of Kiev by incorporating other Slavic-Varangian principalities, before handing over this ever more

Above: Rurik, the legendary Varangian chieftain. Right: Mosaic inside the dome of Kiev's St. Sophia Cathedral.

powerful state to his son Svyatoslav (964-972). By this time Byzantine Christianity had already taken root in Kiev; in a politically astute move, Svyatoslav's son Vladimir I, later to be canonized as Saint Vladimir, married a Byzantine princess in 988 and simultaneously embraced Christianity. Henceforth, the Byzantine form of Christianity became the religion of the people and the state, and the hitherto "heathen" Russia joined the ranks of Christian nations. At this time the Cyrillic script, still used today in Russia, Bulgaria and Serbia, came into common use, having been derived from the older Glagolitic script of the Slavs, combined with the Greek minuscule alphabet from Byzantium. This was probably the work of Cyril and Methodius, two 9th-century Greek monks, known as the Apostles of the Slavs.

It was during the rule of Vladimir's son, Yaroslav the Wise (1019-1054), that the Byzantine-influenced culture of Kiev achieved its greatest heights: Greek and Armenian architects and artists were brought in and magnificent churches and cathedrals were created. In 1037 work was started on the five-naved Sophia Cathedral, which was to be Russia's answer to the famous Hagia Sophia in Constantinople. The years 1037 to 1089 saw the building of the Uspensky (Assumption) Cathedral in Kiev. It should be noted that these religious buildings were virtually the only ones built of stone; the people lived in wooden houses, and even the palaces of the princes and nobles were built of wood, of which there was no shortage in the vast forests round about.

Inside these churches we see for the first time mosaics and frescos in the Byzantine style, and also the icons which, though initially influenced by Byzantium, developed over the centuries into a uniquely Russian art form. Book illustration also reached its first high point with the *Ostromir Gospel* (1056-7). In the course of the 11th century a native Rus-

sian literature emerged, written in Old Church Slavonic, of which the most notable achievements are the *Chronicle of Nestor* (1110-1120) and the *Song of Igor* (1185-7). The tonality and melody so typical of old Russian church music also took shape during the age of Kiev Rus.

These early days saw the creation of a social structure which became characteristic of Russia over the next centuries, and which remained essentially unchanged until the middle of the 19th century: the boyar class, the Russian aristocracy, evolved from a mixing of the original Slav ruling class with the Swedish courtiers of Kiev, and drew its power from the hereditary ownership of land. In the following centuries, the boyars played an important role, since they were able at any time to withdraw their support from the ruler, without forfeiting their lands – unlike western Europe in the Middle Ages, Russia had no system of feudal obligations. This made the boyars unpredictable and often dangerous to all Russian princes, rulers and Czars. The boyars also had control over a veritable army of laborers – starting with slaves and serfs, who were dependent on them, up to the yeoman farmers, who lived in village communities and, initially, were not bound to any landlord.

But first let us bring the story of Kiev to its end: after Yaroslav the Wise, the state enjoyed a second great age under Vladimir II Monomakh (1113-25), who was able to rule as Grand Prince over all the old and new principalities. After his death, Kiev went into a rapid decline as a result of quarrels between his successors, and the appearance of new principalities around its borders. Thus it was eventually possible for Andrei Bogolyubsky, prince of Vladimir-Suzdal and son of Yuri Dolgoruky, to capture and plunder Kiev in 1169. He then made Vladimir the capital of his new realm.

Russian history following the fall of Kiev in 1169 is a story of fragmentation and of violent and bloody fighting for supremacy between the old and new principalities, whose rulers all considered

themselves the true successors of Rurik, and indeed were either sons, brothers, uncles or nephews. The brutality of the house of Rurik weakened Russia seriously at a time when old and new enemies were appearing on the scene, both in the west and the east. From the Carpathian mountains came the Poles and Hungarians, from the Baltic lands the German knights of the Teutonic Order, while Swedish armies marched south and south-eastwards. At that time, the beginning of the 13th century, the principality of Vladimir-Suzdal had once more lost the predominance it had gained under Andrei Bogolyubsky, and was split up into smaller fiefs. Parts of the principality of Galich fell to Hungary, Poland and Lithuania. Only the principality of Novgorod in the north, still an important crossing point of trade routes between Scandinavia, Russia and Byzantium, enjoyed re-

Above: Alexander Nevsky receives ambassadors. Right: Nevsky defeats the Knights of the Teutonic Order.

markable economic growth. Evidence of this is seen as early as the 11th and 12th centuries, in the building of fine churches such as the five-domed Sophia Cathedral (1045-50), which was closely modeled on its namesake in Kiev. Furthermore, Novgorod had evolved into an oligarchic republic, in which the real power lay with merchants and financiers, while the prince fulfilled only a ceremonial function. This did not change until the beginning of the 13th century when the Mongol invasion severed the trade routes to the Black Sea, and at the same time Danes, Swedes, Lithuanians and Teutonic Knights advanced on Novgorod from the west, thus threatening all of Russia. Novgorod and Russia needed a heroic leader – and he was waiting in the wings: Prince Alexander Yaroslavich, better known as Alexander Nevsky, the honorary title which he was later given. In 1240 he decisively defeated the Swedes on the river Neva, and in 1243 beat the German knights at Lake Peipas. Finally, in 1256, he drove back the Lithuanians. The danger was thus averted in the west, but by not in the east.

The Scourge of Russia

The warlike Mongols had, since 1206, posed a threat to the whole of Asia, Russia and even western Europe, which was to last for two centuries. For it was in 1206 that Genghis Khan had united all the tribes of Mongolia. In the following year, armies of Mongolian horsemen had brought all the people of southern Siberia under their yoke, and in 1211 even the mighty China was unable to withstand their onslaught. They then overran the central Asian empire of Kharizmia which dated back to the age of Alexander the Great, before finally conquering northern Persia, Armenia and Georgia. After this they moved on to attack the Polovtsians, who inhabited the south Russian steppes. Though supported by the Russian princi-

palities of Kiev, Chernigov, Volhynia and Galich, the Polovtsians suffered an annihilating defeat on the river Kalka. At first, however, no direct political consequences followed from this.

The death of Genghis Khan in 1227, after an unsuccessful Mongol attack on the Volga Bulgars, gave the quarreling Russian states a breathing space. But in 1237 the Mongol armies rode right into the heart of Russia. In that year, Batu Khan, a grandson of Genghis, defeated the Volga Bulgars and launched an attack on the principalities of Ryazan, Moscow and Vladimir, whose leaders were this time unable to unite. In 1238 Batu Khan conquered the entire regions of the Oka and upper Volga, including the still young and ambitious principality of Moscow. It was razed to the ground, a third of its population were slaughtered and many taken into slavery.

The planned breakthrough to Novgorod, where Prince Alexander Nevsky had been dealing with the previously mentioned attacks from the west, never materialized, because the frozen rivers had begun to melt. But the very next year the Mongol cavalry pressed forward once again and conquered the principalities of Pereyaslav and Chernigov. In 1240 they took Kiev and in the next two years Volhynia and Galich.

Novgorod, alone, was never attacked again, thanks to the shrewd policy of Alexander Nevsky, though, like the others, it had to pay tribute. After all these conquests, Batu Khan divided up the Mongol empire and drew together all the lands west of the Urals as "the empire of the Golden Horde," with its capital at Saray, on the Volga. He even allowed a Russian bishop to reside there. Though continuing to rule Russia, the Mongols were careful to respect the customs, laws and religion of the subject people. They did not depose the Russian princes but submitted them to a form of investiture by the Great Khan, an obligation to pay an often onerous tribute as well as having to provide contingents of soldiers for the Mongols campaigns of conquest further westwards into Europe. Between 1242 and 1430, the Russian princes, still as quarrelsome as ever, had to make no less than 130 journeys of homage to the seat of the Golden Horde at Saray, but apart from that they were free to decide among themselves who really was the successor to Rurik and therefore the Grand Prince of Russia.

The Rise of Muscovy

After the death of Alexander Nevsky in 1263, his son Danil became the first prince of Moscow, and from this moment on, the city was the chief center of power in Russia. Following the conquests which Danil and his son Yuri made, by the beginning of the 14th century the principality of Muscovy, as it is known in history, embraced the whole valley of the river Moskva and stretched into the Upper Volga region. But it was still just one of a number of small Russian states. It was the annexation of the principality of Tver by Ivan I Kalita (1325-40) which made Muscovy the new focus of power in a fragmented Russia.

For Ivan Kalita ("Moneybags") was a cunning tactician; he realized that through high tribute payments he could buy the goodwill of the Great Khan, who then empowered him to collect the tribute of all the other principalities. In 1328 the Great Khan nominated him Grand Prince, whereupon he moved his seat of government from Vladimir to Moscow, in order "to gather Russian earth," in other words to subjugate the other principalities to the Grand Principality of Muscovy. At the same time he took with him the Metropolitan, the ecclesiastical representative of the Patriarch of Byzantium. From now on political activity crystallized around Moscow, which also became the religious center of the gradually

Right: The Russians, under Dimitri Donskoi, defeat the Tatars.

emerging nation of Greater Russia. In 1328, under Ivan Kalita's direction, Moscow's first stone church, the Cathedral of the Assumption, was built; the Metropolitan had his residence right beside Ivan's wooden citadel, which for the first time bore the name Kremlin, and which, after a devastating fire in 1331 was rebuilt from massive oak timbers. The population of Moscow at that time was about 30,000.

When Dimitri Ivanovich, known as Donskoy ("Victor of the Don"), became Grand Prince of Muscovy in 1359, his realm had already become so strong that in 1380 he was emboldened to challenge the Golden Horde. The Mongols still wielded supreme authority over Russia, but he engaged them in open battle and defeated them on the field of Kulikovo, 155 miles (250 km) south of Moscow. Although this victory did not, in itself, rid Russia of its scourge – a punitive expedition by the Mongols in 1382 left Moscow once again in ruins – Donskoy's achievement unleashed a wave of patriotic enthusiasm even among the rival principalities. The Golden Horde had finally lost its aura of invincibility, and no other Russian prince could challenge the Victor of the Don.

Henceforth, every Russian looked to Moscow, which by now boasted 14,000 houses and a Kremlin built of white limestone. From now on all the successors of Donskoy bore the undisputed title of Grand Prince of all Russia, which Ivan Moneybags had arrogated to himself.

Alas, right up to the mid-15th century, the Grand Principality of Muscovy was crippled by a bitter and bloody power-struggle between the sons and grandsons of Dimitri Donskoy. The man who finally emerged victorious was Vasily II, who enlarged and stabilized the Muscovite state. He also succeeded in making Moscow the stronghold of the Orthodox Church and thereby enhanced its status as the unifying force of the Russian people.

At the Council of Florence the Byzantine Church entered into a short-lived marriage with the western Catholic Church, something which was greeted with horror in Russia. When the Metropolitan of Moscow, Isidor, returned from Italy, Vasily had him arrested. In 1448 he convened a synod of all the bishops, which elected bishop Yonas as "Metropolitan of Moscow and all Russia," for the first time without the official blessing of the Patriarch of Byzantium.

Ivan the Great

Yet Russia was still not united and the Mongol peril still lurked in the east, while to the west Lithuania gnawed away at the power of the Grand Prince of Muscovy. It fell to Vasily's son, Ivan III (1440-1505), later, with justification, called Ivan the Great, to complete the task of "gathering the Russian earth" and thus to become the founder of the modern Russian state. In rapid succession he subjugated the important principalities of

Yaroslavl (1463), Rostov (1474), Novgorod (1478), Tver (1485) and *de facto* also Pskov and Ryazan. In so doing he extended his realm so far that it now bordered with western Europe.

In 1494 he closed the Hanseatic trading post in Novgorod and began constructing the fortress of Ivangorod on the river Narva, in order to put a stop to the expansionist ambitions of the Teutonic Knights. He then successfully took up arms against the Grand Duchy of Lithuania in order to regain Russian territory which Lithuania had conquered a century earlier. All these triumphs were made possible by the fact that Ivan II had already been able finally to liberate the whole of Russia from the yoke of the Golden Horde – without a sword being raised! For when he came to the throne, the Mongol empire had already broken up into small, fragmented khanates: Ivan, a shrewd tactician, allied himself with the Khanate of Crimea and then, in 1480 on the river Ugra, staged such an impressive show of combined military might, that

the Mongols withdrew without a fight. After 240 years of supremacy they disappeared from Russian history for ever.

The union between the Byzantine and Roman churches had long since been dissolved, and Byzantium itself was conquered in 1451 by the Ottoman Turks. Ivan III married the daughter of the last Byzantine emperor, Constantine XI, who had fled to Rome, and this demonstrated that Russia regarded herself not merely as the legitimate successor of the Byzantine empire, but as the "third Rome" – a claim which was officially formulated for the first time by the monk Filofei in 1510, five years after Ivan's death.

It was logical, therefore, that the two-headed eagle – the arms of Byzantium – should become the Russian national emblem, and that Byzantine court ceremon-

ial should be adopted together with title "Tsar," the Russian version of the Roman "Caesar."

With such unchallenged new power, Ivan the Great could now apply himself to resolving internal problems. Firstly, the tenacious power of the boyars had to be broken. By cleverly intervening in their internal disputes, Ivan succeeded in gradually reducing them to a court aristocracy, which became merged with the class of newly ennobled retainers to whom he had personally given preferment, and thus obtained their loyalty in the way western monarchs had done through the feudal system. In return for this, however, Ivan was forced to abolish the existing rights of the free and partially free peasant-farmers. This meant that they were for ever bound to the soil; the serfdom which was to be their wretched destiny for centuries, had begun.

Undeterred, Ivan turned to the task of giving his "third Rome" a suitably magnificent aspect. He summoned architects and artists from Renaissance Italy and

Above left: Czar Ivan III. Above right: The czarist coat-of-arms with the double-headed eagle comes into fashion. Right: Czar Ivan IV, the Terrible.

20

gave them the task of rebuilding the Kremlin, which during the years 1485 to 1508, took on essentially the dimensions and appearance it has today: the 1 1/4 mile (2km) long stone wall around the Kremlin was between 13 and 16 feet (4-5m) thick, and between 26 and 56 feet (8-17m) high. Nineteen watchtowers, the river Moskva on one side and a moat round the remaining sides, rendered the fortress virtually impregnable.

The tremendous building program under Ivan drew in thousands of merchants and craftsmen: armories, blacksmiths, foundries, goldsmiths, potters, dye works and brickyards all sprang up in the bustling city. By the end of the 15th century Moscow covered an area of more than 2 square miles (5.4 sq. km) and had a population of about 100,000. It was the undisputed political and economic capital of Russia, and one of the biggest cities in the world.

Ivan the Terrible and the Time of Troubles

Ivan III was succeeded by his son, Vasily III, who brought Ryazan, Novgorod, Pskov and Smolensk under Muscovite sovereignty.

He was in turn succeeded by Ivan IV, know to Russians as Ivan *Grozny,* a word which is wrongly translated in the west as "terrible," but whose meaning is closer to "severe" or "awesome."

When his father died, Ivan was only three years old, and his mother was murdered only four years later. During his minority, the boyars seized power, plundered the state treasury and intimidated the young heir to the throne – an experience which was to leave a permanent scar on his character. Although he was one of the most highly educated men of his age, he had a tendency towards persecution mania, outbursts of rage and the inflicting of brutal punishments. In 1581 he even killed his own eldest son in a fit of anger.

In 1546, at the age of only sixteen, he assumed the reins of power, and in the following year was crowned czar by the Metropolitan Makary. He was the first Grand Prince of Muscovy to assume this title. Showing great astuteness and self-confidence he began his reign with a series of reforms, all aimed at further centralizing and reinforcing his power. First, he convened the *Zemsky Sobor* (Assembly of the Land), a kind of parliament made up of senior representatives of the clergy, high government officials (aristocratic courtiers), and provincial administrators. Then, by establishing a regiment of archers (*streltsy*), paid from his own purse, made himself militarily independent of the boyars. Later the *streltsy,* like the Roman praetorian guard, played an important role in Russian history.

Ivan's military reforms enabled him to defeat the Tatar Khanate of Kazan in 1552, and four years later the Khanate of Astrakhan – victories which expanded his empire as far east as the Urals and the Caspian Sea, and gave him control over

21

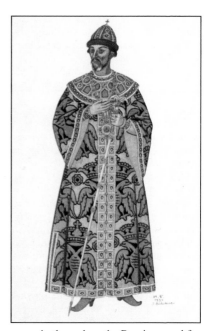

the entire length of the river Volga. He also succeeded in expanding eastward into Siberia, by granting a charter to a powerful merchant family, the Stroganovs, who from 1582 onwards used troops of Cossack horsemen to drive out the Tatars.

Meanwhile the face of Moscow was changing considerably: following his victory over the Tatars, Ivan ordered the construction of St. Basil's Cathedral on Red Square (1554-60). This was the first stone church to be built outside the walls of the Kremlin and was a quintessentially Russian building – a seemingly unplanned jumble of towers, spires, domes and buttresses, built on a foundation in the shape of a Greek cross. According to legend, Ivan had the two architects blinded so that they could never again build anything so beautiful. The name of the Red Square itself has nothing to do with communism, but is so called be-

Above: Boyars in the dress of the late Middle Ages.

cause in those days the Russian word for "red" and "beautiful" was the same. It is first mentioned in the 15th century as a market place. In 1534 a circular platform was built from which for centuries afterwards the *ukaz* or decrees of the czar were read out to the people.

Beyond the walls of the Kremlin, Moscow at that time was still a jumble of wooden houses, the streets had no names, and often changed their alignment as a result of devastating fires. Whenever these occurred, the Muscovites simply went to the timber market and bought rough-hewn tree trunks, doors and roofs, and in a few days had rebuilt their houses.

It is said that following a serious illness as early as 1553, Ivan showed the first signs of persecution mania. With his bodyguard, the sinister, black-cloaked *Oprichnina*, he carried out campaigns of extermination against the princely and boyar families. Nor did he shrink from massacres among the ordinary people. And if any church leaders dared to oppose him he banished them or had them murdered. By the time he died, in 1584, he had led Russia into a deep economic, social and political crisis.

Ivan was succeeded initially by his mentally defective son Fyodor. With his death in 1598, in unexplained circumstances, the legendary dynasty of Rurik died out. The Zemsky Sobor, without the participation of the boyars, had chosen Boris Godunov to rule the country as regent while Fyodor was alive, and in 1598 Boris was elected as the new czar. He was not a boyar, but an aristocrat of Mongol origin, whose family had been courtiers since the 14th century. During his regency, Godunov had cleverly gained the support of the church by unambiguously severing the connection with Constantinople in 1589 and installing the Metropolitan of Moscow, Iov (Job), as the first Patriarch of the Russian Orthodox Church. With the might of the church behind him, Godunov was able to hold in check the ambitious boyars, who felt themselves slighted by his preferment.

However, the system of feudal serfdom was becoming more and more widespread (just the reverse of what had happened in western Europe), and this led to unrest, particularly among the Cossacks. These were originally free or partly free peasants, who, faced by the threat of serfdom under Ivan III, had fled eastward into the steppe where they adopted the lifestyle and fighting techniques of the Tatars.

The boyars, anxious to avenge themselves against Godunov by overthrowing him, put about a rumor that Godunov had intended to murder the youngest son of Ivan IV, Dimitri (d. 1591), but that the young man had miraculously survived and reappeared in Poland. It was a lie which soon bore political fruit among the credulous Russians. A disaffected boyar named Otrepyev gathered support in Poland and in 1605, shortly after Godunov's death, this "false Dimitri" arrived with a Polish army augmented by dispossessed Cossacks and with the help of treacherous boyars, entered Moscow. So began the *smuta*, or "Troubles," and events took a rapid turn for the worse.

Godunov's son Fyodor II briefly succeeded him but was murdered, and the False Dimitri (Grigory Otrepyev) briefly became the czar. However his retinue of Polish Catholics made him unpopular with the people, while his liberal reforms displeased the boyars, and in 1606 a revolt, led by a boyar, Vassily Shuisky, drove the Pretender out of Moscow. Two days later Shuisky was elected czar by the boyars, and with support from Sweden, managed to hold on to the throne until 1610, though he was gradually crushed by opposing forces: on the one hand were the boyars, who for centuries had been trying to win back their former power; on the other was an increasingly restless peasantry, who wanted to throw off the shackles of serfdom and free themselves from economic oppression.

A peasants' revolt, led by Bolotnikov, threatened to topple the czar in 1606-7, but was put down with much bloodshed by the czarist nobility. A second "False Dimitri" appeared, again backed by the Poles, but Shuisky was able to keep this "Thief of Tuzhino," as he was called, from entering Moscow until 1610, when a Polish army, aided by boyars, captured much of western Russia, deposed Shuisky and put Vladislav, the son of the Polish king Sigismund III, on the throne as the next czar.

But this Polish interlude did not last long, for anarchy reigned throughout the land: Sigismund III took arms against his own son, the Swedes invaded Novgorod, and Cossacks and Tatars plundered the land at will. Finally, in 1612 a volunteer army led by Minin, a merchant, and Prince Pozharsky from Nizhni-Novgorod, was able to relieve Moscow from a Cossack siege and drive the Poles out of

Above: From its beginnings, Moscow was laid out as a mighty and magnificent capital city. This engraving is from about 1650.

Russia altogether. In Moscow, steps were taken to put the Russian state back on its feet. In January 1613 the Zemsky Sobor, now including Cossack representatives, elected as the new czar the sixteen-year-old Mikhail Fyodorov Romanov.

The rise of the Romanov dynasty

The ancestor of the Romanov dynasty, which was to determine the history of Russia from now until 1762, was a Muscovite boyar named Kobyla, whose descendant, Nikita Romanov, made an unsuccessful bid for the throne, in opposition to Boris Godunov, in 1598.

It was not until 1619 that his son, the first Romanov czar, succeeded in bringing Nikita back to Moscow from imprisonment in Poland. Michael then appointed his father Patriarch of Moscow, under the name of Filaret.

Michael himself did not cut a particularly impressive figure as a ruler. Nor did his successor Alexei (1645-76), while Fyodor III (1676-82) was only a minor, and Ivan V (1682-89) was mentally retarded. The 17th century saw renewed threats from beyond the borders of Russia as well as within. The empire now extended, in 1654, to include the Ukraine on the left bank of the Dniepr. Five years earlier, the Cossacks had crossed the whole of Siberia and followed the Amur river as far as the Pacific Ocean. In the west, wars with Sweden and Poland had been dragging on since 1655; while to the south the Russo-Turkish war raged from 1677 to 1681.

At home, social tensions were building up in a threatening manner, since Czar Alexei had introduced a code of laws (the *Ulozhenie*) which put serfdom into a rigidly institutional framework, whereby the whole of society was divided into a hierarchy of 14 occupations, "from royal councilor to lowliest musketeer." The growing economic oppression suffered

by the lowest ranks of society led to numerous uprisings, including the Moscow Revolt of 1648, the so-called Revolt of Copper Money (1662) and riots in 1674 against a drastic increase in the salt-tax. But above all, the peasantry, by now bound in complete serfdom, were sinking into ever greater poverty, and allied themselves with the Cossacks. Their rebellion lasted four years before being bloodily suppressed. The leader, Stenka Razin, was executed in 1671, a fact which only succeeded in making him a folk hero.

Even the *streltsy* mutinied; and another pillar of state authority, the Orthodox Church, began to totter. The ecclesiastical reforms of Patriarch Nikon in 1653 were intended to bring about a return to Byzantine Greek orthodoxy, and thus ran counter to the previously won independence of the popular Russian tradition. This led to a *raskol* or schism in the Russian church and the Old Believers, henceforth known as *raskolniki*, were oppressed and persecuted.

Peter the Great

When Peter I assumed the reins of power in 1689, he was only 17 years old, but officially he had already been czar for seven years, sharing the throne with his mentally retarded half-brother, Ivan V. During this period, Peter's half-sister, Sophia, ruled Russia as regent, but as soon as Peter had attained the age of majority, he quickly dispatched her to a nunnery. For the next 35 years he gave Russia a greater shake-up than any czar before or after him. For Peter ruled with an iron hand and ruthless determination.

Even as an adolescent, his curiosity had taken him into the "German quarter" of Moscow, the Nemetskaya Sloboda, where at that time there lived a large number of intellectuals, technicians, military experts and craftsmen from all over western Europe. As a young man, Peter's greatest ambition was to open Russia up to western influences and bring her out of the isolation which history had hitherto forced on her. With this in mind he made

25

his first journey incognito in 1697-8, to Prussia, Holland and England, principally to learn the science of shipbuilding. For he realized that Russia could only become a great power by gaining access both to the Black Sea and the Baltic. Even before setting out for Europe, he had built a strong battle fleet and captured the Turkish stronghold of Azov, the gateway to the Black Sea. Returning from his European journey, Peter met the Polish King Augustus II, who in fact was a German, the Elector of Saxony, and they agreed on a joint campaign against Sweden. Thus began, in 1700, the 20-year long Great Northern War against Sweden, from which, in spite of early defeats, Russia finally emerged victorious. In the same year he put an end, once and for all, to the payment of tribute to the Crimean Tatars, and conquered large parts of what is today Azerbaijan.

Above: Czar Peter's reforms demanded many sacrifices. Right: Topographical representation of St. Petersburg, around 1712.

In every way, he reformed the state from top to bottom: in place of the *ukases* (royal commands) he instituted, in the years 1718-22, a centralized system of administration which was divided up into "Colleges" or ministries dealing with key areas such as defense and foreign affairs. He had already established a Senate in 1711 and now built this up into the supreme government authority, acting for the czar in his absence, collecting taxes and serving as an ultimate court of appeal. This effectively made the boyars' *duma*, or assembly, redundant. In 1719 Peter divided Russia up into eleven governorships, which were directly accountable to him. His plan to create a strong, effective and centralized state was further served by his politically inspired religious reforms, aimed at reducing the influence of the church.

After the death in 1700 of the Patriarch of Moscow, Hadrian, the post of patriarch was left vacant and eventually replaced by the Holy Synod, a college of clerics more in the nature of a government department. The power of the church was thus definitively curtailed. Peter's economic and financial reforms were spearheaded by the introduction in 1721 of a poll tax on every adult male peasant, to replace the former household tax, and he also did much to encourage manufacturing industry. When he came to the throne there had only been 13 factories in Russia; by the time he died there were 191.

Peter also laid the foundations for educational reform in a country whose people were largely illiterate. In 1697 the Slavonic, Greek and Latin Academy was founded in Moscow, the first institution of higher education in Russia. It was followed in 1701 by the School of Mathematics and Navigation and in the same year Peter pushed through the establishment of mathematically orientated elementary schools. The year 1702 saw the opening of Russia's first theater.

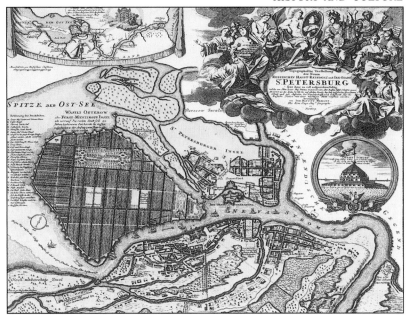

A century later, Alexander Pushkin, the father of Russian literature, wrote:

"Peter I was no lover of Moscow. With every step he took there he was reminded of earlier rebellions, or encountered resistance among the superstitious and bigoted Muscovites."

Nevertheless Peter did enlarge and modernize Moscow along western lines: the city's population was then around 600,000 and it was one of the largest in Europe. But its citizens still walked the sandy or muddy streets wearing caftans and shoes made of straw. The houses were built of wood, and the first paved street was not built until 1693. Close to the Nemetskaya Sloboda Peter ordered the construction of western-style palaces and barracks, nearly all of which were destroyed in the great fire of 1812. But again and again he came up against the resistance of the Muscovites who saw their historical and cultural independence threatened. He finally got tired of it all, and in 1703 ordered work to start on the building of a completely new capital.

The birth of St. Petersburg

The city he built spread over 44 islands, crossing 65 arms of the Neva delta and numerous canals, with 600 bridges. It was the place where the Varangians had once forced their way into Russia, in order to open up new trade routes to Byzantium. When, on 27th May 1703, Peter the Great laid the foundation stone of the Fortress of Peter and Paul, on an island called Hare Island, in the midst of marshland, he knew what he was doing.

The Swedes had repeatedly tried to capture the delta of the Neva and the surrounding area, in order to cut Russia off from the Baltic. To this end they had constructed the fortress of Nyenschanz in 1617, not far from Hare Island. When Peter came to the throne, Sweden controlled the whole of the Baltic and its coastal region, which is why he launched the Great Northern War against Sweden in 1700. In 1702 he regained the fortress of Noteborg, to which he gave the German name of Schlüsselburg, because it

27

was the key (*Schlüssel*) to the Baltic. Two weeks later the foundation stone of Sankt Pieter Burkh was laid, at the narrowest point of the Neva delta, where the arms of the river join and all shipping could be controlled. For this purpose 120 cannon were mounted on its bastions. At the same time, Peter built the fortress of Kronstadt on the Gulf of Finland. Under the eye of the cannons, there began what is probably the largest and most costly – both in money and lives – construction project of modern history: the creation of a new capital out of nothing, Russia's "Window on the West."

In the midst of a mosquito-infested swamp, Peter's city literally rose out of the earth. Countless thousands of soldiers, serfs and craftsmen were drafted to St. Petersburg from every corner of Russia; armies of *muzhiks* carried earth to the marshes in sacks, on mats, even in their pockets, in order to provided a solid

Above: River view from Nevski Prospekt in 18th-century St. Petersburg.

foundation. Possibly as many as 30,000 died and were buried in that same earth. In a very short space of time there arose fortifications, palaces, shipyards, residential blocks, workshops and factories. As early as 1705 the Admiralty was completed, in whose dockyard Russia's first ocean-going warship was built.

By this time, as many as 40,000 people were already living in the city. Peter wanted to give his new metropolis a western appearance, but since there was a shortage of stone, he decreed that no stone houses should be built anywhere else in Russia, and landowners were all obliged to build one stone house in St. Petersburg. Peter met the huge demand for skilled craftsmen by arranging for the permanent settlement of masons, bricklayers, carpenters and others, who were given their own houses and gardens.

The leading architects of the day were brought to St. Petersburg from all over Europe: in 1710 work started on the Cathedral of St. Isaac and the Alexander Nevsky monastery; then the first stages of the Nevsky Prospekt were laid down, and in 1712 the church of St. Peter and St. Paul was begun. Having built a palace for himself on Vasilevsky Island, Prince Menshikov, Peter's trusted army commander and St. Petersburg's first governor, ordered the building of a Summer Palace for the czar beside the Neva, to which a Winter Palace was later added. In 1712 the court moved permanently from Moscow to St. Petersburg, and Russia had its new, if unloved, capital.

Under Peter the number of factories in Russia increased tenfold and nearly all of them were concentrated in St. Petersburg. This was accompanied by rapid advances in education: in 1711 the first printing-works opened, which published Russia's first newspaper, *Vedomosti* (Bulletin). The general public were given access to Peter's private library, and Russia's first museum, the Chamber of Art, was opened. In 1725 the Academy of Sciences was founded – and St. Petersburg began increasingly to attract men of ideas from the west. From now on, the city was undoubtedly the "head" of the nation, though Moscow remained its "heart" for people of all ranks. Even the court nobility took every opportunity to return to Moscow, which hardly changed during Peter's reign but kept its typical Russian character with wooden houses, narrow alleys and gilded domes.

After his victory over Sweden in 1721, Peter decreed the manner in which the succession to the throne should be decided, and assumed the sole right to nominate the next czar. Yet when he died in 1725 he had in fact failed to do this – he had dispatched his son Alexei to prison in 1716, for the sole offense of lacking interest in military matters. There he died two years later, as a result of deliberate ill-treatment. This is why Menshikov, aided by the regiment of guards, put Peter's widow on the throne, as Czaritsa Catherine I. She had no gift for government and presided over a period of favoritism and political instability, which continued under her successor Peter II, the grandson of Peter the Great from a previous marriage. When he died in 1730 the male line of the Romanovs died out, and he was succeeded by Anna I, the widow of a German duke, and niece of Peter the Great. During her reign, the undue influence of her favorites, who were mostly of German origin, caused disquiet both among the people and the nobility. She weakened the landed aristocracy, who had brought her to power, in favor of the court nobles. This meant serfdom for every peasant in the land.

After the death of the childless Anna I in 1740, the nation's affairs were briefly in the hands of Anna Leopoldovna, Ivan V's granddaughter, whose infant son had been nominated Czar Ivan VI, but in the following year she was toppled in a *coup d'état* led by Elizabeth, a daughter of Peter the Great, who had earlier been rejected as a successor to the throne.

As Elizabeth I she certainly did not make an ideal monarch, but she was very open to the ideas of the Enlightenment which filtered in from western Europe. In 1755 she founded the first university, in Moscow; and in St. Petersburg she established the city's first theater and the Academy of Fine Arts. By now St. Petersburg had a population of more than 100,000 and had replaced Moscow as the political and cultural center of Russia.

Before Elizabeth died in 1762, she nominated her sister's son, Karl Peter Ulrich of Holstein-Gottorp as heir to the throne. This meant that the Romanov dynasty would be extinguished in both the male and female lines, although subsequent monarchs called themselves Romanov-Holstein-Gottorp, in order to preserve a semblance of dynastic continuity

A wife had to be found for the new heir and she was a German princess, Sophie of Anhalt-Zerbst, who, for her Russian role, was re-christened Yekaterina.

The age of Catherine the Great

Peter III was only granted the briefest of reigns: he felt himself to be entirely German and loathed all things Russian. This made him unpopular with the Russians and presented an opportunity to his consort, whom he frequently insulted in public. She had adopted the Orthodox faith and now put herself at the head of the dissatisfied court and army officers. With the help of two Guards regiments she forced her husband to abdicate and then connived in his murder – just six months after his coronation. In spite, or perhaps because of this, she is known to history as Catherine the Great.

In her foreign policy, at least, she was highly successful: in the wars against the Ottoman Empire (1768-92) Catherine II gained the important access to the Black Sea, while capturing the Crimea in 1783.

Above: The empress Catherine was a strong ruler. Right: Field-marshall Kutuzov, who defied Napoleon. Far right: Czar Alexander I.

Through the three Partitions of Poland she was able to to annex the two eastern Polish territories of Ukraine and White Russia, as well as Lithuania and Kurland, to the empire of All the Russias. Russia was now very definitely a major European power, not least in a cultural and intellectual sense, for Catherine had been brought up in the tradition of the Enlightenment, and corresponded regularly with men like Diderot, Voltaire and d'Alembert. In 1764 she founded the Smolny Institute, the country's first educational establishment for women. In 1783 a pedagogical college was opened in St. Petersburg, where by this time a third of the population was made up of noblemen, officials, officers, artists and intellectuals. Fine riverside esplanades were built in the classical style, together with buildings such as the Hermitage, and an equestrian statue of Peter the Great, the "Bronze Rider," was erected. By the time Catherine died, St. Petersburg had become the "Jewel of the North," whose praises have been sung ever since.

ALEXANDER I

Moscow also grew during Catherine's reign, though in 1771 a plague had carried away some 57,000 souls. The inflammable wooden houses were replaced by stone ones, streets were paved and lit with streetlamps, and in 1787 work started on a fresh-water system.

Yet this "foreign" czarina was not loved by the Russian people. Firstly, there was her extravagant lifestyle and her numerous lovers and favorites, such as Orlov and Potemkin. The latter was notorious for erecting artificial villages to fool her on her tours of inspection.

Secondly, she was responsible for perpetuating and aggravating the serfdom, which drove more and more people into destitution. At the same time the nobility became ever wealthier and more privileged; they built themselves luxurious residences in St. Petersburg and smashed their champagne goblets ostentatiously against the walls.

This led in 1773 to a great uprising in the Urals and Volga region, of Cossacks, factory workers, serfs and Moslem peoples under the leadership of the Cossack, Pugachev. It was suppressed with great bloodshed.

Like all absolute rulers in Europe, Catherine greeted the ideas of the French Revolution with utter disdain. After 1789 her policies became openly reactionary. This culminated in Russia taking sides against the revolutionaries and directly challenging Napoleon. So began one of the darkest hours in Russian history.

Napoleon in Russia

Catherine's son, Paul I, reigned for barely five years (1796-1801). He pursued his mother's expansionist policy by annexing Georgia but withdrew from the anti-Napoleonic coalition. He was a capricious and obsessive man, with a secret admiration for Bonaparte, and in 1800 briefly formed a League of Armed Neutrality with Denmark, Sweden and Prussia, aimed at defying Britain's naval blockade of France. This enraged the nobility. In the course of a palace revolution he was murdered, possibly with the knowledge of his own son and heir, Alexander I, who reigned from 1801 to 1825 and became Napoleon's great adversary.

Czar Alexander had inherited from his father a secret treaty with Napoleon, but after 1805 he entered into alliances with Britain, Austria and Prussia in order to halt the victorious progress of the Grande Armée. However, after the bitter defeats of Austerlitz (1805) and Friedland (1807) he changed sides again and at the Peace of Tilsit in 1807 made separate terms with Napoleon. This treaty did not last long: in May 1812 the Grande Armée began advancing into Russia. "To take Kiev is to tickle Russia's feet; to attack St. Petersburg is to scratch her head, but to capture Moscow is to strike her heart," so Napoleon is reported to have said.

This was the beginning of the "Patriotic War" which gave rise to a wave of national unity and fervor. At first the Russian army retreated until, under Kutuzov, it faced Napoleon at Borodino. The battle was inconclusive and Napoleon continued his advance on Moscow, which he reached on 2nd September. He found the city deserted, for the Russian commanders had decided to sacrifice it in order to conserve their forces. But no sooner had Napoleon moved into a suite in the Kremlin than the first fires broke out among the wooden houses, and soon almost three-quarters of the city was reduced to rubble and ashes.

Only with great difficulty was Napoleon able to escape and order the retreat. In the bitter cold of the Russian winter, harried by partisans and advancing Russian troops, crushed, starving and decimated, the legendary Grande Armée met a miserable end.

After Napoleon's forced abdication in 1814 Czar Alexander I was hailed as the "liberator of Europe."

Right: In St. Petersburg the army charges against the Decembrist rebels.

But "Mother Russia" had suffered sorely and there was much to be done, especially in Moscow. Immediately after the retreat of Napoleon extensive reconstruction was begun under the architect Giuseppe Bove, in a suitably splendid imperial style. Whole residential districts were built for the nobility, and in 1824 the Little (Maly) and Great (Bolshoi) Theaters were built. The city was habitable once again and the people returned; soon trade, business and industry were blossoming again.

St. Petersburg, on the other hand, had hardly suffered at all during the Napoleonic Wars and continued to bask in an imperial and classical grandeur that surpassed even Paris. After 1812 Alexander commissioned the architect Carlo Rossi to design new squares, streets and groups of buildings, such as the General Staff headquarters, the Mikhailov Palace and the theater that is now the Pushkin Theater. St. Petersburg became one of the finest cities in the world and its harbor one of the most important.

Oppression and resistance

The people paid a high price for all this. Alexander, brought up by his grandmother, Catherine the Great, to be an enlightened despot, attempted, through internal reforms, to create a state based on principles of justice and order, which were modern for their day, though he was careful not to put his autocratic power at risk. Thus, he founded four new universities between 1802 and 1805, and another in St. Petersburg in 1819. In 1802 he set up specialized ministries reporting directly to him. In order to counter the nobility's appetite for power, he subordinated the (aristocratic) senate to a new imperial council, in 1810.

In 1803 he had already issued a *ukaz* permitting landowners to make their serfs free peasants – but it was no more than permission. Thus, until the death of Alex-

ander, there was virtually no change in the conditions of the peasantry, workers and servants, who continued to live like slaves in grinding poverty, while the nobles went on swigging champagne.

The grumbling of the people became ever louder and was heard by intellectuals, minor nobles and young officers. In 1817 the first secret society was formed in Moscow, opposing the monarchy and serfdom. Soon it was joined by others in St. Petersburg and all over Russia. In the brief power vacuum following Alexander's death in St. Petersburg on 14th December 1825, the Decembrist Rebellion broke out, with the object of preventing Nicholas I from being crowned czar, and replacing him with their own candidate, the Archduke Constantine. But Nicholas was able to rally support among the army and used artillery swiftly to put down the rebellion in St. Petersburg. Five ringleaders were executed. Hundreds of other rebels were put into labor camps or banished to Siberia. No sooner had Nicholas ascended the throne than he showed what

was to be expected of him: unlike Alexander I, he was from the outset opposed to reform, and his policies made this abundantly clear.

In order to stifle any modern, democratic aspirations, in 1826 Nicholas created the notorious "Third Department" of the czarist chancellery, a mixture of secret police and censorship, which ruthlessly persecuted anyone with dissident views. At his death he bequeathed a sophisticated military and bureaucratic apparatus, whose chief purpose was the maintenance of serfdom, the monarchy and the expansion of Russia's economic and political power.

Under Nicholas, Russian manufacturing achieved technical standards comparable with the west, especially in St. Petersburg, which had developed into the industrial center of an otherwise largely agricultural country. As early as 1831 the first All-Russian Industrial Exhibition was opened in Moscow and a year later, the first agricultural exhibition. In 1843 the first steam locomotive left the Putilov

works in St. Petersburg; and in 1851 the first railroad line, between Moscow and St. Petersburg, was inaugurated – at that time the longest in the world. In the same year the first cast-iron bridge over the Neva was completed.

Nicholas applied his police-state methods abroad as well as at home, and after crushing the Polish revolt in 1830 and one in Hungary in 1849, he became known as the "gendarme of Europe." But it proved impossible for him to close the "window on the west," which had been thrown open by Peter the Great; the intelligentsia continued to grow more radical despite official suppression and persecution. For the "westernizers" the ideals of the French Revolution, of German idealism and French utopian socialism could not be ignored. The Slavophiles, on the other hand, forged a nationalism based on an idealized past.

Above: Czar Nicholas I. Right: A country fair in 1906, painted by Boris M. Kustodiyev.

As often happens in times of political repression, literature blossomed. Nicholas' reign saw the emergence of the first Russian writers of world rank: Alexander Pushkin, Mikhail Lermontov and Nikolai Gogol. The next generation of celebrated authors also lived their early adult lives under Nicholas: Ivan Turgenyev, Leo Tolstoy and Fyodor Dostoyevsky.

Alexander II, who succeeded Nicholas, ascended the throne of the czars in 1855, the year of Russia's defeat at Sevastopol in the Crimean War. This brought to an end Russia's hegemony in Europe, but she compensated for this by becoming a great power in Asia. In quick succession Alexander annexed the Amur-Ussuri region, where Vladivostok was founded in 1860, then the Cherkessia region and the peninsula of Sakhalin. By the end of his reign the Russian empire bordered with Persia, Afghanistan and China. Even Japan felt threatened. At the same time, to tidy things up, Alexander sold Russia's American outpost, Alaska, to the USA for a derisory $7.2 million.

The defeat at Sebastopol had already highlighted the backwardness of Russia's administration, army and economy, the chief reason for this being serfdom, which continued to condemn the peasantry to a life of misery and apathy. Domestic reform therefore became a matter of life and death for the monarchy. Thus Alexander declared in an edict of 1861, that the peasantry was henceforth free, and could belong to self-governing village or town communes (Russian: *mir*) though they could not leave their *mir* without a passport. At least, though, the yoke of serfdom was removed from some 47 million Russians.

There was, however, one major catch: the land farmed by the serfs remained the property of the landowners, who were usually noblemen. It is true that the peasants were given limited rights to exploit the land, and even to buy it outright, but how many could afford that? Although

the state contributed one-fifth of the purchase price, the balance had to be paid back over 49 years at 6% interest. Thus the emancipation of the penniless serfs drove most of them further into poverty, or into big cities like Moscow and St. Petersburg, where, thanks to investment by the state and by far-sighted aristocrats, industry was booming. But this soon produced a rapidly growing proletariat; by 1869 the population of St. Petersburg was 668,000, while that of Moscow grew from 364,000 in 1864 to 754,000 in 1882.

In rural districts, local councils, or *zemstva*, were introduced, with limited autonomy in health, education and communications. After 1870, self-governing city councils were established on the basis of a three-class electoral system. In the same year military conscription was introduced by decree. Earlier, in 1864, Alexander II had reformed and modernized the judicial system.

The face of the big cities was also changing, especially Moscow and St. Petersburg. In Moscow, the world-famous Conservatory was opened, where Tchaikovsky lectured before becoming celebrated as a composer. From 1867 the main streets were lit with gaslamps, which were replaced by electricity as early as 1883. In 1872, the first horse-drawn tramway went into service, and in the same year the first higher education institute for women opened. A telephone network was inaugurated in 1882.

The tottering throne of the czars

There is no doubt that under Czar Alexander II "Mother Russia" changed profoundly and rapidly due to the invasion of western capitalism. In the cities the number of large companies with more than 500 employees rose dramatically, and the steadily growing and ever more dissatisfied working class created new problems. Thus the social and political conflict came close to boiling-point even during the repressive reign of Alexander II.

The czar, in common with all his predecessors, was fundamentally op-

posed to democracy, and hesitated to introduce a constitution that would establish a system of government based on the separation of powers on the western model. A second rebellion in Poland (1863) and the first, unsuccessful, attempt on his life only reinforced his increasingly reactionary attitude. The attempted assassination was not a random occurrence, for the alienation of the Russian intelligentsia, which had begun under Nicholas I, became more acute under Alexander. The Pan-Slavism, which was rampant chiefly among the nobility, and which Alexander had tried to satisfy with his Russification at home and his expansionist foreign policy, competed with the utopian ideals of the *Mir* socialists, who were strongly influenced by Alexander Herzen. At the same time, two aristocrats, Prince Kropotkin and Mikhail Bakunin were illegally spread-

Above: Fyodor Dostoyevsky, banished by the czars to Siberia. Right: The assassination of Alexander II.

ing their anarchist-communist ideas. These gave rise to debates among the intelligentsia, of the kind which their contemporary, Dostoyevsky, captured in his novel *The Possessed*. Revolutionary clubs, groups and organizations sprang up like mushrooms. Finally, into this fertile ground, the seeds of Marxism were sown by Plekhanov.

In 1865, under the influence of Herzen, the *Narodnik* (Populist) movement, led by Chernyshevsky and Lavrov, began propagating a nationalist, agrarian socialism in opposition to western capitalism. This led, in 1873, to the "mad summer," when thousands of young intellectuals went "to the people" in the countryside. The peasantry, however, were no more interested in *Mir* socialism than in overthrowing the czar. This failure in turn gave rise to revolutionary anarchist clubs, who sought to put an end to the rule of the czars by terrorist means. In 1866 the *narodnik* Karakozov had tried to shoot Alexander II; in 1879 a *narodnik* terrorist organization called *Narodnaya Volya* (People's Will) was formed, and in the following year they smuggled a bomb into the Winter Palace. The czar only escaped death by a miracle. However, on 1st March 1881 another bomb attack in St. Petersburg succeeded in killing him.

The new czar, Alexander III, lived in permanent fear of assassination and sealed himself off almost completely from the world. His domestic policy measures were, unsurprisingly, reactionary; the self-governing powers of the *zemstva* were curtailed in favor of the nobility, as was the autonomy of the universities. Censorship was made more severe and around the periphery of the huge empire Pan-Slavist and anti-Semitic policies were the order of the day.

During this period Marxism was spreading, not only among the intellectuals, but also in the industrial working-classes of St. Petersburg and Moscow.

In 1895 the Moscow intellectuals and

workers joined forces in the "Workers' League." In the previous year, Nicholas II, the last Romanov, had come to the throne. He was a weak-willed man, unable to cope with the crisis which was engulfing the nation. What is more, he fell under the malign influence of the monk and charlatan Rasputin and increasingly ignored the signs of impending disaster.

The man who called himself Lenin

Why should the czar, as he drove around St. Petersburg, take any interest in an undersized law-student named Vladimir Ilyich Ulyanov? Yet it was this young man standing on the kerbside – and not the bomb-throwing terrorists – who would successfully challenge and eventually bury czarism. He later took the name Lenin.

During his student days Ulyanov had immersed himself deeply in Marxism. In St. Petersburg in 1895 he founded the "Campaign for the Emancipation of Labor," with Plekhanov and Axelrod. In 1897 he was arrested for agitating among the workers of St. Petersburg and exiled for three years to Siberia, where he wrote *The Development of Capitalism in Russia*. In this he put forward the theory that since Russia was already a fully capitalist society, it could miss out the bourgeois-democratic revolution that western Europe had already gone through, and proceed straight to the proletarian revolution postulated by Karl Marx. This viewpoint put him in direct conflict not only with the Narodniki, from whom the Social Revolutionary Party later evolved, but also with Plekhanov, Axelrod and Martov, who, during Lenin's exile in Siberia, had founded the Russian Social Democratic Labor Party in Minsk, in 1898. This fundamental divergence of views later led in 1903 to the split between the *Mensheviki*, or minority party, and the *Bolsheviki*, or majority party.

What condition was Russia in at the turn of the 20th century? Despite the apparent industrial progress, the economy was still 80 per cent agricultural, and the

life of the peasantry, despite the abolition of serfdom, was appalling. Hunger, poverty and the loss of their land continued to drive millions of peasants into the industrial centers, causing the urban population to rise from 6.7 million in 1876 to 23.8 million in 1913. Largely due to the forcing of the pace of industrialization by the finance minister, Sergei Witte, the number of industrial workers in Moscow and St. Petersburg grew from 1.42 million to 2.37 million. The normal working day was "reduced" to 11 1/2 hours in 1897 only by dint of much pressure on the capitalist employers.

Thanks to Witte's policy of imposing tariff barriers and raising immense foreign loans, Moscow and St. Petersburg enjoyed a real boom, which for example made it possible to build the Trans-Siberian Railway (1892-1902). By 1900 St. Petersburg had a population of 1.3 million, and Moscow just on 1 million. Electric streetcars had been running in Moscow since 1890, and in 1894 the department store which later became known as GUM (State Universal Store), first opened its doors.

In 1898 the first telephone link between the two cities was installed, and in 1902 the first subway trains began running under the streets of St. Petersburg.

Cultural life was also blossoming as never before: 1897 saw the opening of the Russian Museum with works by many great native artists; plays by Anton Chekhov and Maxim Gorky were put on in the theaters, the great singer Chalyapin and the prima ballerina Pavlova had their first triumphs. New works were performed by the composers Glazunov, Scriabin and Rachmaninoff. But this economic prosperity and artistic achievement was bought at the price of unbelievably wretched conditions for the urban workers and the rural peasants – aggravated by a reactionary domestic policy enforced with totalitarian rigor. The

Above: The October Revolution, 1917. Lenin speaks on Red Square in Moscow.

much-hated Interior Minister Plehve ran a police state and abolished the autonomy of the *zemstvo* councils. He also persuaded the czar to occupy Manchuria, a move which led to war with Japan in 1904-5, and the crushing defeats at Port Arthur, Mukden and Tsushima.

With the war lost and a tense political situation at home, revolution was in the air. Plehve was assassinated in 1904, but all the demands from virtually every level of society for a greater degree of self-government, a constitution and a parliament, were met by stonewalling on the part of the czar. The workers of the Putilov factory in St. Petersburg responded by going on strike, and this broadened into a general strike. On 22nd January 1905 about 150,000 people, led by a priest, Father Gapon, demonstrated outside the Winter Palace with crucifixes, church banners, pictures of saints and of the czar himself, from whom they peacefully petitioned a constitution, basic rights and relief of poverty. It seems almost certain that Gapon was an *agent provocateur,* working for the secret police. At all events, czarist troops fired indiscriminately into the huge crowd and killed or wounded some 4,500 people in this "Bloody Sunday." This event irrevocably severed any ties between the people and the "Little Father," the czar. Unrest, revolts and acts of violence shook the empire of the czar with increasing frequency, and Russia did after all go through a bourgeois-democratic revolution, with the growing participation of sections of the army.

In June 1905 a general strike was called in Odessa, which spread nationwide in October. It became ever clearer that the czar's throne was tottering. And so Nicholas II finally gave in to the growing pressure: in his October Manifesto of 30th October 1905 he promised basic civil rights, universal franchise and the setting up of a parliament with legislative powers, which met for the first time in May 1906. But the manifesto was very quickly revealed as a tactical maneuver, aimed at bringing the situation under control. The Duma was really only a sham parliament whose rights were progressively reduced. Ultimately all decisions by the Duma required the assent of the czar and of the government, which he controlled, and this led to the dissolution, in June 1906 and June 1907, of the 1st and 2nd Dumas, which were nominally opposed to the czar.

Political unrest continued to grip the country, culminating in an armed revolt of the Moscow workers in December 1905, led by the Bolsheviks. In the same year the first "Soviet" (the Russian word for "council") was founded in St. Petersburg. On 1st February the first All-Russian Trade Union Congress was held.

By introducing new electoral laws Czar Nicholas and "his" prime minister, Stolypin, succeeded in assembling the pro-czarist third Duma (November 1907 - June 1912). The growing discontent throughout the country and the terrorism that fed on it, were met by Stolypin with the creation of military tribunals with powers of summary justice, but in 1911 he himself fell to an assassin's bullet. The fourth Duma (November 1912 - March 1917) was also a willing instrument of czarist policy, and that is how matters stood in Russia at the outbreak of the First World War on 1st August 1914.

The collapse of czarism

Ironically, czarist Russia fought on the side of republican France and democratic Britain, together with Italy and Japan, against the Kaiser's Germany, the empires of Austria-Hungary and Ottoman Turkey. But she was not strong enough, militarily or economically, to meet the challenge. Heavy defeats quickly made conditions worse for the Russian people, who had initially shown a certain degree of enthusiasm for the war.

On 3rd March 1917, the Putilov workforce in Petrograd (the city was so named from the beginning of the war until 1924) went on strike once again, and this developed into a general strike on 9th March. In the night of 11th March, units of the troops which had been mobilized by the czar, allied themselves with the strikers, and Russia experienced a second bourgeois-democratic revolution, which, under the old Russian system of dating, was known as the February Revolution.

On 15th March 1917 Nicholas II, under pressure from all sides, abdicated. The rule of the czars had finally collapsed. There followed a period of "dual rule." On the day after the abdication the executive committee of the fourth Duma formed a Provisional Government under Prince Lvov. It proclaimed civil rights, made a commitment to convene a constituent assembly, and declared its intention to continue the war against Germany and Austria. This prompted the Germans to make the clever move of dispatching Lenin, who was opposed to the war, in a sealed train from Switzerland to Russia. He arrived at Petrograd's Finland Station where he was ecstatically greeted as the "Peacemaker."

On arrival, he found the Provisional government in a state of paralysis, largely incapable of making policy, and since 16th March opposed by an executive committee from all the workers' and soldiers' soviets. For every thousand workers and each army company there was a representative in a soviet. The people wanted peace, bread, land and democracy. The whole of Russia was in a ferment; everywhere soviets (literally "councils") were springing up, strengthened since the February revolution and modeled on the first soviet in St. Petersburg. They all disputed the claim of the Provisional Government to be running the country. Lenin realized that he had returned at precisely the right moment.

Above: The storming of the Winter Palace on 7th-8th November 1917. Right: One man who changed the world: Lenin.

In his famous April Theses, attacking the Provisional Government, his watchwords were: "Peace to all nations, land to the peasants, factories to the workers and power to the soviets!" His demands met with broad approval among the population and led to an armed uprising in St. Petersburg on 16th July, which was put down by the Minister of War, Kerensky. Lenin had to flee, and Trotsky and Kamenev were arrested. However, the new government, which was shortly afterward formed by Kerensky, would not and could not keep its promises to end the war and put through the long overdue agrarian reforms. The people's impatience grew, and in September the Bolsheviks achieved a majority for the first time in the Moscow and St. Petersburg soviets. On 13th October a memorable session of the central committee was held, which decided to launch an armed uprising and topple the Provisional Government.

In the dawn of 7th November (25th October in the old calendar, which is why it is called the "Great October Revolution"), the Winter Palace in St. Petersburg was stormed, and the entire government arrested, apart from Kerensky himself, who escaped in a car lent by the US Embassy. The 2nd Russian Congress of Soviets quickly transferred power to the "Council of People's Commissars." Lenin was its chairman, Trotsky was responsible for foreign policy and Stalin for the non-Russian nationalities. At the same time the congress passed a "Decree about Peace" which rejected any annexation of territory or reparations, and also a decree about land, which dispossessed the landowners and handed all land over to the peasants. But this victory did not resolve Russia's problems; new ones were simply added.

Lenin had promised elections to a Constituent Assembly. These were held on 8th December and the Bolsheviks only gained 23.3% of the votes, while the socialist parties won 62% and the liberal parties 13%. When the Constituent Assembly met for the first time on 18th January 1918, Lenin simply dissolved it. In its place the R.S.F.S.R. (Russian Soviet Federative Socialist Republic) was proclaimed on 23rd January. The Treaty of Brest-Litovsk, which was signed with Germany on 3rd March, gave the newly created Soviet Republic a breathing-space in which to meet new challenges at home and abroad. Although the First World War was, for Russia, at an end, a long and terrible civil war, with massive foreign intervention, was still to come. Among other things, the seat of the Soviet government was moved from Petrograd back to Moscow, to the "heart of Russia." The former St. Petersburg, which had been Russia's "window on the west," as well as the revolutionary nerve center since 1905, lost its 200-year old supremacy. In just three years, from 1917 to 1920, its population dropped from 2.4 million to 720,000.

On 10th July the third All-Russian Congress of Soviets approved the con-

41

stitution of the RSFSR, which in 1922, following the amalgamation with White Russia, the Ukraine and Trans-Caucasia, was renamed the Union of Socialist Soviet Republics (USSR). All political power rested with the Communist Party of Russia (Bolsheviks), CPR (B), the new name given to the Russian Social Democratic Labor Party. In 1925 the name was changed again, to the Communist Party of the Soviet Union (CPSU).

The western Entente Powers saw a threat from the young Soviet Union under Bolshevist leadership. They were furious that the new regime refused to honor loans raised under the czars and were busy expropriating industrial plants, most of which had in fact been built with foreign capital. For this reason British and French troops invaded the country, in order to help the "Whites" bring down the Bolshevik regime. The "Whites" was the name given to the forces in Russia at that time who were fighting for a restoration of czarist rule, and were able to make common cause with Mensheviks and Social Revolutionaries who had been sidelined by the Bolsheviks. Thus the revolution slipped without a noticeable gap into a three-year civil war (1918-1921).

Declaring himself Imperial Administrator, General Kolchak advanced from Siberia as far as the Volga; from the Ukraine and the Crimea troops under Denikin headed north; Kornilov's troops came from the lower Volga and southern Russia; Yudenich threatened Petrograd from the north, and in 1920 a Polish army occupied the Ukraine – all with the support of the Entente Powers. The Soviet government was fighting for its life. Lenin therefore proclaimed a policy of "war communism:" nationalization of natural resources, banks and industrial companies on the one hand, and implementation of agrarian reform on the other. This led in the country to the creation of new class of property owners with small to medium sized holdings, who owned 95 % of all the land by the end of the civil war. This in itself was very popular with the farmers – what they did not like, however, was the ban on all private commerce and the obligatory supplying of produce to support the nation during the civil war. They deliberately cut their agricultural activity right down, thus causing a breakdown in food-supplies, which in turn gave rise to strikes and riots in the cities.

To meet these internal and external threats, a secret police force, the *Cheka*, had been founded in 1917 and given the task of ruthlessly hunting down saboteurs and counter-revolutionaries. At the same time the War Commissar Trotsky, with the help of 40,000 former czarist officers, built up the Red Army of Workers and Peasants, which ultimately succeeded in defeating the White forces. But the civil war had left terrible scars on Russia. The Moscow of 1920 presented a miserable picture; and 64 of Petrograd's largest industrial plants had to be shut down in 1921 due to lack of fuel. The sailors at the Kronstadt naval base mutinied and made common cause with striking workers to demand the restoration of basic political rights within a Soviet democracy. The revolt was put down with great bloodshed on 18th March.

At the 10th party congress of the CPR (B) in 1921 Lenin announced his New Economic Policy (NEP), in order to end the persistent food crisis, which reached its climax in the famine of 1921/22.

Under the NEP, a private business sector would be allowed to exist alongside the state-owned sector, the farmers were relieved of their obligation to contribute food for nothing, and this was replaced by taxation on the commercial sale of their produce. Industrial workers were once again paid on the "capitalist" piecework system.

Right: Red Army soldiers and sailors at a mass demonstration in Leningrad in 1920.

It is true that Lenin only intended the NEP to be a transitional phase, on the way to a subsequent total socialization of the economy. In fact, it did solve the severe economic problems caused by civil war, war communism and the over-hasty introduction of socialism: the food situation improved, the economy recovered, industry swung back into action, political and trading relations were re-established, even with the "capitalist nations." However, the western allies were not pleased by the Treaty of Rapallo signed by the Soviet Union and Germany in 1922. Ostensibly a commercial agreement, it contained secret clauses which allowed Germany to carry out military exercises on Russian soil, in return for training the Red Army. High-level army contacts between the two nations continued until the Nazi period.

Following an attempt on Lenin's life in 1922, his health deteriorated and he died, aged only 54, on 21st January 1924. A few days later Petrograd was renamed Leningrad.

The Stalin era

Lenin's premature death led to an intense power struggle within the upper echelons of the CPR (B), which was to culminate in the dictatorship of Stalin. Trotsky held the view that socialism could never be achieved without a successful world revolution; Stalin, who had been General Secretary of the party since 1922, believed that "socialism in one country" was a practical possibility, even if no world revolution took place. The wily Georgian, born Josef Dzhugashvili, had managed, by clever maneuvering and using his powers to the full within the Politburo and the Central Committee, to remove all his opponents. Some he liquidated, including Trotsky, who was exiled first to Alma Ata and later to Mexico, where he was murdered in 1940. The way was now clear for Stalin's vision of "socialism in one country."

In 1927/28 Stalin declared the NEP phase ended and introduced much tighter state control of the economy. The NEP

had been very successful, particularly in industrialization: in 1925 the first tractor left its factory in Leningrad; in Moscow the first Soviet-built motorcar attracted admiring gazes.

But the rural economy had deteriorated further in comparison with the cities. This was because, in the wake of the agrarian reforms introduced by the Bolsheviks, a new class had arisen among the peasants: the *kulaks*, or affluent farmers who employed poorer men and women to till their land and increasingly began to hoard their produce until the prices went up, instead of taking it straight to market. This of course created food shortages. As part of the first Five-Year Plan (1928-32) it was decided that the peasantry should be collectivized. To break the resistance that he expected to meet from the kulaks, Stalin used force to push through this collectivization within

Above: Although a Georgian, Stalin drove Russia's economy forward. Right: Deportation of dispossessed kulaks in 1929-30.

a few years. By the end of the first Five-Year Plan virtually all peasant-farmers were organized into *kolkhoze* (collective farms) or *sovchoze* (state farms). The resistance of the kulaks, and also of those few peasants who had managed to hold on to their parcels of land, was brutally crushed by the GPU, the secret police organization which replaced the Cheka. In 1929/30 the situation in rural regions was close to civil war. In the mass-deportations that followed, several *million* kulaks and peasants perished.

Simultaneously the party was forcing the pace in the Soviet Union's still underdeveloped industrial sector. Since 1929 state-owned industries had been urged to compete with the west through the raising of individual output – piece-work and bonuses were now permitted – in a "Stakhanovite" campaign (named after a miner, Stakhanov, who was made a "Hero of Soviet labor"). Under the direction of the state planning authority, *Gosplan*, the output of raw materials was enormously increased, the transport system expanded, new factories and steelplants built, agriculture mechanized, and the electrification program accelerated by the building of dams. Between 1929 and 1932 the number of industrial workers increased from 10 to 22 million, and industrial output doubled.

The period up to the 2nd World War

During the first Five-Year Plan, the USSR was anxious to ward off any external threat, especially on its western frontier, and pursued a policy of "peaceful co-existence." Between 1928 and 1932 it concluded non-aggression pacts or peace treaties with nearly every European nation and even established diplomatic relations with the USA in 1933. In 1934 the USSR joined the League of Nations.

On the home front, thanks to the undoubted success of the first Five-Year Plan, this was a period of relative calm;

the gulf between city and country, and between the party and the people, had largely been bridged, supplies of food and other essentials had by now been regularized, wages were going up and even free schooling for all was guaranteed. No one was unduly concerned by the fact the new Soviet constitution, passed in 1936, which permanently established the one-party state, confirmed Stalin as General Secretary of the party and thus made him a quasi-legal dictator. But no one knew how ruthlessly he would set about eliminating his real and imagined opponents, both inside and outside the party. Meanwhile, in Germany, Hitler's Nazi Party had seized power in 1933, and while they were forging their plans for world domination, Stalin was staging his notorious purges and show-trials in Moscow, in which not only long-serving Bolsheviks, but many hundreds of thousands, even millions, of others were the innocent victims.

In late August 1939, a few days before German troops overran Poland, Stalin and Hitler signed a non-aggression pact, but this did not prevent Hitler from invading Russia, without a declaration of war, on 22nd June 1941. By this time, virtually all the original Bolsheviks had died or been executed.

Soviet foreign policy had always been influenced by the justified fear that, as the world's first socialist state, they would be encircled and attacked by the western capitalist nations. Hitler's seizure of power revived these fears. The Soviet foreign minister, Litvinov, worked assiduously from 1930 to 1939, to establish a system of "collective security" in alliance with the western democracies and against the Fascist axis of Germany and Italy. But the democracies refused to cooperate, and it was, in particular, the tactical concessions to Hitler's Germany made by Britain and France and embodied in the 1938 Munich Agreement, which finally persuaded Stalin to adopt a new course, in the hope of guaranteeing the security of the Soviet Union against the threat of Fascist ag-

gression: on 23rd August 1939 Litvinov's successor, Molotov met his German counterpart, Ribbentrop, in Moscow to sign the document which has gone down in history as the "Hitler-Stalin Pact," because in a secret protocol added later, Germany conceded the Soviet Union's territorial claims, which dated back to czarist times: those on eastern Poland, Estonia, Lithuania, Latvia, parts of Finland and Bessarabia in Rumania.

The Great Patriotic War

The earlier mass purges within the Red Army, which was in any case inefficient as a military machine, weakened it still further and made it easy for the *Blitzkrieg*-hardened German troops to sweep rapidly into Russia. The Nazi invaders behaved with unbelievable harshness and brutality towards the civilian population,

Above: Leningrad under siege by the German army. Right: A group of Leningraders greet their liberators.

but in doing so, like Napoleon a century earlier, they reawakened that fervent Russian nationalism which Stalin had tried, in a 1934 decree, to convert into "Soviet patriotism."

Stalin was still "only" General Secretary of the Soviet Communist Party, but from May 1941 he was also chairman of the Council of People's Commissars. He now proclaimed that the defense of Russia against Fascism, like that against Napoleon, was the "Great Patriotic War" and thus was able to enlist the support of ethnic minorities and other traditionally anti-Bolshevik elements. Even the Russian Orthodox Church, which had been suppressed since 1917, was willing to come to terms with the communist state, in order to defeat the forces of Fascism. Stalin knew he had to relieve the western powers of the fear of "communist infiltration and subversion," if he was to forge an anti-Hitler coalition involving the USA, so he abolished the Communist International (Comintern), which had been founded in 1939.

British convoys, carrying American supplies, ploughed through the Arctic seas, under constant attack from German aircraft, to the ports of Archangel and Murmansk, and thus helped to sustain the Russian war effort. However, it was largely the Russian people themselves, fighting in partisan groups, combined with the Stalin's scorched-earth policy, that succeeded in halting the German offensive outside Moscow and Leningrad. General Zhukov, who took command of the Russian army in December 1941, assembled a vast army of 100 divisions, spread out along a 200-mile (320 km) front. Some German troops came within sight of the Kremlin, but the Wehrmacht was decisively turned back from Moscow. Meanwhile, Leningrad was under siege, but held out heroically for 900 days, until it was finally relieved by the Red Army. But the cost was appalling: nearly 642,000 of the inhabitants died of starvation, a further 16,750 were killed in the fighting, 33,700 were wounded and 716,000 made homeless.

Further south in Stalingrad (now Volgograd), a German army was encircled by the Russians and after months of bitter fighting through the winter of 1942/3, was forced to surrender. From then on, the fate of Germany's Russian campaign was sealed. The Soviet Union had been responsible for the first decisive defeat of Nazi Germany and thereby considerably strengthened its position within the anti-Hitler coalition. This enabled Stalin to impose his ideas for a new European order upon the western allies, at a series of conferences which were subsequently held, in Teheran (1943), Yalta (1943) and Potsdam (1945). With the capture of Berlin on 2nd May 1945, Stalin pushed the frontiers of the Soviet Union's sphere of influence as far west as the river Elbe.

The post-war period

During the Second World War none of the combatant nations had paid a higher toll in human life than the Soviet Union; the number of its citizens who died be-

tween 1941 and 1945 has been put at anything from 20 to 40 million, to say nothing of the enormous economic and material losses. The greater part of its agricultural land had been devastated or was lying fallow, many millions were homeless, most of its industry had been destroyed or removed by the German armies and turned over to armaments production. Thus the fourth Five-Year Plan (1946-50) had to provide for a massive program of reconstruction: millions of apartments had to be built, gigantic hydroelectric power-stations were constructed on the Volga and Dniepr rivers, heavy industry had to be converted from military to peace-time production, among other things to supply tractors and farm machinery for the ailing agricultural sector. To finance all this, Stalin insisted that reparations be paid by all the states that had waged war against the Soviet Union,

Above: Nikita Khrushchov, who introduced de-Stalinization. Right: Yuri Gagarin – the first man in space.

chiefly Germany; in the Soviet-occupied eastern zone of Germany, and indeed in the whole of Eastern Europe, he had entire factories dismantled and reassembled in the Soviet Union. In the event, the Soviet economy recovered astonishingly fast. As early as 1948 industrial production in Leningrad had reached its pre-war level, and by 1952, in the whole of the USSR, output had doubled. In Moscow and Leningrad thousands of apartment-blocks went up, together with grandiose official buildings in the Stalinist "wedding-cake" style. Typical of these is the gigantic Moscow State University with its tower 787 ft (240m) high. From 1951 the second plan for the reconstruction of Moscow was put into effect, (the first plan had been in 1935); but work started as early as 1947 on a systematic expansion of the subway network, whose first line had been opened in 1935. Yet Stalin's priorities were not entirely peaceful: in 1949 the USSR stunned the world by exploding its first atomic bomb.

All this was only possible because, after the Second World War, the Soviet Union, in contrast to the situation in 1918, no longer stood isolated in a hostile world. Its power and influence extended over a vast area of the globe, from the Elbe to the Pacific, and in the countries of Eastern Europe there was industrial capacity, still largely intact, which Stalin was able to exploit. Everywhere east of the Elbe the Red Army was garrisoned in large numbers, "People's Democracies" on the Soviet model were set up in East Germany, Poland, Hungary, Rumania, Bulgaria and Czechoslovakia; in 1947 the Cominform was founded as a kind of successor to the Comintern which had been abolished during the war, and it provided a forum in which Stalin's chief theoretician, Zhdanov, proclaimed for the first time the existence of a "socialist camp." In the following year the Council for Mutual Economic Assistance (COMECON) was founded as an economic union of all the states mentioned above. In the winter of 1948/49 the Cold War between the "socialist and capitalist camps" reached its first crisis with the blockade of Berlin and the subsequent allied airlift to keep the city alive. But when the Chinese invaded Korea in the "hot war" of 1950-53, Stalin refused to become involved.

Back in 1946, the Council of People's Commissars founded by Lenin was changed into the Supreme Soviet of the USSR, of which Stalin acted as chairman, without giving up his powerful position as General Secretary of the Communist Party. The cult of personality around Stalin was now given a head of steam under the direction of the "chief ideologue," Zhdanov. When Zhdanov died in 1948, there were new purges in the party machine, arbitrary arrests and mass-deportations to labor camps, all on the instructions of the secret-police chief, Lavrenti Beria. In October 1952 the 14th Soviet Communist Party Congress was held in Moscow, the first since 1939. It was to be Stalin's last; he died on 5th March 1953.

From Stalin to Gorbachov

After Stalin's death the Communist Party adopted the principle of collective leadership. In reality this concealed a backstage struggle over succession within the all-powerful party: first of all, a loyal servant of Stalin, Malenkov, took over as Chairman of the Supreme Soviet and General Secretary, but was forced to cede the latter post to Nikita Khrushchov in September 1955, while Bulganin was named Prime Minister.

At the 20th Party Congress, in 1956, Khrushchov denounced Stalin and ushered in a program of de-Stalinization. This sparked off uprisings in Poland and Hungary against their Stalinist regimes. In the same year the Warsaw Pact was created to counterbalance NATO.

In domestic politics, Khrushchov confronted the old Stalinists, Kaganovich, Malenkov and Molotov, stripped them of their offices and declared them enemies of the party. In the same year, the USSR launched the world's first man-made earth satellite, a fact which came as a particular shock to the United States. However, the ambitious targets of the Seven-year Plan (1959-1965) could not be achieved, despite promising early results. The harvests were far below expectations and a nation that had once been an exporter of wheat now had to import it in massive quantities. The chronic problem of Soviet industry since 1917 had always been the imbalance between heavy and light industry, and this even Khrushchov was unable to solve. This weakness could not be concealed, despite another spectacular technical achievement by Russia – the first manned space flight by Yuri Gagarin in 1961. So it was no surprise when, on 24th October 1964, Khrushchov was removed from his position as General Secretary and as Prime Minister.

Khrushchov was replaced by three men: Leonid Brezhnev as General Secretary, N. Podgorny as Head of State and A. Kosygin as Prime Minister. However, Brezhnev soon emerged as the real leader, so that the period up to his death in 1982 is always known as the Brezhnev era, and was an age of notorious stagnation: living standards scarcely improved, while the military-industrial complex consumed huge sums of money sorely needed in other parts of the economy. Furthermore, internal politics were marked by gradual re-Stalinization, which led to stricter control of intellectual and cultural life and to civil rights protests among the intelligentsia. In foreign policy as well, Brezhnev proved to be harsh and unyielding, as when, in 1968, he ordered tanks to crush the demonstrators in the "Prague Spring." The 1980 Moscow Olympics were boycotted

Above: Mikhail Gorbachov, pioneer of glasnost and perestroika. Right: Even in the 1990s communism still has supporters.

50

by the western nations, in protest against the Soviet intervention in Afghanistan.

On his death, Brezhnev left behind a sclerotic bureaucracy whose leadership was aging. His successors, Y. Andropov, died in 1984 and K. Chernenko in 1985. It was a turning-point in the history of the USSR when a member of the Politburo, hitherto almost unknown in the west, was elected General Secretary of the Communist Party. He was Mikhail Sergeyevich Gorbachov.

Glasnost and Perestroika

Immediately after his election as Party Secretary at the 27th Party Congress, Gorbachov began putting into effect his reforms, which rapidly gained popularity under the watchwords *glasnost* (openness) and *perestroika* (restructuring), and even caused a stir in the west. With *glasnost* he wanted to bring more transparency and democracy into politics, while *perestroika* was intended to get rid of economic mismanagement and corruption, dismantle the rigid, planned economy and introduce a regulated market in which private enterprise would be allowed. His reforms initially met with general approval; a mood of excitement and rebirth was in the air.

In 1988, for the first time, there were free elections to the Congress of People's Deputies, in the following year the Communist Party renounced its monopoly of political power, other parties were permitted, and new laws guaranteed freedom of the press, of speech and of religion. Gorbachov was awarded the 1990 Nobel Peace Prize for his successful efforts towards world security: as early as 1987 the treaty providing for the destruction of medium-range missiles had been signed, by 1989 the Soviet troops had been pulled out of Afghanistan, and in 1990 the treaty on a reduction of conventional forces in Europe was signed, making German reunification possible.

In 1991 both COMECON and the Warsaw Pact were officially wound up. But with glasnost and perestroika Gorbachov had initiated a chain of events which soon got out of control and led to precisely the opposite of what he had envisaged. In the state bureaucracy, his policies were boycotted and sabotaged; while for the radical reformers and free marketeers who gathered round Boris Yeltsin, Gorbachov's reforms did not go far enough. The liberalizing of the economy brought profiteers and fraudsters out of the woodwork, who deliberately created food shortages and finally brought the economy to a state of collapse.

Within and between the republics of the Soviet Union, old ethnic conflicts suddenly flared up: the Baltic republics, which had been annexed by Stalin in 1940, demanded independence. The disintegration of the Soviet Union could no longer be prevented; the economic situation was catastrophic, and in August 1991 there was an attempted coup by a group of die-hard communists. The people of Moscow and St. Petersburg (as it was once again called) took to the streets, the army supported Yeltsin and the coup failed. The Communist Party was banned. On Christmas Day 1991 Gorbachov resigned as president of a USSR, which had in reality ceased to exist. Only a rump of the old Soviet empire remained in the form of the CIS (Commonwealth of Independent States). Boris Yeltsin, as president of the Russian Federation, has been juggling with political parties from extreme right to extreme left, miraculously winning just enough in elections to stay in power, while the world watches with bated breath, neither really liking his manner, yet not quite sure who could be better.

Those are the pains of democratization, the feeling of being an "open" country, no longer able to entrench itself behind vast spaces and iron curtains. The war in Chechenya that broke out in 1994, so bloody and senseless, was a perfect example: the world's media came to report, and after a while it had to stop.

MOSCOW: THE INNER CITY

KREMLIN
RED SQUARE
ST. BASIL'S CATHEDRAL
HISTORICAL MUSEUM
KITAY-GOROD
BOLSHOI THEATER
LUBYANKA SQUARE

THE KREMLIN

The Kremlin is the historical heart of Russia and of the former Soviet Union. From the insignificant palisaded fortress on Borovitsky Hill above the Moskva River – Kremlin means "fortress inside a city" – the Russian rulers, over the centuries, conquered a vast empire, which at one time covered a sixth of the earth's surface. The more the Russian Empire grew in extent and importance, the larger and more beautiful were the buildings which its rulers erected in the Kremlin, until its bizarre beauty and dazzling diversity could scarcely be surpassed.

Its beginnings, however, were very modest: the first rulers built a fortress of oak staves, which lasted until the 14th century, when Dimitri Donskoy replaced the wooden fortifications with ramparts of white stone. Only a century later, Ivan III commissioned the Italian architects Ruffo and Solario to erect walls of red brick, which are still as visitors see them today.

The Kremlin was the seat of the Grand Dukes, and later of the czars, as well as of

Previous pages: St. Basil's Cathedral and the Savior Tower, on Red Square. Cathedral of the Annunciation in the Kremlin. Left: The Trinity Tower in the Kremlin wall.

the Metropolitans, the archbishops of the Russian Orthodox Church. At the same time it was a fortress, a prison and torture chamber, a museum and place of coronation, an armory and a treasure chamber, and the venue for important cultural events. Even in the Soviet era and up to the present day, little of this changed. Accordingly one or two areas of the Kremlin are under strict guard and cannot be visited (the Hall of St. George; the Arsenal; and the Presidium of the Supreme Soviet).

A great deal of time and stamina are required to view the Kremlin in the way which its status deserves. If you have time, it makes sense to tour the whole Kremlin complex on foot first of all, in order to gain an overall impression of its size; this involves walking a distance of nearly 1 1/2 miles (2.2 km). The **Trinity Tower** (*Troitskaya Bashnya*) on the west wall would be a suitable starting point. It dates from the year 1495 and at 250 ft (76 m) is the tallest of the Kremlin's 20 towers. It has deep cellars which were formerly used as an ammunition depot. The **Kutafya-Tower** (*Kutafya Bashnya),* which dates from the 16th century, stands in front of the Trinity Tower.

Where the Neglinnaya River once flowed along the Kremlin wall, Ossip Bove created the **Alexander Gardens**

57

(*Aleksandrovsky Sad*) in 1821-24, and also designed the grotto by the Middle Arsenal Tower. In the main avenue of the gardens stands the **Obelisk** erected in 1913 to celebrate the 300th anniversary of the Romanov dynasty. The Tomb of the Unknown Soldier was placed at the north side of the gardens after 1945. The ten dark red porphyry blocks contain earth from each of those "heroic cities" of the Soviet Union, which suffered most severely in the Great Patriotic War of 1941-1945, as the Second World War was known in the USSR. Bridal couples still lay flowers at the Eternal Flame of the Memorial, to remember those who died in the war.

The **Corner Arsenal Tower** occupies the northern corner of the Kremlin wall, and this is followed along the eastern wall by the **Nikolskaya Tower** (*Nikolskaya Bashnya*) and the **Senate Tower** (*Senatskaya Bashnya*), both built in 1492. The most beautiful of the Kremlin towers is probably the **Savior Tower** (*Spasskaya Bashnya*), designed by Pietro Antonio Solario in 1491. In 1624-5 the English clockmaker Christopher Galloway built a chiming clock into it. The present clock dates from 1851-2.

Continuing south, the next tower we come to is the little **Czar Tower** (*Tsarskaya Bashnya*) which rises only 37 ft (11.4 m) above the Kremlin wall. It was from here that the czar's family watched celebrations and occasional executions in Red Square. The 121 ft (37 m) high **Constantine and Helena Tower**, which was built in 1490 to replace a stone gatetower, housed the torture chamber. Its neighbor, the circular **Beklemishevskaya Tower**, is larger and more important. It stands 150 ft (46m) tall and since 1487 has secured the south-eastern corner of the Kremlin overlooking the Moskva River.

The Moskva could be reached from the **Tainitskaya** ("Hideaway") **Tower** which was built in 1485 by Solario, and

GREATER
MOSCOW

0   5   10 km

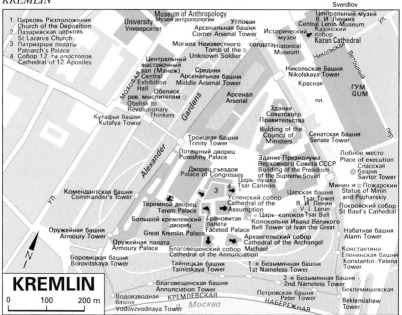

KREMLIN

0   100   200 m

1. Церковь Ризположения
   Church of the Deposition
2. Лазаревская церковь
   St Lazarus Church
3. Патриарши палаты
   Patriarch's Palace
4. Собор 12 ти апостолов
   Cathedral of 12 Apostles

Sverdlov

Museum of Anthropology
Музей антропологии
University   Угловая
Университет   Арсенальная башня
             Corner Arsenal Tower
Могила Неизвестного   солдата
Tomb of the   Historical
Unknown Soldier   Museum
Центральный
выставочный
зал (Манеж)   Средняя
Central   Арсенальная башня
Exhibition   Middle Arsenal Tower
Hall   Обелиск
рев. мыслителям
Obelisk to
Revolutionary   Арсенал
Кутафья башня   Thinkers   Arsenal
Kutafya Tower

Центральный музей
В. И. Ленина
Central Lenin Museum
Казанский
Исторический собор
музей   Kazan Cathedral

Никольская Башня
Nikolskaya Tower
Красная

ГУМ
GUM

пл.

Троицкая башня
Trinity Tower

Потешный дворец
Poteshny Palace

Дворец съездов
Palace of Congresses

Здание
Советского
Правительства
Building of the
Council of   Сенатская башня
Ministers   Senate Tower

Здание Президиума
Верховного Совета СССР
Building of the Presidium
of the Supreme Soviet
Царь-пушка
Tsar Cannon

Лобное место
Place of execution
Спасская
башня
Savior Tower

Комендантская башня
Commander's Tower

Теремной дворец
Terem Palace

Большой кремлёвский
дворец
Great Kremlin Palace

Оружейная башня
Armoury Tower

Оружейная палата
Armoury Palace

Боровицкая башня
Borovitskaya Tower

Успенский собор
Cathedral of the
Assumption

Грановитая
палата
Faceted Palace

Благовещенский собор
Cathedral of the Annunciation

Тайницкая башня
Tainitskaya Tower

Благовещенская башня
Annunciation Tower

Водовзводная   КРЕМЛЕВСКАЯ
башня
Vodovzvodnaya Tower   Москва

Царская башня
Tsar Tower
В. И. Ленин
V. I. Lenin
Царь-колокол
Tsar Bell
Колокольня Ивана Великого
Bell Tower of Ivan the Great

Архангельский собор
Cathedral of the Archangel
Michael

1-я Безымянная башня
1st Nameless Tower

2-я Безымянная башня
2nd Nameless Tower

Петровская башня
Peter Tower

НАБЕРЕЖНАЯ

Минин и   Пожарскiй
Statue of Minin
and Pozharskiy
Покровский собор
St Basil's Cathedral

Набатная башня
Alarm Tower

Константино-
Еленинская башня
Konstantin-Yelena
Tower

Беклемишевская
Beklemishew
Tower

is the oldest surviving tower of the Kremlin site. The **Annunciation Tower** (*Blagoveshchenskaya Bashnya*) was built with limestone blocks from the old 14th century Kremlin. Like all the corner towers, the circular, 194 ft (59m) high "water tower," **Vodovzvodnaya Tower** has particularly strong walls. In 1633 a water pump was installed in it, which provided the Kremlin with water via a system of pipes. The Armory is reached by way of the **Borovitskaya Tower**. The smaller towers, the **Armory Tower** (*Oruzheynaya Bashnya*) and the **Commander's Tower** (*Komendantskaya Bashnya*), stand along the wall facing the Alexander Gardens.

Entering the Kremlin precincts by the Trinity Tower, you pass the Arsenal on the left, and on the right the Palace of Congresses. At the center of the whole complex lies **Cathedral Square**, which is enclosed by the Cathedral of the As-

Right: The main door of the Cathedral of the Assumption.

60

sumption, the Cathedral of the Annunciation, the Cathedral of the Archangel, the Church of the Deposition of the Robe, and the Bell-tower of Ivan the Great. At first sight the churches seem deceptively alike, but closer inspection reveals significant differences. After the failed coup of August 1991, the cathedrals were restored to the Orthodox Church, and since then services have been held in them.

It is impossible to overestimate the part played by the **Cathedral of the Assumption** (*Uspensky Sobor*) in Russia's history. Here, from 1547 until 1894, the czars were crowned, the metropolitans and later the patriarchs were enthroned. Architecture suffered from the isolation of Russia under the Tartars, and so Ivan III commissioned the Bolognese architect Fioravanti to build this church in 1475, an event that was without doubt a great boon for Russian ecclesiastical architecture. By 1479 Fioravanti had created one of the most magnificent cathedrals in Russia, which up to now has survived the passage of time unscathed.

Following the model of the Uspensky Cathedral in Vladimir, Fioravanti erected a simple building of exemplary proportions which was a harmonious combination of the old Russian building traditions and Italian construction techniques. Four slender columns in the main body of the church and two square pillars which are hidden behind the iconostasis support the five gilded cupolas and the flattened out cross-vault of the roof. The **South Portal** is particularly magnificent and opens on to the cathedral square. The impressive 52 ft (16 m) high **iconostasis** separates the altar from the body of the church. Some of the icons date from the 11th century, but the most important ones were painted during the following three centuries. The iconostasis was completed in the 17th century.

The frescoes in the interior date from the beginning of the 17th century and were uncovered between 1922 and 1960 and subsequently restored. Fioravanti created a masterpiece in the Uspensky Sobor. The cathedral was the czars' principal church and as such was decorated regardless of cost. The icons especially are amongst the most beautiful and the most valuable which Russian ecclesiastical art has to offer: the series of intercessionary icons are by Theophanes the Greek, the feast day series above it was painted by several artists including Andrei Rublyov (the left-hand portion), who began his career as an icon-painter in this church. The wall frescoes are the work of Feodosios between 1513 and 1515 and were uncovered in 1947. Ivan IV had the floor of the cathedral tiled with pieces of jasper from the Urals.

The **Church of the Deposition of the Robe** (*Tserkov Rizpolozheniya*) was built by craftsmen from Pskov between 1484 and 1486. The private church of the metropolitans and patriarchs of the Orthodox Church stands on a tall base and is easy to recognize by its single dome. Experts uncovered mid-17th-century frescoes in 1951. The interior is worth seeing for its magnificent iconostasis by Nazari Istomin.

At the same time craftsmen from Pskov were also working on the **Cathedral of the Annunciation** (*Blagoveshchenskiy Sobor*) close to the Palace of the Czars. It ranked as Chapel Royal to the czar's family, which is why there is a bridge from the palace to the gallery of the church.

The **Cathedral of the Archangel** (*Arkhangelskiy Sobor*), built between 1505 and 1508, also represents the successful combination of Renaissance elements with Russian building traditions. The Italian architect Alviso Nuovo decided to create a church with three naves and a domed roof consisting of a main dome and four secondary domes. Here almost all the Russian grand dukes and czars from the 14th century to the time of Peter the Great were buried along with the members of their families. Only Boris Godunov was interred in the monastery

Above: The gilded domes of the Kremlin's cathedrals. Right: Weighing 200 tons, this is the worlds heaviest bell.

of Sergiyev Posad (previously: Zagorsk). In all there are 48 sarcophagi in the church, notably those of the czarevich Dimitri and of Ivan the Terrible.

The original frescoes of Theophanes the Greek and Simeon Chorny were removed during the 17th century when the walls were cleaned. They were replaced by depictions of Russia's struggle to become one nation, and scenes of everyday life. Grand Dukes of Muscovy and the national saint, Alexander Nevsky, can be recognized here. The iconostasis was originally created in 1680 and contains a few icons from an earlier period including the "Archangel Michael" (14th/15th century).

On Cathedral Square the visitor is struck more than anything by the splendid **Bell Tower of Ivan the Great** (*Kolokolnya Ivana Velikovo*) which, with its 21 bells, is one of the most impressive structures of its kind. Built in 1505 by Marco Ruffo the tower consists of four octagonal tiers tapering upwards. In 1600 the bell tower was surmounted with a two-storey spire, so that the building now has a height of 266 ft (81m). Between 1532 and 1543 Petrok Maly constructed a monumental bell-cage and in 1624 the Filaret bell cage was added. The largest bell is dedicated to the Assumption of the Virgin Mary and weighs 65 tons.

The imposing **Czar Bell** *(Czar-Kolokol)*, which stands next to the Bell Tower, is the largest bell in the world, weighing 200 tons – but it has never been rung. During the fire of 1737 the colossus was liberally dowsed with water with the result that a piece weighing 11.5 tons broke away from it. The **Czar Pushka Cannon** suffered a similar fate: not one shot was ever fired from the 40-ton monster, which has a bore of nearly 3 feet (89 cm).

The Czars' Cannon stands in front of the **Patriarch's Palace** with its Church of the Twelve Apostles. Nikon ordered this church to be built following his elevation to Patriarch in 1652. The spiritual leader introduced severe reforms, which should have restored the Russian church to its origins, but which instead provoked a split in the religious community. The **Chamber of the Cross**, measuring 43 ft by 62 ft (13 m x 19 m), in the Patriarch's Palace was used as a reception room and as a ceremonial chamber; it is spanned by a huge vaulted ceiling, unsupported by pillars. At the time of its construction this was a remarkable architectural feat.

The south side of the Kremlin is occupied by the **Great Kremlin Palace** *(Bolshoi Kremlyovsky Dvorets)*. A palace which was the residence of the czars once stood on this site. Following the great fire of Moscow in 1812, Konstantin Thon built the present palace using parts of the old building from the 15th and 16th centuries. The most recent alterations were completed in 1973. Today the large conference chamber is used for meetings of the People's Deputies of the Russian Federation.

The Hall of St. George on the upper floor has an area of 13,500 sq. ft (1250

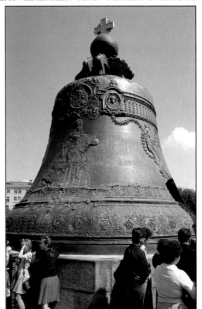

sq.m.); it is decorated with white marble and stucco and is used for prestigious occasions. Adjoining this is the octagonal Hall of St. Vladimir, which leads across to the oldest parts of the building (not open to visitors).

To the north of the Great Kremlin Palace is the **Terem Palace** *(Teremnoi Dvorets)*, which was first built in the 15th century and received baroque additions around 1635. In old Russian mansions the private apartments of the women were called *terem*. The anterooms are decorated in an opulent style, and the room known as the Chamber of the Cross has overpoweringly colorful murals and stained glass windows. The walls of the bedchamber are decorated with floral patterns, while those of the Throne Room are deep red. The **Golden Chamber of the Czaritsa** is heavily painted and has a rather gloomy effect. The palace is only occasionally open to visitors.

The oldest building in the Kremlin is the **Church of the Resurrection of Lazarus**, built in 1393. It is to be found in the undercroft of the Church of the Nativity of the Virgin, and is one of several small churches which were used by the czar and his family. In 1680-1 they were united under a single roof comprising eleven gilded domes.

The first secular stone building to be erected in the Kremlin is the **Palace of Facets** (*Granovitaya Palata*). It was commissioned by Ivan III in 1487 from the Italian architects Marco Ruffo and P. A. Solario. This early Renaissance building derives its name from the faceted limestone façade which faces the Cathedral Square. The upper storey has a room 72 ft square (22m x 22m) whose groin-vaulted ceiling is supported by one single pillar. The walls are almost totally covered with vivid frescoes, all devoted to religious subjects. Heavy chandeliers add to the overall magnificence of the place.

The **Armory** (*Oruzheynaya Palata*), Russias's oldest museum, houses the country's most precious treasures, some of which date back to the 14th century. The Armory was originally a workshop for weapons and armor which gradually changed over to producing magnificent decorative objects. The building was designed and built by Konstantin Thon in 1844-51. Among the oldest exhibits is the treasure of Ryazan from the Middle Ages. Connoisseurs will appreciate the crown which Vladimir II (1113-25) received from the Byzantine Emperor Alexius Comnenus I. The Kazan Crown of Ivan the Terrible and his magnificent wedding regalia are on view, as are the crown, imperial orb and scepter of Mihail Fyodorovich, the founder of the Romanov dynasty. The glitter of fabulous weaponry wrought in gold and silver and thrones inset with precious stones bear eloquent witness to the splendor of the czars. In this museum you can marvel at

Right: Lenin's Mausoleum – the site of a long cult of personality."

the craftsmanship of silversmiths from distant Germany, cloths, tapestries and porcelain from the Royal Factory at St. Petersburg, the coronation robes of the czarinas, as well as magnificent decorative pieces, including the famous golden Easter eggs, snuffboxes and clocks created by the court jeweler Fabergé. In the carriage room you can see how the imperial family traveled and admire the magnificent oriental harness of the czars'' horses.

The Armory also houses the **USSR Diamond Fund**. It is under heavy guard but may be viewed. Here are displayed the largest and most beautiful diamonds in the world including the historic *Prince Orlov* and *Shah* diamonds and the additions from the Soviet era, the *Oktyabrsky* and *Komsomolsky* stones.

The **Palace of Congresses** is the most massive and ugly example of the architecture of the Soviet Union anywhere in the Kremlin. The theater and conference hall built in 1961 holds 6,000 people and is the place where cultural productions are staged for tourists. The banqueting room above the conference hall seats 2,500 guests, and the 800 additional rooms make the Palace of Congresses the largest building of its type in the Russian Federation.

To the north of the Palace of Congresses three secular buildings catch the visitor's eye. The long building to the west is the **Arsenal**, which was built by Peter the Great. It was destroyed by Napoleon in 1812 and rebuilt by Ossip Bove in 1828. It adjoins the **Old Senate** on the eastern side, whose Great Chamber represents a masterpiece of classical architecture. Today it is the seat of the Council of Ministers of the Russian Federation. The triangular building was the work of Matvei Kazakov in 1776-88.

The **Presidium of the Supreme Soviet**, erected in 1932-34 on the site of old monastery buildings, stands by the Spassky Tower.

RED SQUARE,
ST. BASIL'S CATHEDRAL, GUM

Red Square, whose name in Russian is *Krasnaya Ploshchad,* must rank as one of the finest squares in Europe. The huge towers of the Kremlin rise up on its west side and, in front of the imposing Kremlin walls, that most sacred shrine of the former Soviet Union, Lenin's Mausoleum, looks relatively modest. To the south, one's gaze is instinctively drawn to the strange and fabulous beauty of St. Basil's Cathedral.

The façade of the GUM department store stretches for over 800 ft (250m) along the east side of the square, while the massive bulk of the Historical Museum, with its shimmering white roofs, occupies almost all the north side. The aesthetic interplay of the different buildings, whose ages range across five centuries, creates excitement and tension, and is quite simply breathtaking. For the Russians themselves, Red Square is not just a visual adventure – it is deeply rooted in the national psyche, and is part of Russian history, rivaled only by the square in front of the Winter Palace in St. Petersburg.

In Moscow's former times traders used to congregate by the Kremlin to offer their wares. The quarter where the stalls and booths were set up, between the eastern wall of the Kremlin and the Moskva, was called *Veliki Possad* – Great Settlement. The trade routes from all corners of the realm met here. After the great fire of 1403 the Muscovites renamed their market place simply *Pozhar*, "The Fire." During the 17th century the merchants built a number of imposing houses here and once again the square's name was changed, this time to *Krasnaya Ploshchad*, which in the Russian of those days, meant not only "Red Square" but also "Beautiful Square." There was always something happening on this open space – the magnificent processions of the czars or of the patriarchs and their acolytes. The autocratic boyars and rebels were executed on Red square, and Stenka

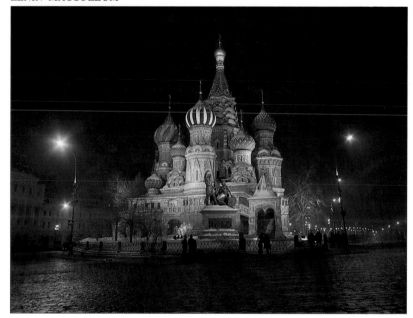

Razin was drawn and quartered here. Following the 1917 Revolution the square, which is 1650 ft by 495 ft (500 m by 150 m), was used for parades and processions, military march-pasts and announcements of national importance.

Each year on Labor Day (first May) and on the anniversary of the October Revolution (7th November) Red Square saw tens of thousands of workers and soldiers marching past the Lenin Mausoleum where the party leaders stood. It was only in 1991 that military parades were finally abandoned.

The **Lenin Mausoleum** stands in front of the Senate Tower and is the most modern building on Red Square – a monument, a tomb, and a grandstand all in one. Vladimir Ilyich Lenin had decreed that no cult should grow up around him after his death: the founder of the Soviet Union always lived an ascetic life and

Above: St. Basil's Cathedral and the memorial to the national heroes, Minin and Pozharsky.

wished to maintain this simplicity in death. Stalin, however, took advantage of the situation to further his own aims and turned Lenin's funeral, in January 1924, into a state ceremony of great pomp. It enabled him to establish himself in the eyes of the people as the champion and guardian of Lenin's policies. Lenin's body was embalmed and initially interred in a temporary wooden mausoleum. A solid oak mausoleum followed in the spring of 1924, already prefiguring the present form of the tomb. It was not until 1930 that Lenin's body was placed in the austere monument of dark red granite and black labradorite, designed by Alexei V. Shchussev. For many decades the world was accustomed to the sight of elderly party leaders saluting parades from the mausoleum. Plans to finally move the body to the family crypt in St. Petersburg where his wife Nadezhda Krupskaya lies have not yet been put into action.

Inside the mausoleum Lenin's embalmed body was preserved in a specially lit crystal sarcophagus. Until the final

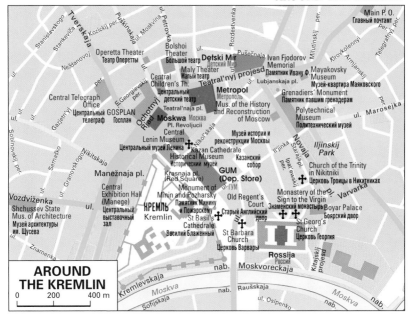

AROUND THE KREMLIN

0   200   400 m

phase of Communism this place was the inner sanctum of the Soviet Union which the visitor approached with bated breath. The endless stream of the curious who filed past Lenin's body day after day was strictly supervised.

In the *Glasnost* era it became known that a team of scientists was dedicated to maintaining the state of Lenin's body and constantly controlled the appearance and condition of the corpse. Few visitors know that in the spring of 1953 Stalin's body was placed alongside that of Lenin and the inscription over the entrance was altered to include Stalin's name. As part of the policy of de-Stalinization, Khrushchov ordered the removal of the dead dictator from the Mausoleum and had his body buried in the Kremlin wall, in the grove of blue spruce trees behind the mausoleum, where he now lies in a pantheon of noted Communist dignitaries. Those paying homage to Lenin's body would, on leaving the mausoleum, pass these graves of revolutionaries and party leaders, in the Kremlin wall.

The **Cathedral of St. Basil** – the dominant feature of Red Square – may rightly be called the most fabulous building in Russia and cannot be surpassed in bizarre beauty, bewildering architecture and deep historical resonance. The poet Lermontov said that "its somber appearance" oppressed his soul. He believed he could see in it the embodiment of the spirit of Ivan the Terrible. The French traveler Astolphe de Custine compared it "with an irregular fruit bristling with excrescences." Arthur Holitscher went so far as to speak of a "porcupine with armored devices on its skin." In short, these writers were dumbstruck at the sight of the cathedral and had to search for the strangest comparisons.

The Cathedral of St. Basil was built by Ivan the Terrible, who ordered the erection of a church on the "Beautiful Square" to commemorate his victory over the Tartars. Since the Russians celebrate *Pokrov* on 1 October, the festival of the Veil of the Blessed Virgin Mary, and the date on which the Cathedral was

67

consecrated in 1559 it was called at first *Pokrovskiy Sobor shto na Rvu*, or the Cathedral of the Veil by the Moat. Ivan IV gave the architects Barma and Postnik Yakovlev a free hand in the design of the cathedral, stipulating only that the church should be beautiful and radiate joy.

Although the external appearance of the cathedral is bewildering, the design of St. Basil's is in fact quite simple: four chapels form the shape of a cross whose intersection is the site of a fifth chapel. Four further chapels occupy the spaces between the arms of this star-shaped structure. The nine churches each have a tower, so that from the outside the view is a confusing one of nine vibrantly colorful cupolas, none of which resembles any of the others. The largest tower in the center culminates in a conical spire with a small onion dome above it. The church was given its present name by Czar Fyodor Ivanovich, who had a tenth chapel added

Above: St. Basil's Cathedral.
Right: Inside the GUM department store.

in 1588, in which the mortal remains of the itinerant preacher Vasily Blashenny were buried. Since that time Muscovites have called the Pokrovsky Sobor (which in the recent past has been restored once more to the Orthodox Church) **Vasily Blashenny Cathedral**. At that period the cathedral was given its decorated onion domes. A bell-tower was added on the southeastern side in 1670. On his withdrawal from Moscow Napoleon wanted to destroy this church too, but the general in command did not carry out his order. In 1954 restorers uncovered wall paintings and carvings dating from the founding of the church. Although the chapels are opulently decorated and covered with frescoes they cannot be compared with the ornate exterior.

In front of the church is the **Monument to Minin and Pozharsky**, the national heroes, who in 1612 were instrumental in the expulsion of the Poles. The sculpture, executed between 1804 and 1818 by Ivan Martos, is the earliest secular monument in Moscow. The inscription reads: "To Citizen Minin and Prince Pozharsky – from a grateful Russia, 1818." Not far from the monument is the **Place of Execution** (*Lobnoye mesto*), which is marked by a round stone platform. This was where decrees from the czar and the Church were pronounced, where the czar addressed the people, and where death sentences were pronounced and carried out.

Red Square is bounded on the north side by the Historical Museum and on the east by the **GUM Department Store**. Both buildings are striking and unmistakable from the outside. In the case of the GUM store it is the unbroken façade which is so evident and is nearly half the length of the Kremlin wall opposite.

GUM's long, low emporium was built by Alexander Pomerantsev in 1889-93 under the name of Upper Trading Arcade. His client was Czar Nicholas II, who rented the shops to merchants. The Upper Trading Arcade was given a transparent roof of iron arches and plate glass. In 1953 the complex was completely renovated and reopened as GUM, the largest store in the Soviet Union. GUM stands for *Gosudarstvenny Universalny Magazin*, which means simply "Universal State Department Store."

The enormous complex consists of three length-wise arcades and transverse arcades, linked with one another by a system of bridges and galleries. In the days of the Soviet Union 300,000 people would pass through the store daily in order to grab from the total of 1 1/2 miles (2.5 km) of shop displays all those things that could be found nowhere else. GUM was for decades a propaganda flagship for the USSR, part of socialist mythology. No foreign journalist would file his report without a stroll through GUM – after all, the whole Soviet Union used to do its shopping there.

In 1973, a German journalist wrote: "One can only say that GUM is overwhelming." He went on: "The store has

corridors, galleries, bridges, dungeons, halls, and little temples, which make it look like one of the architectural fantasies of a Piranesi. Here too there are processions, queues without beginning or end which move slowly forward over floors and up staircases. This is indeed the ideal of a socialist society, where the high-ranking officer stands patiently besides the worker's wife..."

This fine, poetic description may have seemed appropriate enough in Brezhnev's time, but everything changed after *Perestroika*. Firms from the West have opened branches here and GUM is losing its socialist character. Having started life as an upper-class bazaar, GUM is again becoming an international city of shops, a department store with many traders and well-known western companies who certainly give the customers what they want, but do not forget to line their own pockets in so doing. All these have considerably altered the solid, comfortable image of the socialist department store. Little here has anything to do with the state any

more, but, out of reverence and the sense of comfort provided by its name, the old familiar GUM is still called GUM.

HISTORICAL MUSEUM

The red brick **Historical Museum** (*Istorichesky Muzei*) is a particularly pleasing sight because of its white roofs, countless turrets and ornamental gables, called *kokoshniki* after a traditional women's headdress. This was formerly the site of the old town hall, which the scientist Lomonossov intended to turn into Moscow's first university. The Archaeological Society commissioned V. Sherwood (a Russian, despite his name) and A. Semyonov to build the Historical Museum on this site, which they did between 1875 and 1881, and it was to play a significant role in the development of Muscovite architecture at the turn of the

Above: The Historical Museum. Right: The Church of St. George in front of the Rossiya hotel. Far right: A street portraitist.

century. Experts in architectural history say that this museum provided the inspiration for the reconstruction of the center of Moscow. The architects' conception of the building was that it should become a memorial to the epoch and a symbol of Russia. The dominant idea at that time was Russian nationalism which found expression in architecture among other things. Architects sought a counterbalance to the palaces of Italian and French architects, who up until then had put their stamp on St. Petersburg. It thus becomes clear why the design of the museum's façade incorporated old Russian motifs in the form of pyramid-roofs, *kokoshniki,* miniature staircases and other ornamental elements, borrowed from early Russian architecture. The architects' idea was that the whole building should in itself be regarded as a historical exhibit.

Sherwood's task was enormous: Red Square already had a very special aesthetic character, which it owed to the towers and churches of the Kremlin as well as St. Basil's Cathedral. He divided

his massive building into many different stylistic elements which harmonized with the Kremlin and the Cathedral. The great brick building thus blended pleasingly with its surroundings without losing its own particular aesthetic quality The Museum can definitely hold its own alongside the Kremlin and St. Basil's.

The task of the Historical Museum was to document the history of Russia's vast empire, from earliest times to the present day, through objects that were either exceptional or typical, from all the peoples and nationalities of the Russian Empire. Of course this museum is in a situation of considerable difficulty at a time of national upheaval and new consciousness. The vast holdings – more than 4.5 million collected items – must be catalogued again and classified. The things that are to be kept include: Prehistoric man *Sinanthropus*, who lived from 400,000 to 300,000 years ago, the Scythian and Greek finds from the Black Sea coast, documents of early Russian history, such as the *Russkaya Pravda*, believed to be

the oldest book of Russian law. The most diverse historical epochs are documented here – such as the history of Novgorod from the 10th to the 15th centuries, the rule of Peter the Great, and Russia's rise to a world power in the 18th and 19th centuries. For over 10 years the museum remained closed. In 1997, finally, a good dozen exhibition rooms were once again opened to the public.

KITAY-GOROD

Moscow's trades and crafts quarter used to lie on the eastern side of Red Square, behind where the GUM now stands. In the 16th century this district was surrounded by its own town wall with watch towers, which presumably gave rise to the name of the quarter: **Kitay-Gorod** – from the old Slavonic word *kita*, meaning stakes used to fortify a wall. Parts of this wall have been preserved on Teatralnaya Square and on the Kitaisky Proyezd. In the 17th century there were still 72 rows of houses with

approximately 700 businesses and shops. Many of these houses have now disappeared, but the quarter is still worth strolling about in.

The **Nikolskaya Ulitsa** (street) begins on the northern side of the GUM. The pretty little **Kazan Cathedral** was built up here again in the mid-1990s. It had originally been constructed in 1636 to celebrate the chucking out of the Polish invaders from 1612. For over 200 years, the icons of the God Mother of Kazan were kept here, the symbols of Russia's steadfastness in the face of strife. The cathedral was torn down in 1936 because it allegedly stood in the way of parades being held on Red Square.

On the corner facing the Historical Museum stands a house built in 1740 for the Governor and his staff, and beside it the Mint dating from 1697. At No. 7 it is worth making a detour through the courtyard to the Zaikonospassky Monastery,

Above: Some of the spaces in front of Metro stations like veritable free-trade zones.

founded in 1600. In 1687 the monastery opened Russia's first higher education institute, the Slavonic, Greek and Latin Academy, where the polymath Lomonossov was taught.

Another important building in this street is No. 15, with the Synodal Press and the Imperial Printing Works where Ivan Fyodorov printed the first book in Russian in 1564. However he had to flee to Poland where he was better able to pursue his newfangled trade. The memorial sculpted by Sergei Volnukhin in 1909 shows Fyodorov standing erect, holding in his right hand a fresh proof, his left hand resting on the press.

Ilyinka Ulitsa runs parallel to Nikolskaya. This was formerly the principal business street in Kitay-Gorod. The most striking building is the **Old Arcade** (*Stary Gostiny dvor*), built between 1790 and 1805 to plans by Giacomo Quarenghi. The huge façade with Corinthian columns is most impressive. The former Moscow **Stock Exchange** built in 1875 by Kaminski is also well worth seeing.

Parallel to the Ulitsa Ilyinka runs the Ulitsa Varvarka, which formed the boundary of the old Moscow dock area Zaryadye, one of the most overcrowded and dirtiest districts of old Moscow. It was demolished during the 1960s to make way for the **Rossiya Hotel**. With 6,000 beds this hotel ranks among the world's largest. The 23-storey complex is dominated by a 312 ft (95m) high tower and has, in addition to numerous conference suites and many other facilities, a concert hall which seats 2,500.

We should be grateful to Moscow's town planners for thoughtfully leaving untouched the many churches which surround the Rossiya Hotel. Close to St. Basil's Cathedral is the small **Church of St. Barbara** (*Tszerkov Varvary*), built in 1794 in the classical style. The small, solidly built house next to it is the **Old English Inn** (*Stary Angliski Dvor*), which was given to the English merchants in Moscow by Ivan the Terrible in 1556. The white church of **St. Maxim** (*Tserkov Maksima*) dates from 1699.

On the other side of the flyover that leads to the Rossiya Hotel is the **Old Regent's Court** (*Stary Gosudaryev Dvor*), which once belonged to the boyar Romanov family, and also the **Monastery of the Sign to the Virgin** (*Znamensky Monastyr*). After Mikhail Fyodorov had founded the Romanov dynasty, he endowed this monastery, which was built on his estate. Czar Fyodor had the cathedral with its five cupolas built between 1679 and 1684. The House of the Romanov boyars, No. 10, dates originally from the 17th century, but was authentically restored in the 19th. It houses a museum furnished to show how the boyars lived in the 16th and 17th centuries.

St. George's Church (*Tserkov Georgiya*) on the Pskov Hill, built in 1697, completes the list of sites to visit on the Ulitsa Varvarka.

The house (*palata*) of the artist Simon Ushakov, who as the father of *chiaroscuro* had a decisive influence on Russian icon painting in the 17th century, is in the Ipatyevski Pereulok. One of his works can be admired close by: in the neighboring Nikitnikov Pereulok (lane) the visitor will find one of Moscow's most beautiful churches – the **Church of the Trinity in Nikitniki** (*Tserkov Troitsy v Nikitnikakh*). The Moscow merchant Grigori Nikitnikov had the church built between 1635 and 1653 next to his business on the site of a former warehouse. The iconostasis was made by the best artists from the Kremlin armory. The icons "The Trinity of the Old Testament" and "The Annunciation" are worthy of note. Simon Ushakov's work is represented here as well as that of the notable Russian icon painters Yakov Kazanets and Gavril Kondratyev. The church is surmounted by five domes.

FROM REVOLUTION SQUARE TO THE BOLSHOI THEATER

The district between the GUM and the House of the Trade Unions, between Manezh Square and the Metropol Hotel, has much to offer culturally: some of Moscow's most important theaters are to be found here, including the Bolshoi. Students of architecture will find a visit here especially rewarding: the group of buildings are of so many varied styles, that this district could be described as an open-air museum of architecture.

The **former Lenin Museum** is opposite the Historical Museum, set up in the building of the former city *duma* or council. The house was built by D. Shchagov in 1890-92 in a pastiche-historical style, which contrived to outdo even that of the neighboring Historical Museum. Something like 800,000 items were assembled here – first editions, manuscripts, photographs and speeches, as well as objects relating to Lenin's private life – but at no time were more than 13,000 exhibits displayed in the museum's 34 rooms. Now

that the founder of the Soviet Union is disgraced, President Yeltsin had the museum closed in November 1993, without attempting to re-evaluate communist history. On the upper floor a commercial concern now organizes fashion shows.

The short section of the street between Tverskaya (formerly Gorki Street) and Theater Square is now once again called Okhotny Ryad – "Hunter's Row." During the Soviet era this broad street was called Prospekt Marksa. It is dominated by three imposing buildings.

The **Moskva Hotel** was built in 1933-38 as the principal and hence appropriately representativehotel of the Soviet capital. Under the direction of the architect Alexei Shchussev (who planned the Lenin Mausoleum) the building with its several tower-like structures achieved its final form. The 14-storey front façade of the hotel which overlooks Manezh

Above and right: The Bolshoi Theater – synonymous with ballet. Every performance is both a social and an artistic experience.

Square commands attention with its imposing five-storey high portico.

The building of the former State Planning Department **Gosplan** totally dominates the beginning of Tverskaya Ulitsa. It was built in 1936 by the architect A. Langman. The monumental style of its architecture is subtly relieved by echoes of the modern functionalist style.

The **House of the Trade Unions** (*Dom Soyuzov*), one of the most interesting buildings in the metropolis, stands opposite the Moskva Hotel. The main part of the building was erected in 1784-87, in the classical style, by the celebrated architect Matvei Kazakov, for Prince Dolgoruky. It was later bought by the Moscow Assembly of Nobles, which in fact was a gentlemen's club. The building stands on Pushkin street, stretching from Okhotny Ryad to Georgiyevsky Pereulok. The front façade is enhanced by a six-column portico. The architect's masterpiece is the pillared hall whose 28 pillars faced with imitation marble give it a majestic appearance. Above the Corin-

thian columns Kazakov set in huge windows, each tapering to a point, which lend a floating, vaulted effect to the ceiling of the room. The result can truly be described as a great example of classical interior architecture as well as being the best venue in Moscow for classical concerts. Pushkin and Lermontov, Turgenyev and Tolstoy once used to attend the balls held by the nobility here, and it was here that Dostoyevsky made his famous "Pushkin" speech in 1880, which was a call to arms in the intellectual battle for Russia. After the Revolution important political conferences were held here, including the Comintern Congresses. It was in this room in January 1924 that the young Soviet Union took its leave of Lenin. And it was in this same splendid hall, during the 1930s, that Stalin staged the big show-trials of the apparently discredited Bolsheviks, including Kamenev, Zinoviev and Bukharin. The dictator occasionally used to observe the proceedings from the gallery. To the west of the House of the Trade Unions, the oldest

private house in Moscow can be found in an inner courtyard. Parts of it date from the 16th century and it was enlarged in the 17th century by a boyar named Troyekurov to create a small palace on the banks of the Neglinnaya, which in those days used to flow by here.

The Bolshoi Theater, the Maly Theater and the Central Children's Theater lie to the east of the Dom Soyuzov. If one were to name a single place in which Russian culture has been shaped and where it has found expression, it would have to be the **Bolshoi Theater**. The history of the Bolshoi, one of the best and most famous stages for ballet and opera in the world, began on 28th March 1776, when Prince Uruzov was granted the right to stage plays in Moscow. For this purpose he was obliged to build a handsome theater of stone and thus it was that the Petrovka Theater opened in 1781, named after the nearby Ulitsa Petrovka, and where the first actors were his serfs. After the fire of 1805 Carlo Rossi built a new theater on the Arbat which was in turn destroyed by the great fire of Moscow in 1812. Then, in 1825 the theater was rebuilt on the old site near the Petrovka. It was designed by the architects Andrei Mikhailov and Bove, in the classical style with the characteristic eight-column portico and the bronze quadriga of Apollo. When the interior was destroyed by fire in 1853 the architect Cavos remodeled the Bolshoi Theater in the most magnificent style.

First performances of works by the greatest Russian composers including Tchaikovsky, Rimski-Korsakov, Mussorgsky and Glinka were given at the Bolshoi, whose name simply means the "Big" Theater. The world-famous bass, Fyodor Chalyapin, sang here, and it was here that Galina Ulanova danced her immortal ballet roles. However the Bolshoi did not immediately assume its leading role in the world of opera and ballet: for decades it had to survive in competition with the theaters of St. Petersburg. The breakthrough finally came in 1877 with the first performance of Tchaikovsky's "Swan Lake." An evening at the Bolshoi is one that the visitor will never forget, even if only because of the opulent neo-Baroque interior.

The **Maly Theater** is, so to speak, the little brother of the Bolshoi. It was opened in 1824 as a theater staging only dramas and is the oldest establishment of its kind in Moscow. Originally built to house businesses, the building was redesigned in 1838-40 by Konstantin Thon, who had the ground floor arches bricked up and a second portico built on to the north façade, so that the building became strictly symmetrical in form. The "Maly" adopted a deliberately didactic role during the last century and for this reason the theater was called Moscow's "second university." The famous dramatist Alexander Ostrovsky enjoyed a very close association with this theater for thirty years

and almost all his plays were performed here. So it is understandable that a memorial to Ostrovsky by the sculptor Nikolai Andreyev was unveiled in front of the theater in 1929.

Opposite the Maly Theater the visitor will find the **Academic Youth Theater,** which was founded in 1921 as the first professional theater for a young audience.

On the other side of Teatralny Proyezd is the new five-storey Moskva Hotel. It looks deliberately simple and harmonious in design, particularly when compared to the **Metropol Hotel** opposite, which contemporary critics described as "a modern Tower of Babel." Walcot, who designed the building between 1899 and 1903 in the early Art Nouveau style, punctuated the whole façade with countless balconies and bay windows, pointed towers and projections. Large areas of the façade are decorated with majolica and ceramic, which lends the building a whimsical air of dreamy romanticism. The most conspicuous majolica picture depicts Princess Greza and is to be seen on the side overlooking Teatralny Proyezd. It was executed to designs by Mikhail Vrubel, the leading exponent of National Symbolism. G. B. Shaw spent his 75th birthday at the Metropol.

LUBYANKA SQUARE, NEW SQUARE, OLD SQUARE

To the east of the fairy-tale castle of the Metropol, a section of the old fortified wall comes into view, which once screened the mercantile quarter of Kitay-Gorod from the rest of Moscow. Following the wall along Teatralny Proyezd one comes to the memorial to Ivan Fyodorov, the first printer of books in Moscow. From the foot of this memorial there is a good panorama of the circular **Lubyanka Square**, a name that goes back to before the Revolution. It was later named after Feliks Dzerzhinsky, the founder of

Right: New Square – not everything in Moscow has fallen to the pickaxe.

Cheka, the secret police, which was the forerunner of the modern state security service, the KGB. Opposite the memorial is the famous children's store *Dyetsky Mir* (Children's World), which until a few years ago offered everything a child could dream of. The building can be recognized easily by its high portal windows. Like GUM, this store too was one of the great Soviet myths. You would not guess from looking at this imposing building that it was only put up in 1953-57, on the site of the earlier Lubyansky shopping arcade.

At the end of Teatralny Proyezd, opposite the children's store, stands the former insurance building which, from 1947 onward, was the headquarters of the KGB. It was chosen, presumably, because in underground rooms beneath that building, the czar's secret telegraphic service formerly operated. The very name "Lubyanka" spread fear and terror throughout the land for many decades. Czar Paul I had the telegraph office disbanded, but the basements were preserved and put to use once again during the Soviet era as a prison. The memoirs of dissidents of the Soviet regime are full of recollections of this notorious dungeon. After the August coup of 1991 the secret service was split into three, but in essence little has changed: this organization is still the unseen embodiment of power throughout the country.

And yet Lubyanka Square shows visible signs of the changes of the post-Glasnost period: it was here that, following the failed reactionary coup, angry Moscow citizens of all ages demolished the huge memorial to Feliks Dzerzhinsky in front of the world's television cameras. Like all the other bigwigs of the Soviet era "Iron Feliks" found his way to the memorial graveyard at the Central Artists' House opposite Gorky Park, where other Soviet figures have been unceremoniously dumped.

It is not very far from his empty pedestal to the **Mayakovsky Museum** on the Prospekt Serova, which runs parallel to **New Square** (*Novaya Ploshchad*).

Vladimir Mayakovsky, the powerful poetic voice of the Revolution, lived in No. 3 on the square for eight years. His name was synonymous with the bright hopes and bitter disappointment of the October Revolution, and finally, for this and other reasons, the poet who is still popular today, committed suicide on 14 April 1930, bringing to an end a life that had been wrapped in myth. In his memory his house was turned into a museum. Between Prospekt Serova and New Square lies the massive bulk of the Polytechnical Museum, founded in 1872. Various phases of building between 1877 and 1907 can be distinguished.

The **Museum of the History and Reconstruction of Moscow** also stands on New Square and a visit here is essential for anybody who is interested in architecture. It is housed in the Church of St. John the Evangelist, a classical building

Above: Singer and actor Vladimir Vyssotsky captured the soul of Russians from all walks of life.

with French influences. This museum is concerned with the history of Moscow from its beginnings as a small village on a hill above the Moskva, to the metropolis we are familiar with today. Unfortunately the post-Revolutionary period is still under-represented, so that there is very little to study from the important phase of avant-garde architecture during the 1920s and 1930s. Despite this, anyone wishing to acquaint themselves with the thinking behind Moscow's development will want to visit the museum. The **Shchussev State Museum of Architecture** in Ulitsa Vozdvizhenya provides further scope for study.

Old Square (*Staraya Ploshchad*), lies between New Square and Nogin Square, parallel with Ilyinsky Park. The monument in the park was erected in honor of the grenadiers in the battle of Plevna during the Russo-Turkish War of 1877-8. From here there is a view over all the rows of houses on Old Square.

To the right stands the building of the one-time Muskovite traders guild, created in 1909 by Fyodor O. Shekhtel. It shows that beauty can be functional and creates the impression of weightlessness. Beside it stands the imposing neoclassical edifice built by Vladimir Sherwood. This was the HQ of the Central Committee of the Communist Party of the Soviet Union until shortly after the August coup of 1991 and today houses important government offices.

After this comes the so-called **Boyar Palace**, a hotel and business house built in 1901, the design of which was also the work of Shekhtel. Because of the originality of its design this building has been much imitated. The architecture of its lower storeys is simple and plain, whilst the upper floors are emphasized with balconies. The famous architect took care to show the elegant way the framework of the building was constructed. The Church of **All Saints in Kulishki** takes up the south side of the Old Square.

INNER CITY OF MOSCOW

Accommodation

The hotels in Moscow are summarized in the chapter entitled **Travel Information**. See page 243.

Museums / Churches
Sightseeing

Kremlin: A tour of the **Kremlin** gives you an overview of historical and architectural monuments from six centuries (15th-20th.). You should definitely see: The **Cathedral of the Assumption** (*Uspensky Sobor*), the **Cathedral of the Annunciation** (*Blagoveshchensky Sobor*), the **Archangel Cathedral** (*Arkhangelsky Sobor*), and the **Church of the Deposition** (*Tserkov Rizopolozheniya*) with its valuable ikons. Among the secular buildings it is important to mention: The State **Armory** (Czars' clothing, jewels, collection of old weapons, tableware, paintings, sacred objects), the **Palace of Facets**, the **Patriarch's Palace**, **Bell Tower of Ivan the Great and Czar's Bell**, the Czar's Canon, *Czar pushka* as well as the **Museum of Applied Art**; opening times vary; viewing is sometimes only possible in groups, Tel: 921 4720. The **Kremlin Wall** with 20 bastions or towers: The finest are *Spasskaya Bashnya* on Red Square and the *Troitskaya Bashnya* with the *Troitsky Most (bridge)*. By the Kremlin Wall is the **Lenin Mausoleum** (no longer open to the public) and graves of leading communists.

Red Square: St. Basil's Cathedral (*Vassily Blashenny*) and the **Marian Votive and Protection Cathedral** with the memorial to Minin and Pozharsky; **Historical Museum**, only some of the rooms are currently open. Nearby is the **Central Lenin Museum**, also closed at the present time.

In the historic district of **Kitay-Gorod**: The **Kazan Cathedral** (*Kasanski chram*) and the **Old Arcade** (*Stary Gostiny Dvor*) in Ulitsa Ilyinka; the former **Stock Exchange**; in Ulitsa Varvarka in Zaryadye, **St. Barbara's Church** (*Tserkov Varvary*) and the **Boyar Museum in the Old Regent's Court** (16./17th Cent. house at Nr. 10). The **Znamensky monastery**, **St. George's Church** and the sumptuously decorated **Trinity Church in Nikitniki**, Nikitnikov Pereulok 3.

Sightseeing in the rest of the city center:
Central Exhibition Hall (former riding-school), Manezh Square 1-9. Historic **Hotel Metropol** on Teatralny Proyezd. **Shchussev State Museum of Architecture**, Ulitsa Vozdvizhenka 5. **Museum of the History and Reconstruction of Moscow**, Novaya Ploshchad 12. **Vladimir Mayakovsky Museum**, Proyezd Serova 3/6. The legendary **Bolshoi Theater**, to be seen for its remarkable architecture, is on Teatralnaya Ploshchad.

Theaters and Concert Halls

Bolshoi Theater (Opera and ballet), Teatralnaya Ploshchad (Metro: Teatralnaya), Tel: 292 9986. (serious drama) **Maly Theater**, Teatralnaya Ploshchad 1-6 (Metro: Teatralnaya), Tel: 924 4083. **Operetta Theater**, Pushkinskaya 6 (Metro: Teatralnaya). **Chekhov Arts Theater**, (*Khudozhestvenny Teatr*) Kamergersky pereulok 3 (Metro: Okhotny Ryad), Tel: 229 2127. **Molodjoshni teatr** (Young People's Theater), Teatralnaya Ploshchad 2-7 (Metro: Teatralnaya), Tel: 292 0069. **Palace of Congresses** in the Kremlin. **Central Concert Hall "Rossiya"** (Hotel Rossiya), Moskvoretskaya Naberezhnaya 1 (Metro: Kitay-Gorod), Tel: 298 3694. **Concert Hall**, Znamensky Sobor Cathedral), Ulitsa Varvarka 8 (Metro: Kitay-Gorod). **Hall of Pillars in the Trade Union House** (*Dom Soyuzov*), Pushkinskaya 1 (Metro: Teatralnaya).

Restaurants

EXPENSIVE: **Glasur**, Smolenski bulvar 12, Tel: 248 4438. Kropotkinskaja 36, ulitsa Pretschistenka 36, Tel: 201 7500. MODERATE: **Aragwi**, Caucasian cuisine, ulitsa Twerskaja 6, Tel: 229 3762. **Podworje**, ulitsa Marosseika 9, Tel: 923 8505. Praga, ulitsa Arbat, Tel: 290 6171. **Babuschki**, Bolschaja Ordynka 42, Tel: 230 2797. FAST FOOD: **McDonald's**, Gasetny pereulok 6, Tel: 956 9816. In the department store GUM grilled chicken Rostiks, upstairs, third aisle.

Nightlife Bars / Casinos

Manhattan Express (Hotel Rossija, northwest side), Tel: 298 5354/55, 7 p.m.-5 a.m., Disco and live music. **Casino** Club Savoy (Hotel Savoy), ulitsa Roshdestwenka 3 (Metro Kusnezkij most), Tel: 929 8500, 8 p.m.-5 a.m.

Medical Help

Medical Center (AMC), 2. Twerskoi-Jamskoi pereulok, Tel: 956 3366. **International Medical Clinic**, Grocholski pereulok 31, 10th floor, Tel: 280 8374. **US Dental Care** (dental clinic), ulitsa Schabolowka 8, Haus 3, Tel: 236 8106. All with western standards and fees based on US dollars.

Police

Militsiya, Tel: 02. **Accidents**, Tel: 925 5510.

Post / Telecommunications

International post office: Warschawskoje chaussee 37, Tel: 114 4645. Main post office: ulitsa Mjasnizkaja 26, Tel: 928 6311. **Central Telegram Service**: ulitsa Twerskaja 7, ulitsa Wosdwishenka 22, Tel: 927 2002. Fax and modem connections are available in the business centers of hotels.

Tourist Information

INTOURIST, Mochowaja ulitsa 13, Tel: 292 1278.

MOSCOW'S MUSES AND MUSEUMS

TVERSKAYA / PUSHKIN SQUARE
BOLSHAYA NIKITSKAYA
ARBAT / PUSHKIN MUSEUM
OF FINE ARTS
ZAMOSKVORECHYE /
TRETYAKOV GALLERY

TVERSKAYA, PUSHKIN SQUARE

Tverskaya Street, which from 1935 to until 1991 was named Gorky Street after the famous author, is probably Moscow's most important commercial street. The stage-coaches leaving for the cities of Tver and Novgorod, and later St. Petersburg, used this route. Recently Ulitsa Tverskaya has changed a lot. On the ground floors of the solid, granite-clad buildings, many new companies and elegantly appointed hard-currency shops are springing up.

If you start your walk at the lower end of the street, near the Kremlin, you pass two hotels: the Moskva, a gray-brown monolith in the monumental style of the workers' state, and on the left the National, to whose old building a modern skyscraper has been added. On the same side is the **Central Telegraph Building.** Designed by Rerberg in 1930, it is an example of Russian constructivism.

Beyond the memorial to Prince Dolgoruky, Moscow's founder, stands the **Hotel Tsentralnaya** (formerly Lux); with its yellow façade, it has outlived the many alterations to the city center.

Left: The young people of the city show a new awareness – and not just because of western advertising.

The Moscow Arts Theater, in a narrow street opposite the Telegraph Building is fine example of Art Nouveau architecture. This side street takes you past a number of bookshops and to the TSUM (Central Department Store) on Petrovka Street. One block north is Stoleshnikov Lane (*Stoleshnikov Pereulok*) – a pedestrianized shopping-street. Opposite the Dolgoruky Memorial is a tall red building with white pillars, which was built in the 18th century for Count Chernyshov, the Governor of Moscow. The house is now occupied by the city council.

At numbers 12 and 14 on the right hand side you will see an interesting gray-painted town house in the Russian Art Nouveau style with unusual railings, bay windows and balconies. Nearby is Yelisevsky 's famous delicatessen, in a neo-classical building.

In the early 19th century this was the home of Princess Sinaida Volkonskaya, "the queen of the muses and of beauty." A friend of Pushkin, it was in her salon that the literary and artistic élite of Russia used to meet.

One of the capital's largest and most magnificent squares is **Pushkin Square**, with its statue of the great poet, unveiled in 1880. At one time a monastery stood here, but it was demolished by the Bolsheviks to make way for a thoroughfare.

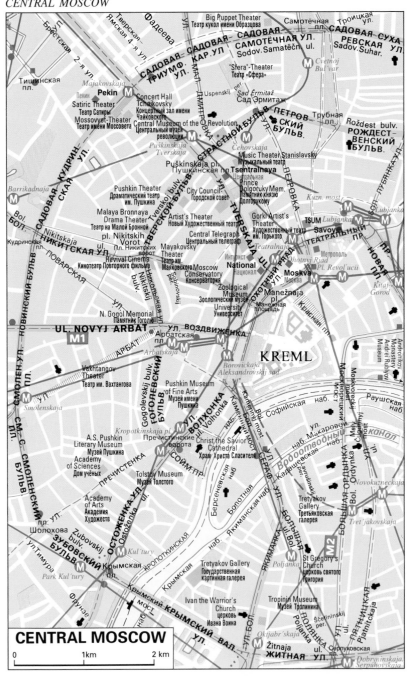

CENTRAL MOSCOW

0   1km   2 km

In the early years of the revolution poets and imagist artists wrote lines of verse on the monastery walls, and illustrated them with little paintings. Their message was unwelcome at the time.

The square is where Tverskaya St.. meets the Tverskoi Boulevard, which boasts two fountains and two theaters: on the left the Artists' Theater (recognizable by its decorative streetlamps) and on the right the Pushkin Drama Theater.

Pushkin Square is famous for its demonstrations and rallies. In the years of "stagnation," it saw the famous gathering of the dissidents, who were protesting against the violation of human rights. However, even in the years of *perestroika*, meetings were again broken up by the police. The editorial offices of many newspapers and magazines are based here. Outside the offices of *Moskovskiye Novosti* something akin to Speaker's Corner in London's Hyde Park has grown up, where people with opposing views on the current political situation shout themselves hoarse in vehement debate. In the long pedestrian subway, hawkers selling newspapers, books and pornographic magazines do a brisk trade. At the other end of Pushkin Square is Moscow's largest cinema, the Rossiya. To the left of the Pushkin Memorial, there is a modern office-block and the newspaper offices of *Izvestiya,* a gray, 1930s constructivist building.

Another attraction, the MacDonald's 'burger house, caused a sensation when it first opened. In spite of relatively high prices, the queues of hopeful customers broke all records. But the fuss has died down a bit now.

Behind some iron railings stands No. 21 Tverskaya, a red house whose gate is guarded by two lions. It was built in the classical style towards the end of the 18th century for Vasilchikov, one of the favorites of Catherine the Great. It was later occupied by Count Razumovsky, arts patron much loved by the ladies.

After the great fire of 1812 it was rebuilt for the Persian prince Khozrev-Mirza, and was later taken over by the British Club. The house has since been converted into the **Central Museum of the Revolution,** with armored vehicles and artillery pieces in the courtyard.

Leading off from Pushkin Square, by the Rossiya, is Chekhov Street, today the administrative heart of the Moscow District. The Art Nouveau house on the corner was the Merchants' Club in Czarist times, and later a famous theater. The church next to it is unusual: it has no façades but, rather like St. Basil's Cathedral, it should be viewed as a piece of sculpture, from every side.

From Chekhov St., you can turn down the narrow Uspensky Pereulok and take a break in the Hermitage Gardens.

BOLSHAYA NIKITSKAYA ULITSA, ARBAT, PUSHKIN MUSEUM OF FINE ARTS

Nearly all the streets in the city center were renamed in the 1920s and 1930s, but today many are being given back their old names. Take Ulitsa Gertsena, for example, which was re-given its former name **Bolshaya Nikitskaya**. It begins at Manezh Square, outside the Kremlin walls. Gertsena recalls Alexander Herzen ("Gertsen" in Russian, which has no letter H), who belonged to that mid-19th century group of intellectuals who devoted their lives to the improvement of conditions for the poor. On the left is the old part of the university and the student theater which was famous in the 1970s for its outspoken views. On the right is the university's **Zoological Museum**, founded in 1791. Its collections include more than 170,000 vertebrates and over a million insects. In pride of place is a dinosaur skeleton.

The nearby Moscow Conservatory is the center of musical culture in Russia. It is linked with the names of famous com-

posers like Tchaikovsky and Rachmaninoff, and leading musicians who have taught or studied here include Sviatoslav Richter and Mstislav Rostropovich.

On the corner of Sobinovsky Pereulok you will find the Mayakovsky Theater and nearby the State Institute of Dramatic Art. The narrow streets leading off Herzen St. to the left and right are particularly popular with the intelligentsia. Many famous actors, writers, painters and musicians once lived and worked here – nearly every house has a commemorative plaque.

As you enter **Nikitsky Gate Square** (*Ploshchad Nikitskiye Vorota*) and look around you, the first thing you notice is the Revival Cinema, where the best films of the past are shown. The modest church on the far side of the square dates from the 18th century. It was here that Alexander Pushkin married Natalya Goncha-

rova, the most famous Muscovite beauty of her day. The town house opposite was designed by Shekhtel in the Art Nouveau style. In the 1930s it was the home of the most important revolutionary author, Maxim Gorky, after whom a park and a river embankment are still named; until recently a Metro station (now called Tverskaya), a street and the city of Nizhny Novgorod all bore his name. Although Gorky lived for years on the island of Capri, he was one of the most influential personalities in the Soviet Union; the destinies of many depended solely on a word from him.

One of the finest theaters in Moscow, the **Malaya Bronnaya Drama Theater** is to be found in a narrow street of the same name. Originally this building housed the Jewish Theater, but in 1948 its director, the outstanding actor Solomon Mikhoels, was murdered by the secret police and the theater was closed down.

On the Tverskoy Boulevard which joins Herzen St. from the right, stands a

Above: Not a theater but the Riga Station.
Right: You should never go out without your shopping-bag.

memorial to the biologist Timiryazev; behind it are some ornamental lamp-posts which have no cultural significance but adorn the entrance to public toilets.

However, we now turn left into Suvorovsky Boulevard and head towards Arbat. In the courtyard of No. 7 stands a **memorial to Nikolai Gogol,** one of the most important of all Russian authors. The statue used to stand at the end of Gogol Boulevard and represented the doyen of Russian letters as a madman, which indeed he was. That is why the statue has been tucked away in the courtyard of the house where he spent the last years of his life. Meanwhile, a healthy-looking but infinitely more boring Gogol can be seen on the boulevard.

An underground footway now brings us to the pedestrianized **Arbat**. The renovated buildings and private houses are painted in bright, glowing colors. Until the end of the 17th century it was the artisans' quarter, as the old names of the side streets still testify. But in the 18th century it became a fashionable place for aristocrats to live. Even today, in the large, chronically overcrowded tenements, you may come across some elderly lady, descended from an aristocratic family, who has miraculously survived the purges of the 1920s and '30s.

Nowadays the Arbat is certainly the liveliest part of Moscow, even though the authorities put a stop to street entertainment by *ukaz* (decree) in the summer of 1993. Until then the Arbat thronged with traders and artists, poems were read out in public and political debates were conducted; actors and musicians to suit every taste would perform here. You could have your portrait painted and pick up souvenirs, books and antiques. Children could be photographed with characters from fairy tales, before pleading with their parents for an ice cream. Until then, orange-garbed young devotees of Rama Krishna danced and played their way through the crowds of pedestrians. Sadly,

all this activity is a thing of the past. The cafés, shops, picture galleries and the Vakhtangov Theater now wait for customers who never come. Returning to the Gorky Boulevardpause for refreshment at the popular **Praga** restaurant.

You now turn right along the boulevard to Kropotkin Square (*Kropotkinskaya Ploshchad*) and from there turn into Volkhonka St. This brings you to the **Pushkin Museum of Fine Arts** (*Muzei imeni Pushkina*) with castings and copies of ancient and medieval sculptures on display, including one of the finest copies of Michelangelo's *David*, and many works from ancient Egypt, Assyria, Babylon, Greece and Rome. Among Russian museums, the Pushkin is second only to the Hermitage in St. Petersburg in its fine collection of masterpieces of western European painting. It possesses more than 3,000 paintings, 350,000 drawings and engravings, as well as 100,000 coins and medals.

In September 1997, right on time for the 850th anniversary of the city of Mos-

cow, the Christ the Savior Cathedral was consacrated. It was completed in 1880 after 40 years work on it, and was intended to commemorate Russia's 1812 victory over Napoleon. But Stalin decided that the Palace of the Soviets should be built on the spot, so in 1934, the church was torn down and excavations made to pour the foundations. The ground, however, was not safe for building, so instead, the authorities built a huge open-air swimmingpool. The rebuilding of the cathedral, with its splendid golden dome, is controversial in light of the country's unsolved social problems. The project cost US$ 250 million, partly from donations, for the most part, however, from state coffers.

Turning right, off the Gogol Boulevard, one enters a street which is traditionally named Prechistenka ("Holy") but was renamed Kropotkinskaya in

Above: A real treasure-house: the Pushkin Museum of Fine Art. Right: Kitsch and art mix freely on the Arbat.

1921, after a revolutionary scholar and writer. Today it looks like a museum of 18th and 19th century architecture.

Between here and the banks of the river Moskva, noble families lived in palatial residences, which have been marvelously preserved. On many of them you can see plaques commemorating the Decembrists, those nobles who took part in the first uprising against the Czars, in December 1925. Famous artists, poets and writers later lived here. Prechistenka is also the address of the Academy of Sciences, the Academy of Arts and museums devoted to two of the greatest figures in Russian literature: Pushkin and Tolstoy.

Though **Alexander S. Pushkin**, the greatest of Russian poets, only lived 38 years, from 1799 to 1837, he remains unequaled in Russia, before or since. Many events in his life are shrouded in mystery and even his death is enigmatic. One of his ancestors, the dark-skinned Abram Hannibal, was brought from North Africa by Peter the Great, as his secretary; and

although Pushkin himself was small and ugly, he captured the hearts of the most beautiful women. A passionate and violent-tempered man, he constantly clashed with officials and even with the czar himself. His barbed epigrams and progressive poetry twice caused him to be exiled from the capital. Documents on his life and work are exhibited in the house where he lived, now the **A. S. Pushkin Literary Museum** (*Dom Pushkina*).

Lev N. Tolstoy is without doubt the best known of all Russian authors. He was a man full of contradictions: aristocrat and farmer, plutocrat and ascetic, devout Christian, yet irreconcilable opponent of the established church, author of complex works of philosophy and aesthetics as well as of simple children's stories. Tolstoy (1828-1910) in a strange way embodied both kindness and despotism, logic and inconsistency. Evidence of all this can be gathered from the countless exhibits in the **Tolstoy Museum** – manuscripts, portraits, personal possessions and memoirs of his contemporaries.

At the end of this long walk you can stop off at **Margarita's** restaurant (*U Margarity*), only a few steps from here.

ZAMOSKVORECHYE – TRETYAKOV GALLERY

South of the Kremlin, on the other side of the Moskva river, lies Zamoskvorechye, the old part of Moscow, which is all under historic preservation. Some of the street names recall the days of Tatar rule from the 13th to 15th centuries. Thus the name of the street running from the Moskvoretsky Most (bridge) to the Little Iron Bridge (*Maly Chugunny Most*), is Balchuk, which is the Tatar word for "mud." Oddly, this name is also that of a smart five-star hotel, owned by the Kempinski chain. The area was indeed once filthy, damp and boggy, but at the end of the 18th century a drainage channel was dug to dry it out.

Once the channel was completed, part of Zamoskvorechye was transformed into a long horseshoe-shaped island, con-

nected to the city center by three bridges. The island is mostly covered with industrial buildings, but contains two important monuments. One is the only building in Moscow that has survived virtually intact from the 17th century. Called Kirillov House, it is rumored to have once belonged to a trusted servant of Ivan the Terrible – his hangman. Today it houses a research institute.

In addition to this group of old Russian houses, there is the church of St. Nicholas and a building from the Stalin era, the **Embankment House** (*Dom na Naberezhnoy*). It was built in 1931 for members of the government and their families, as well as for people who had rendered particularly valuable services to the state. It was not just a house, but an entire town, with its own shops, post office, hairdresser, kindergarten, crèche, bank, gymnasium, canteen, even a theater and a cinema. Here the privileged few could buy

an almost limitless choice of high-quality goods at unbelievably low prices. Yet in spite of its luxurious apartments and many creature comforts, the house has an evil repute. Only now that archives have been opened, is it revealed that there was a secret way in and out, connected to all the staircases via the basement, and through which people who had been arrested were spirited out of the building. The house and the fate of those who lived in it are described in a novel, *The House on the Embankment*, by Yuri Trifonov.

Of the three bridges which link the island to the city center, the **Great Stone Bridge** (*Bolshoi Kamenny Most*) is the most impressive. Strictly speaking, it was only made of stone between the 17th and 19th centuries, after which it had to be replaced by an iron structure. In its present form, it dates from the 1930s. Its cast-iron balustrades are decorated with sickles, flags and other Soviet symbols, and the sides are clad in granite. Before crossing the bridge, you get a wonderful view of the Kremlin from the embankment.

Above: The Great "Stone" Bridge.
Right: Timid attempts at avant-garde art.

Our route now takes us into the "continental" part of Zamoskvorechye, Moscow's mercantile quarter, which is completely different in character from the center of the city. The great 19th century Russian dramatist, Alexander Ostrovsky, called it "a land that no traveler has ever written of." But it was he who, in his plays, portrayed the half-provincial, half-Muscovite life and customs of the merchants of Zamoskvorechye.

Here, perhaps more than anywhere else in Moscow, the streets still look much as they did in the Middle Ages: long, symmetrical rows of modest town houses, all very alike, and many magnificent churches, where, after several decades of silence, services are once again being held. A particularly fine one is **St. Gregory's Church** (*Tserkov Svyatovo Grigoriya*). Dating from the 17th century, it is in the Bolshaya Polyanka, one of the five main streets of the district. There is even a poem about this church, with its decoration of tiles in many bright, glowing colors.

Another beautiful church is that of **Ivan the Warrior** (*Tserkov Ivana Voina*). On the opposite side of Yakianskaya St. you will see a merchant's house looking like a carved wooden toy. It now houses the French Embassy.

In a side street, Lavrushinsky Pereulok, between Ordynka and Polyanka Streets, you will see some remarkably fine wrought-iron railings. Behind them is the Pedagogical Library.

Also in Lavrushinsky Pereulok is the best thing that Zamsokvorechye has to offer – the world-famous old **Tretyakov Gallery**. Many passers-by still do not know how to find it. It was closed for so long that it had been forgotten. The gallery, named after its founder, was opened in 1881. At that time almost all the better known Moscow painters were moving to Zamoskvorechye, where they captured on canvas the tranquil gardens and courtyards and the colorful local community.

Another resident was Pavel Tretyakov, a wealthy industrialist and art connoisseur, who bought up a remarkable collection of works by Russian masters, and in 1892 donated it to the city of Moscow. Since that time the gallery's acquisitions have increased substantially: from 1,200 to 57,000 works, making it the most important existing collection of Russian art.

The gallery building has undergone numerous alterations, and its most recent renovation saved it from complete dilapidation. It now awaits visitors in its new-found splendor. Inside you will see a wonderful collection of old Russian painting, and works by artists of all schools and styles, but with the emphasis on realism.

Do not be disappointed, when visiting the gallery, if you find no catalogue or reproductions for sale. These can however be bought at sales kiosks near the gallery or in the nearby Metro stations of Oktyabrskaya, Dobryninskaya, Polyanka and Novokuznetskaya. Try to leave time to call in at the tiny little shop next to the Tretyakov Gallery, where local art students sell their work. There are some exceptionally fine canvases to be bought there, at well below market prices.

In the wide and usually deserted **Bolshaya Ordynka** street, between impersonal two-storied houses, half-covered by creepers, you can find marvelous examples of architecture from the 17th to 19th centuries: churches in every imaginable style from Old Russian to Classical, and fine old porticoed town houses.

At the **Tropinin Museum** in Shchetininsky Pereulok you can make a closer acquaintance with Russian painting of the 18th and 19th centuries. Its full name is the Museum of Vassily Tropinin and Moscow Artists of his Time, and most of the works are portraits. Tropinin himself was a serf who was not freed until he was fifty years old.

In the old commercial street, **Pyatnitskaya**, with its dozens of shops, stalls and cafés, there is always an alluring smell of fresh bread. But the popular bakery that it comes from is – Australian!

Accommodation

The hotels in Pushkin are summarized in the chapter titled Travel Information. See page 243.

Museums

Pushkin Museum of Fine Arts, Wolchonka 12, Tel: 203 7998; 10 a.m.-7 p.m., closed Mon. **A. S. Pushkin Literature Museum**, Pretschistenka 12/2, 11 a.m.-5 p.m., open until 6 p.m. in summer; closed Mon and Tue. **Lew Tolstoy Museum**, Pretschistenka 11; 11 a.m.-6 p.m., closed Mon and the last Fri of the month. **Tretjakow Gallery** (old), Lawruschinski pereulok 10, Tel: 231 1362; 10 a.m.-7 p.m., closed Mon. **Tretjakow Gallery** (new), Krymski wal 10, Tel: 230 7788; 11 a.m.-8 p.m., closed Mon.

Theater and Concert Halls

Teatr imeni Mossoweta, Bolschaja Sadowaja 16, Tel: 299 3377. **MCHAT imeni Gorkowo**, (Gorky arts theater) Twerskoi bulvar 22, Tel: 203 6188. **Teatr imeni Pushkin**, Twerskoi bulvar 23, Tel: 203 8582. **Musikalny teatr imeni Stanislawskowo i Nemirowitscha-Dantschenko**, Bolschaja Dmitrowka 17, Tel: 229 2835. **Teatr imeni Wachtangowa**, Arbat 26, Tel: 241 0728. **Teatr Satiry**, Triumfalnaja ploschtschad 2, Tel: 299 6350. **Teatr "Sfera," Karetny rjad 3, Sad Ermitash, Tel: 299 0292.** Teatr"U Nikitskich Woro,",Bolschaja Nikitskaja uliza 23/9, Tel: 202 8219. **Teatr kukol imeni Obraszowa** (marionette theater), Sadowaja-Samotetschnaja 3, Tel: 299 3310. **Konsservatorija** (Bolschoi sal; Maly sal/ Large/Small hall), Bolschaja Nikitskaja ulitsa 13, Tel: 229 7412, 229 7446. **Konzertny sal imeni Tschaikowskowo**, Triumfalnaja ploschtschad 4/31, Tel: 299 3957.

Restaurants

EXPENSIVE: **Bojarski Sal**, Teatralny projesd 1/4 (Hotel Metropol), Tel: 927 6089, Russian, **Le Romanov**, ulitsa Baltschug 1 (Hotel Kempinski), Tel: 230 6500, closed Sundays, Russian. **Savoy**, Roshdestwenka ulitsa 3 (Hotel Savoy), Tel: 929 8600, Russian. **Pekin**, Bolschaja Sadowaja ulitsa 5/1, Tel: 209 2124, Chinese. *MODERATE:* Belfiori, ulitsa Petrowka 10, Tel: 924 5423, Italian. **Ispanski ugolok**, Ochotny rjad 2, Tel: 292 0294, Spanish. **Uncle Guilly's**, Stoleshnikow pereulok 6, Tel: 229 2050, grill restaurant. *BUDGET:* **Annushka**, Zwetnoi bulvar 7, bar and grill. Kafe Begemot, Spiridonewski pereulok 10, Tel: 202 9286. **Kafe Margarita**, Malaja Bronnaja ulitsa 28, Tel: 299 6534. *FAST FOOD:* **Pizza Hut**, Twerskaja ulitsa 12.

Casinos

Karo Complex, Puschkinskaja Ploschtschad 2 (Cinema Rossija), Tel: 229 0003, with disco.

Chimki-Chovrino
Medvedkovo
Degunino
Babuškin
Tušino
Goljanovo
Strogino
MOSKVA
Izmajlovo
Moskva
Fili-Mazilovo
Kuncevo
Perovo
Matvejevskoje
Nagatino
Lublino
Z'uzino
Bel'ajevo-Bogorodskoje
Lenino
Orechovo-Borisovo
Čertanovo
Bir'ul'ovo

MOSCOW'S OUTER DISTRICTS

GORKY PARK
NOVODEVICHY CONVENT
ANDRONIKOV MONASTERY / ANDREI RUBLYOV MUSEUM
OSTANKINO
ALONG THE MOSKVA
KOLOMENSKOYE

GORKY PARK, SPARROW HILLS

There can hardly be a westerner who has not heard of **Gorky Park**. American author Martin Cruz Smith wrote a bestselling thriller called *Gorky Park*, featuring a Moscow detective: "Arkady crept from tree to tree along the edge of the clearing, hid behind the trunks and scanned the patches free from snow yard by yard. Just as he was about to move again, the light of a torch flashed in the shallow pit from which the bodies of the murdered men had been recovered. Arkady had ventured about ten yards outside the clearing when the light went out. Who's there? he called. Someone ran off into the darkness."

You may be pleased or disappointed, but in reality nothing very terrible happens in the park – even so, it is not altogether advisable to go walking there at night. During the day, however, and towards the evening, particularly on public holidays, the park is an enjoyable place.

Perhaps Cruz Smith was inspired by another writer, Yuri Trifonov, who the park an "unexplored continent, in which

Previous page: St George fighting the dragon in a 16th-century icon. Left: The towers of the Novodevichy convent.

there are caves and jungle, a place where a shot rings out, shattering the deepening silence, where a rowan thicket may take on a different, more sinister shape..."

The park lies on the right bank of the Moskva and covers an area of approximately 270 acres (110 ha.) The oldest and most beautiful part, with its groves and clearings, is the spaciously laid out **Nyeskushniy Sad** (garden) which spreads picturesquely up the hillside.The park's delightful ornamental architecture includes pillared pavilions, small bridges, fountains and arbors.

This old garden once belonged to the Nyeskushnoye estate which Czar Nicholas I acquired in 1839. Today the Russian Academy of Sciences is housed in the palace and other buildings. In one of the small Empire-style houses is the Museum of Mineralogy, which was founded by Peter the Great. The Museum's collections are fascinating, even for adults, and it is here that childhood dreams of geological expeditions begin and a visit here will inspire children to carry home all sorts of stones.

On the other side the Nyeskushniy Garden extends as far as the Green Theater, (*Zelyony Teatr*) where actors, and rock and jazz groups appear during the summer. In recent years all kinds of youth festivals have been held here and

sometimes competitions too, of the "Miss Lovely Legs" or "Miss Best Boobs" variety, which have met with disapproval from some of the older generation. The amusement park borders on the Nyeskushniy Garden, with fairground attractions, playgrounds, cafés, restaurants and a summer theatre. There are often tremendous crowds here.

The park is the traditional meeting-place for war veterans. Some of these are grey-haired old men, for whom the 1941-45 War is the most important thing in their lives, others are the young men who fought in the war in Afghanistan. These meetings are at once sad and joyful.

When you have had enough of the hustle and bustle you can take a ride on the Ferris wheel and enjoy a view of the city. From a height of about 160 ft (50 m) the whole of Moscow lies at one's feet; this is Moscow seen in the way the Muscovites like to think of their city: vast,

Above: Russian humor is not always very sophisticated.

flourishing, beautiful, and without a care in the world.

On the left behind the *Luzhnikovsky Most* (bridge) is the Central Palace of Young Pioneers and Schoolchildren, which stands out in fine contrast to its hilly surroundings, and offers everything children need in the way of instruction, sport and recreation, even a winter garden with tropical plants. On the right, the Vorobyovskoye Shossé (high-road) leads to the **Observation Point**. It was from here, high above Moscow, that in 1812 the Emperor Napoleon gazed with anticipation over the city, though he did not succeed in conquering it.

There is another spot which provides a magnificent panorama of the metropolis and for this one must drive up on to the Lenin Hills, which have now reverted to their former name of **Sparrow Hills**. The hills are in fact the continuation of Gorky Park and are popular with everyone: it is almost obligatory for newly married couples to come here after their wedding; film-makers have for a long time used this little bit of paradise for location shoots (and in fact, Mosfilm, the country's largest film studio, is one of a number in the area); government ministers also enjoy it, and on both sides of the Vorobyovskoye Shossé, behind a high yellow stone wall, stand large houses which were formerly the residences of members of the Politburo and which today provide accommodation for VIP guests of the government.

On the other side of the river, at the foot of the high ground, is the **Luzhniki Sports Park** with two stadia, a swimming pool and many other facilities – in all about 140 sports resources. At the foot of the bridge, near the stadium, you will see a vast market. Here, as at the other markets in Moscow, a large number of the stallholders are Vietnamese. There is almost nothing you cannot buy here but when you visit the market you should take care to remove cameras and bags

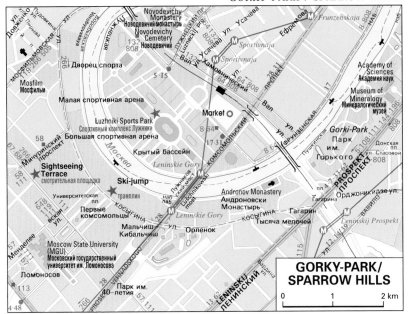

**GORKY-PARK/
SPARROW HILLS**

0   1   2 km

from your shoulder and zip up your pockets, because it is not only the market traders who do business here.

In the lush park below the observation platform are several fine buildings dating from the 18th and 19th centuries: a palace, and monastery buildings which used to house Moscow's first school. But none of these can be seen from above. Towering over the area is a ski-jump.

You should now take a look at the **Moscow State University (MGU)**. It is the best and most highly respected educational establishment in the country. The complex was built between 1940 and 1953 in the so-called "wedding-cake" style of Stalinist architecture. The central section consists of a 788 ft (240m) high tower crowned with a 197 ft (60m) high spire. The buildings of the various faculties lie behind and to the side of the complex, as do the observatory, the Botanical Gardens, the library, a theater, and various shopping-centers. The whole campus is surrounded by parkland where students can relax in their free time.

NOVODEVICHY CONVENT

North-west of Luzhniki is the **Novodevichy Monastyr** (*New Maidens' Convent),* which, in spite of its name, is linked with many bloody events in Russia's history. The convent is in a perfect state of preservation and, together with its church and cemetery, is one of Moscow's most interesting architectural monuments. It is worth devoting quite a long time to your visit. The convent belongs to a ring of fortified monasteries which, from the 16th century onward, were built outside the gates of Moscow. Grand Duke Vassily III had the extensive convent complex erected in gratitude for the liberation of the city of Smolensk from Polish-Lithuanian occupation in 1524. After the execution of the rebel boyars, Ivan the Terrible compelled their widows to enter the convent and to hand over all their possessions to the church. Later on, wives and daughters of czars (czarinas and czaritsas) entered the convent, some willingly, some less so. In this manner the

New Maidens' Convent acquired 36 villages and land totalling some 700 square miles (1800 sq. km), and so became Moscow's wealthiest foundation. The convent's most important benefactress was Sophia, Peter I's ambitious half-sister, under whose seven-year-long regency in the name of Peter, then a minor, and of his mentally defective brother Ivan V, the convent was extended and restored in the style which was later called "Moscow Baroque." She had to take the veil because of her treacherous role in the mutiny of the *Streltsy* of 1697, and the walls she had built became her prison for the rest of her life.

In 1812, when Napoleon was retreating from Moscow, French soldiers had dug trenches and put barrels of gunpowder in place, but at the last moment a nun, risking her life, managed to extinguish the fuses and save the convent.

Above: This stronghold of faith became an actual fortress. Right: The Novodevichy is venerated by the Russians.

After the Revolution, however, the convent fell into disrepair. It was dissolved in 1923 and in 1934 the Party handed the site over to the Historical Museum. It was not until the Brezhnev era that the monastery was restored. It now serves the church again.

The convent is entered by the north gate with its Church of the Transfiguration, built in the Moscow Baroque style. Opposite is the **Cathedral of the Mother of God of Smolensk** with its five domes and magnificent frescoes. The church, which was built by Czar Boris Godunov in 1524-5 stands at the centre of the whole complex. A famous icon of the Mother of God, which was lost during the war, used to hang in this bare and austere cathedral.

The **Bell Tower**, 236 ft (72m) high, stands by itself on the left. It was built in 1690 and lavishly restored in 1988. The distinctive tower, built in the graceful style known as Naryshkin Baroque, by unknown craftsmen, is the most famous part of the convent. To the west of the ca-

thedral is the dining-hall (*trapeza*) with the Church of the Assumption of the Virgin, and adjoining it to the rear is the Church of St. Ambrose. The church of the Veil of the Virgin lies by the south wall of the convent facing the cemetery. Four of the five convent churches serve as museums and services are only held in the Church of the Assumption.

The **Cemetery** (*kladbishche*), which is also simply known as **Novodevichy**, lies adjoining the southern wall of the convent. This is the cemetery for Russia's most eminent departed. A family who has one of its members buried here counts for something these days. This was not always the case, and in former times it was the custom for common people to be buried near the Novodevichy convent, far outside the gates of the city. It was only during the last century that Russia's poets and philosophers, musicians, artists, and scientists chose the Novodevichy as "their" cemetery. The new élite of the Soviet Union, in no way averse to the blandishments of vanity and snobbery, followed this trend. A visit to the convent and its vast cemetery outside the walls is one of the most delightful tourist attractions in the Russian capital.

The cemetery's main entrance is on the Luzhnetsky Proyezd. Only a few years ago uniformed guards curtly turned tourists away. Today, by contrast, visits have been promoted commercially: anyone willing to pay may go in.

Every grave in the Novodevichy Cemetery has its own story. For example, the simple grave of the celebrated author Mikhail Bulgakov, who wrote *The Master and Margarita*, had no headstone for twelve years. His widow, Yelena Sergeyevna, could not come to terms with this and one summer's day in 1952 she took a stroll past the shed used by the graveyard attendants, where she saw in a corner a black, pitted lump of stone. A workman explained that this was "a darned nuisance" – the centenary of the death of the famous author Gogol in March 1952 had been marked by a refurbishment of his grave: the great eccentric of Russian literature had received a worthy memorial for this special day, a suitably fine bust had been sculpted by N. Tomsky (this stands in the Novodevichy) and Gogol's old gravestone, (the"darned nuisance") had been thrown on to the rubbish heap. Yelena Bulgakova scarcely needed time to consider the matter and made an offer for the stone. A few days later the monstrosity was heaved on to her husband's grave. Graves need headstones, after all. Admittedly, secondhand gravestones are rather an exception, even here. Gogol winks mischievously across from his pedestal, as if to say: "The story of the gravestone could be one of my own..."

The reason why Bulgakov had no gravestone for such a long time is simple: people were scared to do anything. After 1940, no cemetery director or sculptor wanted to have anything to do with the disgraced writer. Bulgakov had ridiculed Stalin's Moscow in his novel *The Master and Margarita* as no other writer had dared. He made the Devil and his monstrous cat Behemoth perform their mischief in the capital! Because of this Bulgakov became a non-person and, as such, he could not have a headstone.

In the Soviet Union even the dead were a political issue and history pursued them right to their graves. Someone who was particularly shabbily treated was Nikita Sergeyevich Khrushchov, removed from office in 1964. When he was buried in the Novodevichy in 1972, his successor Leonid Brezhnev ordered that the cemetery be closed, for fear of demonstrations. Today things are different and – in principle – the cemetery is open to everyone. The **Khrushchov monument** by Ernest Neizvestny is *the* tourist attraction. The sculptor used black and white granite in order to express the contradictory nature of the party leader. Nikita Khrushchov, a

zealous pupil of Stalin, also had a lot of skeletons in his cupboard, although he denounced the crimes of the great dictator in his famous secret report of 1956.

A long, leisurely stroll through the Novodevichy is at the same time a unique journey through the history and culture of Russia. The opera singer Fyodor Chalyapin is buried here, as are the pianist Emil Gilels, the composers Alexander Skriabin and Dimitri Shostakovich, the film directors Sergei Eisenstein and Dziga Vertov, the painter Valentin Serov, as well as the art collectors Pavel and Sergei Tretyakov. The visitor who can read cyrillic script is at an advantage.

Between all these graves runs an invisible dividing line of ideology and aesthetics, for it was not only the Russian intellegentsia who were buried here. A place was given here after death to anyone who had held a high position in the Communist Party, in the Red Army, or in the field of Soviet science. The proud relatives would usually have a lifelike image of the deceased carved in stone, looking as he would have done in the prime of life, and the likeness would be mounted on a high plinth. Consequently, the cemetery sometimes looks like a garden of larger-than-life sculptures – and the effect can be rather overpowering. Generals and scientists, members of the Party hierarchy and Admirals of the Fleet, in immaculate uniform and with erect posture, scrutinize the visitor with a penetrating gaze, as though they were still alive and might climb down from their pedestals at any moment. Generals of the tank corps would be allowed a stone tank on their gravestone, air-force generals a jet fighter.

In contrast, the old intelligentsia is represented in an understated way. The grave of the Symbolist poet Andrei Bely, a follower of Rudolf Steiner, is adorned with a small, slender column. It is impossible to imagine that he would have wanted to be placed there, larger than

Right: A Sunday artist works on a painting of the Novodevichy convent.

life, in a rhetorical pose. The last resting place of the lyric poet Alexander Tvardovsky is marked by nothing more than a heavy boulder – connoisseurs of the literary scene will appreciate this allusion to the oppressive burden of his work as editor- in-chief of the literary journal *Novy Mir*. Anton Chekhov's grave is a simple white stone with a metal roof. In contrast to this the dazzlingly white memorial of the singer Fyodor Chalyapin on the main avenue seems rather ostentatious. In the mid-1980s his relatives had his mortal remains brought over here from Paris. Every grave in the Novodevichy Cemetery tells its own distinctive story. The convent and cemetery can be reached by Metro (Sportivnaya Station).

ANDRONIKOV MONASTERY AND ANDREI RUBLYOV MUSEUM

There is another part of Moscow with a distinctive atmosphere and which fortunately benefits from a preservation order. It begins at the Ustyinsky Most (bridge) and is called **Zayauzye**, because it lies (*za*: beyond) on the far side of the river Yauza, a large tributary of the Moskva.

In old travel guides nothing favorable was ever said about Zayauzye: the streets there were crooked and bad, they ran steeply down to the riverbank, and it was dangerous to drive down them even in summer; there were many beggars and homeless, and "decent people" had no reason to go there.

Now a great deal has changed there, even though Zayauzye has in many respects retained its earlier character: the same low, ugly houses in the crooked little streets interspersed with attractive churches and palaces.

The whole area is dominated by a giant high-rise building nearly 600 ft (176m) high, on the Kotelnicheskaya Naberezhnaya (embankment). To the east of it, on the Yauza, the **Andronikov Monastery** has stood for more than 600 years. The Musocovite Metropolitan Aleksei founded it in the 14th century in memory of his amazing rescue from a terrible storm,

which caught him by surprise on his way back from Constantinople. However, the monastery is named after its first abbot, Andronik, and it became famous because of the legendary monk and painter Andrei Rublyov, who lived there at the beginning of the 15th century.

Oddly we know very little and yet a great deal about this outstanding artist. We know where he lived and worked, even what he looked like and the people with whom he was acquainted. Yet up till now neither his grave nor one single icon bearing his signature has been found on the monastery site. The frescoes he painted in the Cathedral of Our Savior, built 1410-27, are irretrievably lost. Andrei Rublyov was a very modest and unassuming man and since he usually did not work alone, but always together with his pupils, he never signed his own name on the icons. He commanded unusually

Above: The Andronikov monastery and its museum of Russia's greatest icon-painter. Right: Triumph in space – a nations' pride.

high respect within the monastery because of his just and pious life, and after his death he was depicted on icons with a halo. During his lifetime he was evidently little known, only achieving fame as an artist at the very end of his life. Yet soon after his death people began to copy his work, for he was from then on held in the same high esteem as the famous Byzantine masters.

It is no surprise, then, that he should have given his name to the **Andrei Rublyov Museum of Early Russian Art**. Although there are no icons here which were painted by Rublyov himself, those icons which hang on the walls of the monastery museum are true treasures. In Moscow the only icons which are believed to be Rublyov's work are in the Kremlin cathedrals and in the Tretyakov Gallery.

The view of the monastery from the river is wonderful. Behind the white-walled battlements of the fortified monastery on the hillside towers the magnificently decorated Church of the Archan-

gel Michael, which was used by the noble family Lopukhin, relatives of Peter the Great, as a funeral chapel. Almost every building of the monastery, which has been under a preservation order since 1947, is constructed in a different style. Of particular beauty is the **Cathedral of the Savior** (*Spassky sobor*), which was built in white stone, between 1410 and 1427. Originally it was a church built on a four-pillar design with three apses and a cross dome.

Unfortunately the church suffered damage during various rebuilding works and the in great fire of Moscow in 1812, when Napoleon entered the city. The refectory (1504-6), which resembles a small fortress, also deserves a visit.

The Andronikov Monastery has always been a center of culture. Now, as a museum, it continues its old traditions. But rumors that the former monastery will be returned to the church abound, and if you visit Moscow it may be that the seat of spiritual instruction behind these walls will again be welcoming pos-

tulants, and services will be held in the cathedrals. Perhaps the tombs in the monastery necropolis will be restored to their former glory – many important Russians are buried here.

Do take advantage of the services of the museum guides, because they are true scholars steeped in Russian culture.

OSTANKINO: VDNKh – MUSEUM OF SERF ART

The next tour takes us far into the northern part of the city, to **Ostankino**, including visits to the place where the country's glorious past is documented, for decades hidden behind the abbreviation **VDNKh**. It stands for "Exhibition of Economic Achievements". Only a few inordinately large reminders remain of the earlier exhibition, which was intended to symbolize the power and greatness of the world's first socialist state and of the largest country on earth: for example the 80 ft (25m) high entrance gate decorated with sculptures, and a number of pavilions and fountains. Someone described the exhibition most appositely as the memorial to a country which no longer exists.

Yet this exhibition complex offers a unique opportunity to see the culture and symbolism of the vanished communist era, to experience its grand dreams and also its delusions, and to get a feeling for the belief of the people that the life it offered was the best one possible. Here you can recapture in your mind all the optimism that is summed up in a popular song of the period: "Today will be better than yesterday, and tomorrow will be even better than today."

Many details of the exhibition appear in retrospect to be a mockery of reality – for example the showpiece of the exhibition, the fountain of "International Friendship" with fifteen female figures representing the republics of the Soviet Union and their steadfast friendship with one another. One only has to think now of the bloody fighting in Armenia and Georgia, the resentment against the Russians in the Baltic states and Ukraine, the rumblings in Central Asia...

In the 1960s, when the exhibition was in its heyday, there really was something worth seeing there. In the "Cosmos" pavilion for example there were – in contrast to many of the other exhibition halls – genuine achievements on display. But even at that time it was an open secret that almost everything that was displayed was the only one of its kind in existence. Today, however, at of the entrance to the Space Pavilion, you can admire a multistage rocket just like the one which made the first ever manned space flight, in 1961 – and man in question was a Russian, Yuri Gagarin.

Leaving the exhibition site by the north exit, the visitor will see the most famous work in Soviet art, Vera Mukhina's

Right: "Factory-worker and Woman from a Collective Farm," by Vera Mukhina.

sculpture *Worker and Woman from a Collective Farm*. This sculpture embodies the ideological union of the industrial workers and the farming community, and in 1937 it adorned the Soviet pavilion at the World Fair in Paris. Of course when Mukhina was working on this piece, which was intended to enhance the reputation of the Soviet Union, during the late 1930s, she was under the strict supervision of the security services. One night she was suddenly arrested. It turned out that one of her guards had somehow got the impression that the face of Trotski, Stalin's archenemy, was leering out from the steel folds of the dress worn by the woman from the collective farm. Fortunately the misunderstanding was quickly cleared up.

Behind the sculpture stands another symbol of the former strength of the USSR: the Soviet pavilion from the 1967 Montreal World Fair. The Canadian press of the day described this as the best designed pavilion in the entire history of world fairs. The hall was brought back here from Canada.

All these things are the supposed successes and genuine achievements of the past. Right now Russia does not, unfortunately, have any grand projects to get excited about, but surely a nation with so much energy, intelligence and imagination will come up with something before too long.

Today a number of the buildings are rented out to various firms who use them as offices and for sales exhibitions, but chiefly as shops for the trade in goods from China, South Korea, Taiwan, and India. Dozens of cooperative kiosks over the whole site now trade in the produce of the "economic achievements of the peoples of Asia."

The restaurant, 985 ft (300m) up, near the top of the Ostankino **Television Tower** is called "In Seventh Heaven." This tower, 1770 ft (540m) high in total, is the tallest structure in Europe, and can

be seen from every part of Moscow. Completed in 1967, it was an attraction which, despite its high prices, enjoyed great popularity in the first few years after it opened. The restaurant occupies three floors and rotates on its own axis once every forty minutes. On a clear day, or more precisely on a smog-free day, one can see over the whole expanse of Moscow.

The engineer N. Nikitin drew up plans for the original TV tower in a few days. He required more time to work out the static equilibrium, but the construction of the tower, together with the television center which stands next to it, was completed in what was, for Russia, a short time: only five years. The tower looks elegant and almost weightless, though it weighs 50,000 tons and is built to withstand even the most violent storm. At any rate it has so far withstood the onslaught of crowds of visitors every day.

It is only in the last thirty years that the name of Ostankino has been synonymous with television in the minds of Musco-

vites, but for more than 300 years it was the name of a former aristocratic estate famous for its 17th- and 18th-century monuments which have been given the name of the **Palace Museum of Serf Art**.

The **Church of the Trinity**, a red brick building with five green onion domes, dates from the 17th century, and is the oldest of the buildings preserved here.

When, a century later, the estate came into the possession of the nobleman Nikolai Sheremetyev, one of the enlightened princes who were patrons of the arts, he had a palace built on the site which was exclusively the work of serf architects, craftsmen, and artists.

Sheremetyev founded a theater with 200 serfs as actors, singers, dancers and musicians. His theater company was reckoned to be one of the best in Moscow, and its repertoire included more than one hundred dramas, operas and ballets. The star of the company was the gifted singer and actress Praskovya Kovalyova-Zhemchugova, a young serf

with whom the prince was madly in love. His love was so intense that he broke all the conventions of the time, gave Praskovya her freedom and married her. Long before the wedding the prince began to build a theater for his beloved, and spared no cost or effort in the process. Italian architects were invited to draw up the plans for the building which was to be in the main section of the palace, but its true creators were the native serf architects Mironov, Dikushin and Argunov.

It was a wonderful palace, constructed entirely in wood, but with a plaster rendering designed to make it look like stone. The whole of the mosaic floor is made of wood, as are the chandeliers and the *faux-marbre* colums. The laurel branches and the gilt furniture show some of the finest wood carving by the nobleman's serfs. In the palace there were galleries for pic-

Above: Stalin's "wedding-cake" architecture.
Right: Apartmentblocks, considered a great achievement of Socialism.

tures, etchings and sculptures, as well as banqueting halls, but the central space was occupied of course by the theater. This was technically equipped in an unusual way for its time which permitted not only special scenic effects but also the conversion of the auditorium in the space of a few minutes into a ballroom – for dances were also held here.

However, the happiness of the prince and the actress was shortlived. Praskovya died at the age of 26, leaving behind an inconsolable Sheremetyev. He lost all interest in his theater and had the buildings turned into a home for the sick and destitute. The hall was restored not long ago, and is now used for holding exhibitions of works by Russian and west European artists, and to show the chandeliers and works of art created by the serfs. Sometimes concerts are held there.

The palace is surrounded by a **French Park** with many sculptures. Paths laid out in the form of a star lead through the park, to the ponds, beyond which lies the main botanical garden of the Academy of Sciences. Flowers and trees not found in our latitudes flourish in the warm, damp air of the orangery, lianas twine upwards and the huge green leaves of exotic water plants float in the pools.

ALONG THE MOSKVA

The visitor who seeks respite from the wearying tours of the city and the noise of the traffic can, for a change, sit back and let the city drift past. There are many steamer trips along the Moskva river, which flows through the city and its suburbs for 37 miles (60km), forming a large semicircle. The most pleasant trip is the one that leaves from the Ustyinsky Bridge and finishes at the Kiev Station (*Kievsky Vokzal*). It enables the visitor to appreciate many of the sights described elsewhere, from another perspective.

Immediately to the right, beyond the jetty on Moskvoretskaya Naberezhnaya

(embankment) is the Rossiya Hotel. It is the largest hotel in Europe and even has a concert hall and the Zaryadye Cinema (named after the old craftsmen's district that used to be situated here). The steamer passes beneath the Moskvoretsky Bridge and then on the left one can see Sofiyskaya Embankment with its palatial mansions, the most beautiful of which is the British Embassy. From here there is a wonderful view of the Kremlin – it is the best place from which to photograph it.

The whole of the left bank is one huge island lying between the Moskva and the drainage channel and forming part of the Zamoskvorechye district. Passing the last bridge which links the island with the "mainland," the **Great Stone Bridge**, you can see on the left a large grey building on Bersenevskaya Embankment. This houses the **Variety Theater** which is the most important element in a space designed for multi-functional use.

To the right, the Kropotkinskaya Embankment is lined, as one so often finds in Moscow, with buildings of many different styles and periods colorfully juxtaposed: classical columns and the stylized architecture of old Russia, murals in majolica with water nymphs, strange plants and creatures in the Art Nouveau style. Behind the green of the trees hides the Moskva public swimming pool and next to it the exclusive Chaika sports club with swimming pool, tennis courts, sauna, and other recreational facilities. Opposite, on the Krimskaya Embankment, you will see the white "Artist's House," a club with exhibition rooms, where pictures from the vaults of the Tretyakov Gallery are are put on display for the first time. These all date from from the Soviet period, after 1917, and give a vivid impression of life and work under communism.

The **Krymsky Bridge** is quite unlike any other bridge in Moscow. The city's only suspension bridge, it is held aloft by two cables, and used to be considered an engineering miracle in the 1930s. Beyond it is the beginning of a completely

105

different Moscow. Gorky Park lies along the left bank and one can see the giant Ferris wheel towering above it. The park runs down to Pushkinskaya Embankment. Opposite lies the elegant Frunzenskaya Embankment, once a run-down area of wasteland and rubbish tips.

After the railway bridge the landscape of parks occupies both banks. From the river one has an excellent view of the park on the Sparrow Hills, the Andreyevsky Monastery and the Mamonov Dacha, a palace nestling amidst the greenery which used to be the home of the eccentric Count Mamonov, who took a voluntary vow of silence.

The steamer continues under the two-tiered bridge which carries the Metro and a roadway. Unfortunately the Metro part has been closed for a long time for repairs (but the upper deck of the bridge can still be used by cars). The glazed, step-like terrace on the slope, used to be the exit of the Metro station, which led directly into the park and to the beach. Today the bathing place can only be reached by unofficial footpaths.

It is hard to believe that anyone should want to bathe in the Moskva at all, let alone be allowed to, for the water is unbelievably filthy. Most of those who do bathe are students; the joke at the university is that "man has survived as a species because he knows how to adapt." Maybe that's the secret.

There is a sharp bend in the river here. On the right the walls of the Novodevichy Convent now come into view, and on the left the bank rises steeply to the Mosfilm film studios, then slopes gradually down to form the Berezhkovskaya Embankment. In the very smart Slavyanskaya Hotel at the end of this street, you are only served if you can offer for foreign currency.

Right: The restored outer gateway to Kolomenskoye dates originally from the 17th century.

KOLOMENSKOYE

An excursion to **Kolomenskoye** is something to look forward to when you have become tired of the hectic activity of the city and would like to relax a little. It lies 12 miles (20 km) south-east of the city centre and in the Soviet era was called the Museum-Reserve of Kolomenskoye. You can walk or take a taxi from the Metro station Kolomenskaya.

Kolomenskoye was a summer residence of the Russian czars from the 16th century onwards. The wooden palace of the czars, built in the 17th century, is no longer standing, but the open-air museum in the extensive and charming parkland situated on the steep bank of the Moskva has much to offer. It is a very peaceful place and, during the week, practically deserted. You should allow a good half-day for a visit here.

To the left of the entrance stands the **Kazan Church**, its blue and gold domes shimmering among the trees. It is named after the Kazan Icon of the Mother of God and was built in the 17th century. The icons on the iconostasis inside also date from that period, while the murals are 19th century.

To the south of the church is the former processional approach which leads to the main gate. Its architecture, with its clock tower surmounted by a pyramid roof, is austere and yet graceful. Side wings were added later at both sides with rooms which today house the **Museum**. They were once used as ecclesiastical offices and the furniture from that time can still be seen. Apart from this the museum contains tiles, icons, and wood carvings. Note the bull's-eye windows of naturally transparent mica. The pride of the collections is however a model of the former Palace of the Czars. Like the gateway and the Church of the Kazan Mother of God it dates from the time of Czar Alexei Mikhailovich (1645-76). With all its towers, stairs and linking corridors, its 280 rooms

with windows of mica, as well as its technical equipment (lifts and running water) it was regarded in its day as the eighth wonder of the world.

The later Czar Peter the Great spent part of his childhood at Kolomenskoye. At the behest of Catherine II the palace was demolished because of its dilapidated condition, but before this was done she asked for detailed drawings to be made. These were used by the woodworker Smirnov as the basis for his accurate model, which he took nine years, up to 1867, to complete.

As you pass through the front gate the **Church of the Ascension** comes into view, a masterpiece of old Russian architecture. Grand Duke Vassily III had the church built in gratitude for the birth of his heir, who grew up to be the Czar Ivan the Terrible. It was the first cathedral to be built in stone on the lines of the native wooden pyramid-roof churches. It provided the prototype of a style of building which became standard in Russia. The delicately structured undercroft, the tall,

narrow windows below the three tiers of *kokoshniki* (blind or decorative gables in the form of an ogee arch) and the pyramid roof decorated with rhombuses create the impression of movement striving heavenwards.

Next to the church the massive water tower with its drum-roof and the falcon tower are still standing, as is also the summer house of Alexander I, a short distance upriver, which houses a small collection of Russian oil paintings.

In good weather, artists of all ages sit in front of the church on the slope down to the river Moskva, capturing on canvas the panorama of the bend in the river and in the distance beyond it, the towering highrise buildings. In the autumn the scene positively glows with the golden yellow of the maple trees.

A footpath leads along the steep bank downstream to the fish ponds, which once belonged to the home farm of the czars' estate. If you cross the little stream at the bottom of the gully and follow the footpath further up the other side, you

reach the woodland cemetery of the village of **Dyakovo** with the **Church of John the Baptist** built in 1529. This church is older than the Church of the Ascension and creates an impression of great solidity with its large central dome above an octagonal apse.

From here one can continue the circular tour by walking downhill, and crossing the stream once again by a small bridge. It is worth walking a little way upstream on the other bank, for this brings you to a spot where several small springs bubble up and feed the stream. They are partially dammed and people bring jugs and bottles and fill them here. You are now a long way from the noise of any traffic. Rest a while here and enjoy the special kind of tranquility which envelops this spot. You may see someone scooping up a little of the water and crossing themselves before drinking from the springs.

Above: The Church of the Ascension in Kolomenskoye.

The czars' estate of Kolomenskoye was declared a "museum-reserve" in 1924. Since then many examples of Russian **wooden architecture** have been assembled here. The most interesting of these is the **Cabin of Peter the Great** dating from 1702, which originally stood on the island of Markov at the mouth of the Northern Dvina. Peter lived in the three lower rooms while he was supervising the building of the fleet at Archangel. Today the cabin is furnished with everyday items from that period. The square **Gate Tower** from the Monastery of St. Nicholas of Karelia is also impressive. Built in 1692, it also came from the White Sea coast.

Beneath the trees in the park there is also a roughly hewn stone sculpture of a female torso, whose shape recalls a heathen fertility goddess. She is the so-called **Woman of Polovets** dating from the 12th century. Some of the trees are several centuries old and shrouded in legend – like so much else, both sacred and profane, in the land of the Russians.

OUTSIDE THE GARDEN RING ROAD

Accommodation
The hotels are summarized in the **Guidelines** at the end of the book. See page 243.

Museums and Churches
Andrei-Rubljov-Museum for old Russian art in the Andronikov convent, Ploschtschad Andronjevskaya 10, Tel: 278 1489, 278 1467; open 11 a.m.-6 p.m. closed Wednesdays and the last Friday of the month.

M. I. Glinka (Central City Museum of music culture), ulitsa Fadejeva 4. Tel: 972 3237, daily, except Monday, 2 p.m.-5 p.m.

New virgins convent (*Novodevichi monastyr*), Metro Sportivnaya, Tel: 2468526; the convent is again open for purpose of religious services, daily 8 a.m.-6 p.m..

Ostan cinema: 1. Ostankinskaya ulitsa 5, in the palace **Museum for artwork of the serfs** , one part of the palace is currently closed for renovations, for information call Tel: 283 4645.

Kolomenskoje: The open-air museum on the edge of the city is easily reached with the Metro to station *Kolomenskaya*. Prospekt Andropova 39, Tel: 115 2713, daily, except Mon. 11 a.m.-5 p.m., however, opening times are often changed without notice.

Theater and Concert Halls
Konzertny sal w Olympiskoi derevne, Mitschurinski Prospekt (Metro Prospekt Wernadskowo), Tel: 437 5650.

Teatr na Taganke, ulitsa Semljanoi Wal 76 (Metro Taganskaya), Tel: 915 1015.

Teatr Satirikon, ulitsa Scheremetjevskaya 8 (Metro Rishskaya), Tel: 289 8698.

Teatr Sovremennik, Tschistoprudny bulvar 19a (Metro Tschistyje prudy), Tel: 921 1790.

Restaurants
EXPENSIVE: **Brasserie** in the Hotel Olimpik Penta, international cuisine, Olimpiski prospekt 18/1, Tel: 971 6101.

Business-klub, Krasnopresnenskaya nabereshnaya 12 (*Sovinzentr*), French cuisine, Tel: 253 1722.

Manila, ulitsa Vavilova 81, Philippine cuisine, Tel: 132 0055.

Mei Hua, Russakovskaya ulitsa 2/1, Chinese food, Tel: 264 9574.

Seoul Plaza, Serpuchovski wal 14, Korean food, Tel: 952 8117.

Tren Mos, American cuisine, ulitsa Ostoschenka 1/9, Tel: 202 5722.

Valeri, Kalushskaya ploschtschad 1, Tel: 238 5848.

Westfalia, Leninski prospekt 87, German food, Tel: 134 3026.

Zolotoi, Kutusovski prospekt 5/3, Tel: 243 6213.

MODERATE: **American Bar & Grill**, 1. Tverskaya-Jamskaya ulitsa 32/1, Tel: 251 7999.

Danilovski, Bolschoi Starodanilovski pereulok 5, Tel: 954 0566, hotel restaurant of the same name on the convent grounds.

Le Chalet, pereulok Korobeinikov 1/2, French-Swiss cuisine, Tel: 202 0106.

Pescatore '90, Prospekt Mira, Italian cuisine, Tel: 280 3582.

Rasgulyai, Spartakovska ulitsa 11, Tel: 267 7613.

Santa Fe, Mantulinskaya ulitsa 5/1, Tel: 256 2126, Mexican food.

Taganka Blues, Verchnaya Radishtshevskaya ulitsa 15, Tel: 915 1004, folklore and jazz music.

U Josefa, Dubiniskaya ulitsa 17, Tel: 238 4646, Jewish cuisine.

U Pirosmani, Novodevichi proyesd 7/3, Tel: 247 1926, Caucasian cuisine.

BUDGET: **Gurija**, Komsomolski prospekt 7/3, Tel: 246 0378, Caucasian cuisine.

Nemetskaya Sloboda, Baumannskaya ulitsa 23, Tel: 267 4476.

FAST FOOD: **Kombi's**, Prospekt Mira 46/48, Tel: 280 6402, and Prospekt Mira 180, Tel: 283 0651.

McDonalds, Bolschaya Bronnaya 29, Tel: 200 0590.

Pizza Hut, Kutuzovski prospekt 17, Tel: 243 1727.

Music Cafés
B. B. King, Sadovaya-Samotetschnaya ulitsa 4/2 (Metro Zvetnoi bulvar), Tel: 299 8206, Thursdays from 9 p.m. Blues, cover charge 10 dollars.

Crybaby, Profsojusnaya ulitsa 100 (Metro Belyayevo), Tel: 335 8322, Friday and Saturday from 7 p.m. with live music of all varieties, cover charge 7 dollars.

Jazzland, ulitsa Generala Yermolova 6 (Metro Kutusovskaya), Tel: 251 4990, Wednesdays from 9 p.m. concert, cover charge 10 dollars.

M-Club, Nikolo-Yamski pereulok 62A (Metro Kurskaya), Tel: 272 6438, daily 11 a.m.-5 a.m., entrance free until 9 p.m., concerts start from 11 p.m.(15-35 dollars).

Soho-Club, Trochgorni Wal 6, Tel: 205 6209, nightlife bar, restaurant, discotheque; stays open 24 hours.

Nightlife bars / Casinos
Golden Palace (Zolotoi Dvorez), 3. Yamskovo Polja ulitsa 15 (Metro Belorusskaya), Tel: 212 3909.

NEW MONUMENTS FOR OLD

On Moscow's Krymsky Val, near the House of Artists, there is a remarkable sight: a cemetery for statues, a potent symbol of the changing political times. Here lie the monumental remains of the onetime big names of the Soviet Union; broken-off heads, scattered limbs, and some still intact statues. They command no respect from the children who clamber over them. On some figures the eyes have been painted in lurid colors, so that they look truly demonic. You will find here, among others, statues of Kalinin, the USSR's nominal head of state in Stalin's time, and of Sverdlov, who reportedly, as chairman of the executive committee of the Soviets, gave the orders for the tsar and his family to be murdered. Particular loathing is reserved for Dzerzhinsky, who founded the Cheka, the forerunner

Above: Hated even in his lifetime: Feliks Dzerzhinsky, founder of the KGB. Right: The poet Yesenin used to stay at the Lux.

of the KGB, and was responsible for the death of thousands of innocent people. His larger-than-lifesize bronze statue stood for decades in the middle of Lubyanka Square, in front of the headquarters of the KGB. After the failure of the conservative coup in August 1991, young people started to dismantle the monument. The city authorities had hastily to dispatch a crane to the square, to prevent the statue, weighing many tons, from toppling over and damaging the important communications cabling buried beneath it. To the cheers of tens of thousands of onlookers, "Iron Feliks" swayed down from his plinth on ropes. In his place there stands today a large cross, which was spontaneously raised by the people and bears the inscription in Old Russian: "With this Thou wilt prevail."

It is no coincidence that a new memorial stands in the same square, a little to one side under the trees; one which does more than anything to raise the spirits. It is a massive stone which has been put up here in memory of the many millions of victims of Stalin's reign of terror. Fresh flowers always lie on it. At the end of the 1980s more than 150 artists from all over the country submitted designs for the memorial, and huge crowds streamed into the exhibition to see them. But the jury felt that none of the designs adequately conveyed the message and so they settled for the simple stone. A monument that should be seen for its artistic quality is the one to the former party leader Nikita Khrushchov, by E. Neizvestny, which stands in the cemetery of the Novodevichy Convent. Once, at an exhibition of Russian painters, Khrushchov coarsely insulted Neizvestny in public for his avant-garde style. Later he apologized to him.

In 1991, the Moscow City Council decided to remove 62 of the 68 statues of Lenin. Anyone who is still interested can see one on Kalushskaya Ploshchad (Metro: Oktyabrskaya Ploshchad).

HOTEL LUX

In the days of communist rule, the Hotel Lux, today the Tsentralnaya, was the top address for communist and left-wing politicians from all over the world.

The ground floor of the building at 10, Ulitsa Tverskaya, was built in the 19th century by a baker called Filipov, who ran a café there. His son built a hotel on to it, which was completed in 1911 to a design by Eichenwald.

When the first Bolshevik government moved to Moscow from Petrograd, the Hotel Lux was occupied by party functionaries, operatives of the Cheka and for a time even the poet Yesenin. In 1920 the Lux, in common with many hotels, convalescent homes and hospitals, was closed to the public and put at the exclusive disposal of the Comintern. European communist leaders lived there temporarily or permanently; even the spy Richard Sorge stopped by sometimes. German and Austrian emigrés also lived there, with whose help Stalin wanted to establish "democratic" regimes after the war. Among these were Herbert Wehner, the West German socialist politician, Walter Ulbricht, East Germany's Communist leader for many years, and several other East European figures of the Cold War. Many communists who sought refuge in the Soviet Union from the terrors of Nazism, were arrested in the Hotel Lux and fell victim to Stalin's purges. Various books have been written about life in the hotel, which was like a small city within a city, with its restaurants, laundry, shoemaker and tailor. It had its own out-patients clinic and a unit of the militia. In 1943 a complete cloak of secrecy was imposed on the Lux and the activities of its occupants. The last "internationalists" did not leave the Lux until the end of the 1940s.

After being renovated from top to bottom the hotel was reopened in 1953 under the name Tsentralnaya. The interior of the restaurant with its magnificent Art-Nouveau decor still recalls the elegant atmosphere of the early 1900s.

THE METRO AND ITS
UNDERGROUND PALACES

Most great cities of the world have a subway, usually a rather mundane affair. However, Moscow's Metro is far from mundane – it is magnificent. Many of its stations should be on your sightseeing schedule. From the outset, the Metro was the pride of the capital and of the Party, which quite deliberately exploited its subterranean splendor for propaganda purposes.

Shortly before the inauguration of the first section in 1935, it was boasted that the Metro had been built without foreign assistance, with native hands and materials, and in record time – it was "the best in the world, a Metro worthy of our proletarian capital." The first line was 6 1/2 miles (11 km) long; today the total network comprises nearly 150 miles (240

Above: A Metro station is a palace under ground. Right: Many Metro stations are decorated with true craftsmanship.

km) of track with about 150 stations. The Communist Party has since lost all significance and the Bolshevik oratory has fallen silent – but the Metro keeps running. Without it the whole of Moscow would come to a grinding halt. Every working day it carries over 8 million people. In the tunnels the blue trains reach speeds of 55 m.p.h (90 k.p.h), while the passengers cram together in the rush hours, or sit in the half-empty carriages, in the early morning or late evening, musing, dozing, or, most often, reading.

Everything is electric: the trains themselves, the ventilation (the air is changed four times each hour), lighting, signals, surveillance, nearly 500 escalators with something like 125,000 steps and a total length of 33 miles (55 km). Not surprisingly the Metro is Moscow's biggest consumer of electric current, burning up more than 4 million kilowatt hours per day. These facts and many more can be learnt in the small **Metro Museum** on the top floor of the south building of the Sportivnaya station.

The museum, which used to be for staff only, has been open to the public since 1985, and entry is free. But let us leave statistics and museums aside – the subway tells its own history through its decoration.

The oldest stations, built before the Second World War, are dedicated to the revolution, and the development and technical achievements of socialism – for example, **Revolution Square** (*Ploshchad Revolyutsi*y) with its eighty bronze sculptures of workers and soldiers, or **Mayakovskaya**, named after the revolutionary poet, Vladimir Mayakovsky. It has stainless steel arches and a ceiling mosaic depicting the development of aeronautics.

After the war construction work continued, and at the beginning of the 1950s the *Koltsevaya Liniya* (Circle Line) came into service. Its twelve stations are among those most worth seeing; all are appointed in the grandeur of the "Stalin Empire" style. In many places the theme of victory comes to the fore, whether in idealized ceramic relief portraits of soldiers and partisans in the **Taganskaya** station, or in the gold-spangled ceiling mosaics of **Komsomolskaya**, where such renowned military leaders as Alexander Nevsky or Marshall Kutuzov are portrayed. By contrast, a more peaceful impression is given by the illuminated glass mosaics of **Novoslobodskaya** station.

In the 1950s and 1960s designs became simpler and cheaper. Several lines were extended, and the stations in the outer suburbs, dating from this period, are often quite plain halls with tiled walls – but still with polished stone floors: both hygenic and long-lasting.

With the more recent stations of the 1980s, greater imagination was once more brought into play. The decor no longer evokes revolutionary emotions, but is often related to the name of the station concerned. **Mendeleyevskaya**, named after the Russian chemist, Dmitri

Mendeleyev, who devised the Periodic Table of elements, is lit by lamps in the form of molecular models. The walls of **Chekhovskaya** are inlaid with with colored stone pictures illustrating the plays and stories of Chekhov. **Borovitskaya** takes its name from the Borovitsky Hill in the Kremlin; it has been built of the same red brick as that of the Kremlin walls.

All the stations are designed differently, but all are astonishingly clean. This is not only attributable to the great army of cleaners who are on duty day and night, but also bears witness to the special relationship between the Muscovites and their subway. Yet you will look in vain for a litter-bin. They were removed in the 1970s, when a number of homemade bombs exploded in them.

So, now you have bought your token and have pushed it into the slot in the turnstile. This entitles you to travel around for as long as you like, get out at any station, take a look around, and then continue your journey.

THE MOSCOW CIRCUS

How would you like to visit somehere full of blissfully happy children, and grown-ups who are just as happy as the kids? In Moscow there are two places like this. The Old Circus in the city center – on Tsvetnoy Boulevard – began life, as Salamonsky's Circus, at the end of the 19th century, but today it does not look any older than the New Circus. It opened its doors once again in 1989 after a face-lift. Its more spacious counterpart, the New Circus in the Vorobyev Hills (Sparrow Hills), has 3300 seats, compared with the Old Circus' 2000. When it opened in 1973 it was a true wonder of technology. Even today there is nothing like it anywhere in Russia, or even in Europe. In a matter of minutes the ring can be transformed into a railway or a pool filled with water. Yet the Muscovites still prefer their old circus. True, it is not so spectacular, but it has retained a very special atmosphere of its own.

Neither of the Moscow circuses have permanent troupes; you can see the same artistes on the Tsvetnoy (Flower) Boulevard as on Sparrow Hills. Back in the days of the Soviet Union, tickets for citizens were subsidized and were distributed in a big way in kindergartens and factories. Tourists could only acquire tickets for many times the ruble value in hard currency. Nowadays, anyone can buy them at the box office, but at prices determined by the market. Every performance lasts nearly three hours, but one is oblivious to the passing of time because every act is an exciting, enchanting experience.

That someone can achieve the peak of technical skill and coordination through rigorous training, is understandable. But how one can teach an elephant to stand just on its front legs is a real mystery! Incidentally it was in the Moscow circus that, for the first time in the world, the principles of a humane method of training animals were worked out and applied. Rough methods are strictly forbidden, and that approach pays. So it was that Yuri Kuklachev, a first-class clown and trainer, succeeded in doing something unique: training domestic cats. They do just about everything, except speak.

The circus is a special form of art. For those who make it their career, it is not just a profession, it is a state of mind and a way of life. But circus artists are neither sportsmen nor bohemians. They have a great respect for the centuries-old traditions of their craft; they have very strong family ties – usually the entire family takes part in presenting a circus act and their secrets are bequeathed to the next generation. Most of them lead an extremely modest, almost ascetic life; the work totally involves and preoccupies the circus artist, but the financial rewards are not very great.

Above and right: Russian circus artistry is quite simply the best in the world.

Not many years ago the Moscow Circus had to make a number of guest tours abroad, under contractual terms that amounted to robbery, since the artists were paid nothing for their performances but merely given their board and lodging. At the beginning of the 1980s there was a court case about this, which attracted a lot of attention. The circus management who had signed these contracts were found guilty of wilful corruption and given severe sentences.

Yet in spite of all these difficulties, it is a passionate devotion to their art which drives the acrobats, animal tamers and tightrope walkers to put their lives and health at risk night after night. Very few leave the circus voluntarily; an artist is more likely to switch to another genre: an acrobat might become an animal trainer or simply work behind the scenes. The circus attracts them with a tremendous magnetic force.

The Moscow Circus has for years enjoyed world renown for its great performers. Representatives of the old circus dynasties, which go back to the 19th century – great animal tamers like the Durovs and the Filatovs – still add luster to the programs of today. Members of the older generation still remember the sad clown Karandash, who modelled himself on Charlie Chaplin, and had a tiny black dog called Klyaska. After him came a clown with a sunnier disposition – Oleg Popov, then the wonderfully philosophical Leonid Yengibarov, who died young. Then there was the unfathomable illusionist Kio. What an act! The jugglers, tumblers, bare-back riders – there were so many of them and there still are! Whether today, yesterday or 50 years ago, a circus performance is an event, just as it was in ancient times: with lights, daring artistes and unusually well-trained animals.The art of the circus is a democratic one. It requires no interpretation or translation. It is intended for people who take pleasure in life and have not forgotten how to laugh.

7 p.m. The performance is about to start. A drum-roll, then... allez-oop!

THE GOLDEN RING

SERGIYEV POSAD

VLADIMIR

SUZDAL

YAROSLAVL

ROSTOV VELIKY

PERESLAVL-ZALESSKY

The Golden Ring

In a decree issued by Lenin in 1919, the new Soviet state was urged "to liberate the working masses from religious prejudices by means of comprehensively organized, scientifically enlightening and anti-religious propaganda," which should, however, "avoid injuring their sensitivities, because this only leads to a strengthening of religious fanaticism." Nevertheless, the magnificent churches and monasteries to be found in a "Golden Ring" of ancient towns around Moscow, have long been promoted by INTOURIST as the crowning glory of tourism in Russia. It must be said that there is a lack of suitable hotels in these towns, though in some places floating hotels provide good accommodation. It is essential for any foreign tourist to visit these centuries-old monastic sites, because they provide a key to understanding Russia's historical greatness. The deterioration, both internal and external, suffered by these buildings in an age of soulless bureaucracy, has been halted, and once again they bear glowing witness in stone to an imperishable Christian faith.

Previous pages: Suzdal is well worth the long journey. Left: The Cathedral of the Assumption in Sergiyev Posad.

SERGIYEV POSAD

No one should miss out a visit to Sergiyev Posad (called Zagorsk during the Communist era, after a party offficial), in order to see the famous **Monastery of the Trinity and St Sergiy** (*Troitse-Sergieva Lavra*), the principal shrine and spiritual center of the old Muscovite state. **Lavra** is a special name given to particularly important monasteries. In old Russia there were only four Lavras.

For a long time the Troitse-Sergieva Lavra was the richest in Russia, with many vast estates worked by over 100.000 serfs. In the course of the centuries it became a treasure chest of indigenous Russian art and architecture, and grew in splendor and magnificence. But its origins were humble.

In 1345 Sergius of Radonezh, a monk, built a simple wooden church on the hill where the monastery now stands. It was attacked by Tatars, who drove out the community which had grown up there, and destroyed the church. In the following century Sergius' corpse was discovered amidst the rubble, miraculously almost unscathed, and soon the village became a place of pilgrimage. A new and active monastic community was founded, which in 1422-24 built the **Cathedral of the Trinity** (*Troitsy Sobor*).

119

This limestone church is today the oldest in the monastery. It has a single gilded dome, and a decorated, gilded *kokoshnik* roof. It stands on the site of the old wooden church, over the grave of the monastery's founder. Sergius was canonized in the year of his death and declared the patron saint of Russia. A shroud bearing his portrait is to be seen in the monastery musuem.

The **iconostasis** in the Trinity Cathedral is the work of Andrei Rublyov. With the help of his apprentices, he created 42 icons for this screen, some of which are now in the Kremlin cathedrals in Moscow, and others – such as his famous *Trinity* – are in the capital's Tretyakov Gallery.

However, the principal church of the monastery is the **Cathedral of the Assumption** (*Uspensky Sobor*), which was built by Ivan the Terrible in between 1559 and 1585. Its five onion domes, of which the middle one is gilded, announce the monastery's presence from afar. The four other domes are a brilliant blue and spangled with golden stars.

To attend a service in this spacious and richly decorated church with its ornately carved iconostasis, is a memorable experience. Three masses are usually celebrated here every Sunday, to which the devout come streaming in and stand crammed shoulder to shoulder.

Despite the atheism offically imposed by the state for seven decades, many Russians, even of the younger generation, are familiar with the words and chants of the liturgy. Towards the end of the service one of the clergy collects little slips of paper from the congregation, on which have been written the names of people to be included in the priest's prayer of intercession.

During the 16th century the monastery was extended and fortified. It was given a massive brick wall with twelve towers, eleven of which are still standing. This enabled the monastery to withstand a siege from 1608 to 1610, laid by the Poles under the "False Dimitri," the pretender to the tsars' throne. As a result, the place grew in importance and came to symbolize the Russian will to resist foreign incursions.

Of the four corner bastions of the defensive wall, the octagonal **Duck Tower**, which is today surmounted by a golden duck, is the one with the greatest architectural charm and interest. Peter the Great is said to have shot a duck from the tower.

One of the fortified towers apparently contains Russia's largest collection of victory trophies from the Second World War. It is said that 16,000 works of art are kept here, which were brought back from Germany by the Red Army. Some of these are priceless items that are part of the world's cultural heritage. For decades this was a taboo subject, but since the end of the Cold War it has been brought into the open.

In the monastery courtyard, next to the Uspensky Cathedral, the body of Boris Godunov rests in his family crypt. He was tsar from 1598 to 1605 and it was under his rule that the Russian Orthodox Church became independent of Constantinople. Boris, who has been immortalized in Pushkin's poetry and the opera by Mussorgsky, was not, however, popular with the Russian people.

The nearby **Chapel over the Well** dates from the late 17th century. The spring which rises inside it has unusually pleasant-tasting water, said to have healing properties. The chapel with its little ornamental pillars, is painted in many colors, giving it a charming, whimsical atmosphere. It is an example of the Naryshkin style, or Russian Baroque, as is the **Refectory**.

This building has a long gallery running round it and pilasters decorated with vines and sea-shells. Most of the work dates from the period 1686-92. Inside is a large hall with a sumptuously decorated,

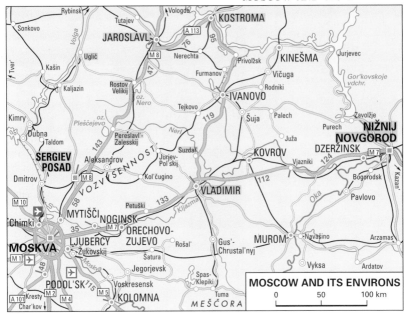

MOSCOW AND ITS ENVIRONS
0   50   100 km

vaulted roof. A wrought-iron gilt screen separates it from a church where services are held.

Among the monastery's other buildings, the following are worthy of mention: the **Metopolitan's Residence**, also known as the House of Centuries, because each of its three storeys was built in a different century, from the 16th to the 18th; the **Tsar's Chambers**, a two-storey building where the tsars and their numerous courtiers would stay when they visited the monastery; and the **Bell Tower**, 289 ft (88m) high, which was built by Rastrelli in 1777. It has 42 bells and, when the monastery is seen in silhouette, it towers above all the other buildings. The pyramid roof of the Church of Saint Zosima and Saint Savvatiy is architecturally interesting.

After the monastery had been acquired for the state by the Bolsheviks in 1917, its buildings fell into gradual disrepair. The fact that the Lavra still exists today, restored to its former splendor, is largely due to one man, Viktor Baldin, a histo-

rian, architect and rescuer of historic buildings. He dedicated almost his entire life to the preservation and restoration of the fifty or so buildings which make up the monastery. He studied the original plans, removed disfiguring additions to the buildings and supervised the training of skilled restorers. During World War Two he painted the golden domes in camouflage colors to protect them from air attack. For his outstanding achievement in preserving the monastery, Baldin was awarded the Europa Prize for the Preservation of Historic Monuments, in 1992.

Some idea of the richness and variety of Russian art can be gained from a visit to the Museum of Historical Art. Here are icons from the 14th to the 17th centuries, including *The Last Supper*, by Simon Ushakov, liturgical objects, priceless embroideries, exquisite pieces of gold and silverwork, and small sculptures, to mention only the more important items.

An important theological college is also to be found within the monastery complex. At present there are 500 semin-

arists training here for the priesthood, because once again every parish in Russia may have its own priest. In charge of the monastery is the Archimandrite, or abbot, who is responsible in turn to the Metropolitan in Moscow. Among the crowd of pilgrims, tourists and, sad to say, beggars, in the monastery courtyard you will quite often pass one of the bearded priests wearing the typical ankle-length clerical robes and tall, black headgear.

The monastery fathers have forbidden the selling of souvenirs within their precincts, but they can be found in the square outside the main gate, where a colorful selection of *matryoshka* dolls, postcards, books and other souvenirs are on offer. However, the range of prices one would expect in a free market economy cannot be found here: the gentlemen who "take an interest" in these matters

Above: The refectory building in Sergiyev Posad, a jewel of "Russian Baroque."
Right: Tower of St. Demetrius Cathedral in Vladimir.

(let's be frank, the Russian Mafia) ensure that uniformly high prices are charged, with no undercutting.

In the little town of Sergiyev Posad there are two factories turning out *matryoshky* and other toys. There is also a **Toy Museum**.

VLADIMIR

The route from Moscow to Vladimir passes through the peaceful landscape of central Russia. Look out for the quaintly named little town of Petushky, meaning "roosters," which has a place in Russian literature. This is because one of the most brilliant authors of Moscow's *samizdat* (underground publishing) movement, Venedikt Yerofeyev, immortalized the town in his novel *Moscow to Petushky*. It reflects the attitude to life of a hard-drinking intellectual who frequently drives along this road from Moscow to visit his girlfriend.

The highway from Moscow to Nizhny Novgorod (Lower Novgorod), which one takes to get to Vladimir, is the ill-famed *Vladirmirka*; for this was the route to the notorious *gulags,* or labor camps in Siberia and the far north, which countless thousands of prisoners had to take – under the tsars as well as under the communist regime that followed.

The prison in Vladimir itself was in particular reserved for political prisoners, and had already become notorious for this in the 19th century. Today the list of prisoners who were incarcerated there reads like a history of the dissident movement in the Soviet Union. The artist I. Levitan painted a famous picture of the Vladimirka, which is now included in the collection of the Tretyakov Gallery in Moscow.

The city of Vladimir, which was founded at the beginning of the 12th century by Vladimir II Monomakh, Prince of Kiev, stands on the high left bank of the Klyazma river. This is a region of forests which has always been famous for its fish and animal pelts.

In the mid-12th century Vladimir became the capital of one of the largest principalities in old Russia. Superbly ornate palaces and churches of white stone were built here. A chronicle records that in a fire at the end of the 12th century as many as 32 churches were destroyed. The town was rebuilt but captured by the Tatars in 1238, plundered and put to the torch. At that time Moscow was capital of Greater Russia and not only strove to emulate the art and architecture of Vladimir but also appropriated for itself the principal shrine and the icons of the Mother of God (of Vladimir).

The town was hardly affected by the sweeping reforms of Peter the Great in the early 18th century, apart from seeing its first secular school opened. The money in the city's coffers dwindled, and despite the occasional attempts of the local authorities to create some sort of order – by surfacing the pavements, laying water pipes, lighting the streets

and organizing the traffic – it fell further and further into disrepair.

Vladimir's ancient buildings are indeed beautiful. Traditionally, a tour of the town begins at the Golden Gate, a massive fortification dating from the 12th century, with a church built on top of it. In days gone by, the copper hinges of the gate were gilded, hence its name. Many inscriptions written on its wall by former inhabitants have been preserved, including one that dates from the 12th century. The Golden Gate has suffered at the hands, not only of foreign invaders, but also of the city fathers, who kept trying to widen or alter it.

Around the Golden Gate are several more recent buildings: the **Church of the Trinity** (*Troitskaya Tserkov*) built in 1913, where painted miniatures from the village of Mstery and the work of the master glass blowers of the town of Gus-Khrustalny are displayed; the Knyaginin monastery and its Church of the Ascension of the Virgin Mary, the Church of the Savior and the Church of St Nicholas.

High above the Klyazma stand the famous Cathedral of the Assumption and the Cathedral of St Demetrius, whose foundation stones were both laid in the 12th century. Both cathedrals are built of white limestone, which was commonly used at that time for churches and royal palaces, and are decorated with stone carvings.

The **Cathedral of the Assumption of the Virgin Mary** was, from its consecration in the 12th century, a focus of the religious and political life of medieval Russia. It was here that until the 15th century the princes of Vladimir and Moscow were elevated to the rank of Grand Prince. The frescoes have been saved, but at great expense, and in the course of restoration some fragments of frescoes by Andrei Rublyov came to light – in the vaulted ceiling of the north nave, his *Entry of the Righteous into Paradise*, and

Above: Frescoes in the Assumption Cathedral in Vladimir. Right: The Prophet Elijah Church in Suzdal.

in the west nave, *Angels Sounding Trumpets*. The **Cathedral of St. Demetrius** also survived unscathed, though only by pure chance. Surprisingly, it was in the 19th century that it suffered its worst damage. Czar Nicholas I visited the town, was most displeased with its shabby appearance and ordered that it be improved. His zealous subjects immediately set to work on these supposed "improvements." They removed the gallery and the towers from the cathedral, so that it almost collapsed. However, not only this cathedral but many other buildings in Vladimir and Suzdal were rescued in the 20th century by an architect named Stoletov. The many figurative carvings on the façades have a richness and disciplined delicacy which puts them among the most beautiful religious buildings not only in Russia but in the whole of Europe.

Compare the frescoes, especially the *Last Judgement*, first in St Demetrius Cathedral and then in the Cathedral of the Assumption. In the first, the faces of the apostle are painted in the Byzantine manner: they are stern and tense, leaving us in no doubt that the Judgement will be truly terrible. But in the Cathedral of the Assumption, which was decorated in the 15th century by painters under the guidance of Andrei Rublyov, the kindly, compassionate faces of the Apostles seated in judgment arouse the hope of salvation.

Also preserved are several buildings from two 12th century monasteries, but local guides will provide you with the best account of these silent witnesses to Russia's turbulent history. If you have time, you should drive out to the **Pokrovsky Church** on the river Nerl. It is probably the most perfect work of 12th century Russian architecture.

SUZDAL

Prince Yuri Dolgoruky's master builders chose the high river bank offering an unusually fine view, for the site of the prince's residence. Needless to say, strategic considerations also played a role in this choice: it was necessary to secure this important waterway. Tourists today can still see the magnificent architectural ensemble of the old village of Kideksha, first mentioned in the chronicles in 1015, which stands where the road crosses the Nerl. And although Suzdal is still 3 miles (5 km) away, your acquaintance with the town starts here. Behind the low wall of its Kremlin are a number of churches built between the 12th and 18th centuries.

Suzdal emerges beyond a bend in the road, a small city which is preserved as a historic monument and has in a miraculous way retained the atmosphere of those times when, in dividing up their estates among their heirs, the Russian Grand Princes regarded Suzdal as the prize. At the beginning of the 12th century Suzdal was the capital of the principality, but this privilege soon passed to Vladimir. The number of merchants and craftsmen grew rapidly, the monasteries expanded and acquired great wealth. In

the 13th century the city was destroyed by the Tatars and did not recover for almost two centuries. However, from the 15th century onwards the city was the religious center of Russia. Its monasteries had since earliest times served as the instrument of spiritual and temporal power. Towards the end of the 17th century, depite the ravages suffered by Suzdal during the occupation by the Poles and Lithuanians, the city entered a period of remarkable economic prosperity. With its paved streets and squares, its substantial houses, its markets and rows of permanent shops, Suzdal became known as "the Merchants' Province."

In 1862 the railroad line from Moscow to Nizhny Novgorod was built, bypassing Suzdal. Overnight Suzdal lost its position as a trading center and went into rapid decline. It would have been left to decay had it not been for some farsighted and courageous people who managed, even in the years after the Revolution, to preserve most of Suzdal's treasures and turn the city later on into one of

the principal tourist attractions of northeast Russia.

A 19th century historian wrote of Suzdal: "It is the city of churches, belltowers and spires, arcane folk traditions and memorials to the dead." Throughout history the city has been famous for its icon painters and its master builders; it also had a reputation for being a city of outcasts, where "living corpses" ended their days in the monasteries. In the Monastery of the Savior and St Euthymios there was until recently a prison for mentally disturbed criminals; but more recently, perfectly sane people with dissident views were also held here, both priests and laymen. The **Pokrovsky Convent**, which from a distance looks like a fairy-tale city, was, from the 14th until the 16th century, a normal, unremarkable convent, until the Grand Prince's family chose it as a place in which to

Above: Cathedral of the Nativity, Suzdal.
Right: This wooden house has been preserved as a museum.

exile troublesome women of noble blood. Thus it came about that this convent in remote Suzdal was richly endowed with money and estates, which enabled it to put up fine stone buildings.

The most important of Suzdal's four monasteries and nearly two dozen churches are briefly mentioned here. The **Cathedral of the Nativity** *(Rozhdestvensky Sobor)* was built in the 13th century and substantially altered in the first half of the 16th century. Only a few frescoes and fragments, and gilded copper doubledoors with biblical scenes, were preserved from the original building. Also from the 13th century is the **Monastery of the Deposition of the Robe** *(Rizpolozhensky Monastyr)*, which has several churches within its walls. Rising up above the low Kremlin wall is an architectural curiosity, a bell tower dating from the last century, which is the "Leaning Tower of Suzdal." Many legends surround the town's Holy Gate, whose two entrances are each adorned with tentshaped towers. The monastery of the Sa-

126

vior and St Euthymios, mentioned earlier, is called in Russian **Spasso-Yefimevsky Monastyr**. Immediately recognizable by its twelve spires of varying heights, it was built in the 14th century and bears the name of its first abbot. Integrated into the complex, the **Cathedral of the Savior** was built in the 14th century but enlarged in the 16th. It holds a very special place in the hearts of the Russian people: for here is the grave of Prince Dmitri Pozharsky, who played such a distinguished part in the war against Poland in 1612.

The Pokrovsky Convent, whose history has already been described, stands high above the Kamenka river. Its principal church was built of stone at the beginning of the the 16th century. In the 17th century, an onion dome was added, in the typical Moscow Baroque style. The church is dedicated to St Nicholas. The former **Palace of the Metropolitan**, (built 1682-1707), has an almost whimsical quality in the architecture of its galleries, staircases, porches and belltowers.

The southwest part of the palace dates from the end of the 15th century and was incorporated into the later 17th century building.

The whole complex is covered with high, hipped roofs. The collection of religious treasures, valuable silverware, embroideries, old manuscripts and miniatures, is worthy of any musuem and is unique in Russia.

In the **Church of the Intercession of the Virgin** – a perfect example of the 18th-century style of building in wood – you will not find a single iron nail! The churches here were built with the physical as well as the spiritual needs of the congregation in mind: most of them were built in pairs, of which one is cold, and the other "warm," that is to say, it can be heated.

Today all the monasteries are museums and contain wonderful examples of the nation's craftsmanship, such as embroidery and paintings on wood. On the bank of the Kamenka, opposite the town's oldest and most important historic building, its Kremlin, or fortress, there is an **Open Air Museum of Wooden Architecture and Peasant Life**, where churches, farmhouses and windmills from the surrounding villages have been assembled.

YAROSLAVL

In ancient times a heathen shrine stood on the bank of the Volga, where it is joined by the little river Kotorosl. The local inhabitants, descendants of Finno-Ugrian tribes, tilled the land, fished and hunted. As their principal deity they worshipped a she-bear. However, in the 11th century, the warriors of Yaroslavl the Wise, Prince of Rostov, invaded the place, struck the sacred bear dead with an axe, burned down the sanctuary, and at the prince's command built in its place a small wooden stockade, which they named Yaroslavl after their leader.

Sadly, except for a few superb icons and old books containing miniatures, nothing has survived of the oldest buildings of the town, from the period when it was capital of the principality.

The rise of Yaroslavl first began in the 16th century with the opening up of the trade route to Europe. Even the Polish-Lithuanian occupation did nothing to hamper this development: Yaroslavl minted its own coins and was in effect the capital of Russia. From this period dates the **Cathedral of the Transfiguration** (*Preobrazhensky Sobor*) within the monastery of the same name. It was built in the ten years 1506 to 1516.

By the late 17th century Yaroslavl was one of the largest cities in the whole of Russia and a center for craftsmanship, trade and culture. One in six of the country's wealthiest merchants lived here and the fame of Yaroslavl's master icon-painters spread far and wide. In the fifty

Right: Frescoes in the church of the Prophet Elijah in Yaroslavl.

years follwing the great fire of 1658, in which the city built of wood was reduced to ashes, local architects did their finest work: the Church of Elijah the Prophet, the church of the Epiphany and other religious buildings.

Most of Yaroslavl's churches are richly and colorfully decorated and there is no hint of asceticism in their murals. They were built by rich merchants who had seen at first hand the brilliant colors of the Orient; the frescoes depict scenes from real life. Some of the merchants played a significant role in the economic life of the country, and the relatively well-preserved 16th century frescoes are intended to portray the piety of their ancestors. The richness and magnificence of the 17th century murals in the nave and galleries of the **Church of Elijah the Prophet** take one's breath away: dozens of biblical episodes and scenes of everyday life in Russia adorn the walls; the denseness and profusion of the painting has the effect of a vast carpet covering the walls and ceiling. The iconostasis is in the Baroque style.

In 19th century Yaroslavl, merchants' houses were built, and decorated with wooden carvings. They have made the **Embankment** (*Naberezhnaya*) into the most beautiful promenade in all the towns along the Volga. In the early years of the 20th century the city became an important center for the Bolshevik party, and played a decisive role in establishing the power of the soviets in this region. During the rebellion of the White Guard in 1918, the fabulously beautiful church of the Epiphany suffered considerable damage from artillery fire.

The two most important museums in the town are the **Museum of History** and **Architecture**, in the Spassky Monastery, and the **Museum of Art**, which dates from the 1820s. Both have fine collections.

Yaroslav is full of surprises. Despite the large number of churches, the place

has a very light-hearted atmosphere. It is a center of commerce and industry, yet it was here that Russia's first professional dramatic theater was founded, in 1750, here that the first newspaper was published, outside Moscow and St Petersburg, and here that one of Russia's earliest universities was established.

Yaroslavl is the birthplace of scholars, writers and composers, and is also where the first woman in space, Valentina Tereshkova, spent her childhood.

If you have time, take a steamer to Yaroslavl. There are some lovely cruises on the Volga, lasting between 6 and 12 days, which will also take you to other towns in the Golden Ring, such as Kostroma and Uglich. Life in these old Russian towns moves at the same leisurely pace as the Volga itself.

ROSTOV VELIKY

In historic Rus only two cities called themselves *veliky*, "great. " One was the "capital of the north," Novgorod, and the other was Rostov, which lies like a fairy-tale kingdom between two old monasteries on the shores of Lake Nero. Rostov is first mentioned in the chronicles almost three centuries before Moscow, in AD 862. By the 10th century, it was already a large city by the standards of those days, with a monastery, a royal palace and a Kremlin.

At the beginning of the 13th century Rostov became the capital of a separate principality; stone churches and cathedrals were built here, and cultural life flourished. The ruler at that time, Prince Konstantin, was known as a patron of the arts and sciences, while one of his contemporaries was the scholarly Bishop Kyril, from whose library manuscripts have survived to the present day. However, no one knows how many valuable books were destroyed during attacks by the Tatars, who harassed the city for a hundred years, from 1238.

But the wars finally came to an end and there was a revival of cultural life. The fame of Rostov's libraries attracted

129

people with a thirst for knowledge. Later, philosophers and writers of the Enlightenment were educated here. A school of painting rapidly developed, whose works are today considered to be Russia's greatest, and it was here that Dionissi, one of the finest Russian painters of the 15th and 16th centuries, lived and worked. Rostov's architects and stonemasons were responsible for many important buildings in neighboring cities.

Trade between Russia and Western Europe began in the 15th century, through the northern port of Archangelsk, on the White Sea; and since Rostov lay on the route from there to Moscow, it enjoyed a great economic boom.

While the city fathers of Rostov were keenly fostering the arts and sciences, they gave no thought at all to measures for the defense of the city. This led, in 1608, to Rostov being plundered by Pol-

ish and Lithuanian troops, who made such a good job of it that even ten years later, when moves were made to introduce taxation, it was soon realized that the townspeople had nothing left to tax.

So everything had to be started from scratch. But the city which had always been famous for its building, now had to call in help from outside. Firstly, under the guidance of a Dutchman, Jan Cornelius Rodenburg, the central part of the city was enclosed with huge earthworks, and later, on the initiative of the Metropolitan Yona, a Kremlin was built on the shore of the lake. There is almost nothing in Russia that can compare in beauty with this group of buildings.

History has passed down to us the name of the greatest of the stonemasons who gave the city this treasure: he was Master Pyotr Dossayev. To be famous in his own lifetime was not often granted to a simple working man, but Dossayev's name stands in the parish register among the foremost citizens, and second only to the Metropolitan himself!

Above: Partial view of the religious buildings and the Kremlin of Rostov Veliky. Right: The prophet Elijah, an icon painted about 1700.

Almost all the buildings in this Kremlin are linked to one another by galleries, staircases or bridges. The principal building is the **Cathedral of the Assumption** (*Uspensky Sobor*), which resembles the cathedral of the same name in the Moscow Kremlin. The Metropolitan Yona is buried here. Next to the cathedral is an unusual, four-arched belfry with 13 bells. Each of the bells has a highly individual tone and can be heard at a considerable distance from the city. The bell-ringers of Rostov created their own special musical art form. The carillon is a complex, polyphonic instrument, which could only be performed by true virtuosi. It was not enough for them to possess musical abilty and no mean physical stength, they also had to know the particular secrets of performing this peal. In medieval Rus, bells were held in great awe, indeed they were worshipped. But the foreign invaders, who despite its long and bitter resistance finally captured the city, used to like to "execute" a bell by wrenching out its clapper.

The churches of the Kremlin are, each in a different way, unusually fine: in the Church of the Resurrection, the Church of the Savior, the Church of St John the Evangelist and in other Kremlin buildings, wonderful frescoes have been preserved. In the Church of the Savior they even replace the traditional wooden iconostasis. In two of the churches there is an unusually high and wide podium in front of the altar, almost like a stage. They were built on the orders of the Metropolitan Yona, who loved his services to be sumptuously celebrated and made true spectacles out of them.

The Rostov Kremlin is indeed beautiful and awe-inspiring; the monasteries of Jakob and Abraham down on the lake shore are magnificent, and the other architectural monuments of the city are equally unforgettable.

However, Rostov is also famous for its enamel painting, an art which has been preseved down to the present day. There is scarcely a tourist who can resist the temptation to buy a souvenir from among the highly individual miniatures, pendant earrings and brooches, or the bracelets with the pink, mauve and blue flowers on a milk-white background.

PERESLAVL-ZALESSKY

The word *zalessky* in Russian means "beyond the wood," and indeed the old road to Pereslavl does run beneath tall trees. Then you emerge from the woodland to see Lake Pleshcheyevo glistening in the sunlight. The city was founded on the banks of the lake in 1152 at the behest of Prince Yuri Dolgoruky. Pereslavl was once the capital of a great principality, whose most famous ruler was Alexander Nevsky, one of the greatest names in Russian history. His honorary title, Nevsky, came from his victory in the battle of the river Neva in the 13th century, when he led the armies of Russia and routed the Swedish and Lithuanian knights.

Above: Faith and work – certainly, work – have not changed for centuries in Suzdal.

He was canonized by the church for his services to the nation, and the Lavra in St Petersburg was later named after him. However, as the last prince of Pereslavl, he died without an heir and in 1302 the principality was annexed by Moscow.

Ever since then the czars have had a special fondness for Pereslavl and often visited the city. They gave money to build churches and monasteries here, and although the city was laid waste many times by foreign invaders, it was always rebuilt afterwards.

As a young man, Peter the Great lived here for some years towards the end of the 17th century, and it was on the shores of Lake Pleshcheyevo that he began to build Russia's first flotilla. Only one of its ships has survived, the *Fortuna*, which can be seen in the local musuem.

However, it was Peter who, unintentionally, caused the second and final decline of the city. When he moved the capital from Moscow to St Petersburg, Pereslavl faded out of history. Industry only developed slowly and the new railroad passed it by. Perhaps it is precisely this fact that preserved the city as a historic treasure, even though not all its monuments have survived.

The oldest buildings are the **ramparts**, which date from the 12th century. The Cathedral of the Transfiguration belongs to this period as well. The ramparts are 1/2 mi (2.5 km) long, 50 ft wide and 26 ft high (15m by 8m), and are among the most impressive fortifications in Russia. The earthworks were surmounted by a double palisade of oak stakes and twelve watch towers. At the northern end is the **Cathedral of the Transfiguration** (*Preobrazhensky Sobor*), built of white limestone. Massive, unshakeable and austere, it has survived all the ravages of war, and seems to be hewn out of a single rock, so carefully have its walls been fashioned. Sadly, the 12th century frescoes inside the church are in a poor state of preservation; there is only a rather stylized iconostasis of a much later date, which contrasts uncomfortably with the austere lines of the cathedral.

Some wonderful churches from the 16th to 18th centuries have been preserved both inside and outside the ring of fortifications. Some of them are the remnants of once wealthy monasteries, of which four still survive: these are the Daniel, the Fyodor, the Nikita and the Goritsky monasteries.

The first three of these are linked with the name of Russia's ruthless czar, Ivan the Terrible: the main cathedral of the Daniel monastery was built to mark his birth, and the oldest building in the Fyodor monastery commemorates the birth of his son. The Nikita monastery, founded before the city itself, was completely rebuilt on his orders, in a mere three years. It was rumored at the time that the czar had earmarked the Nikita monastery as his own future residence in case he was overthrown.

The **Goritsky monastery** stands on a hill and flourished later, during the 17th and 18th centuries. When the original buildings from the 14th to 16th centuries threatened to collapse, they were demolished, and the monastery became the residence of the Metropolitan. The finest craftsmen were brought in to improve the interiors. They also built the outwardly plain monastery cathedral, which, inside, was a showpiece of ecclesiastical magnificence. The carved and gilded iconostasis and the Baroque stucco ornamentation are stunning in their extravagance.

Another of the Goritsky monastery's treasures is the Holy or Golden Gate. This work of an unknown master has the appearance of lace carved in stone and its beauty has been wondered at for nearly four centuries. Today the monastery houses the **Museum of Art and History,** one of the most richly stocked provincial museums in Russia. Its exhibits include works of art and items illustrating the daily life of the peasantry.

THE GOLDEN RING

Yaroslavl: This preserved historic city 160 mi./ 260 km from Moscow has become famous for its **Icon-painting** and the **Spassky monastery**. Two richly decorated 17th century churches are: the **Epiphany Church** and **Prophet Elijah Church**. Open 9am to 5pm, in summer until 6pm. The **merchants' houses**, with their carved wooden frontages, on the Volga Embankment, give a picture of the 19th century. This industrial town on the Volga is easily reached by electric train from *Yaroslavsky Vokzal (Metro Komsomolskaya Ploshchad)*.

Pereslavl-Zalessky: The **Cathedral of the Transfiguration** and the **ramparts** from the 12th century are the main attractions within the area beside the Pleshcheyevo Lake. The **Goritsky monastery** and the **Golden Gate** are two further sights, set in attractive landscape. Distance from Moscow: abt. 80 mi./130 km. Open 9am to 5pm, in summer until 6pm.

Rostov Veliky: The **Kremlin** beside Lake Nero is without equal anywhere in Russia. The **monasteries** (Abraham, Jacob) and **churches** (Savior and John the Evangelist) are important architectural monuments. The best way to visit Rostov Veliky (124 mi./200 km from Moscow) is with an organized tour. Open 9am to 5pm, in summer until 6pm.

Sergiyev Posad (formerly *Zagorsk*): The open-air museum is one of the most frequently visited tourist attractions outside Moscow. The **Lavra of the Trinity and St Sergius** lies 47 mi. / 75 km northeast of Moscow. The most important buildings in the monastery complex: The **Trinity Cathedral**; the **Cathedral of the Assumption**; the church of **Sts Sossima and Savvaty**; the **Czar's Palace**; the **Palace of the Metropolitans** and the **Ikonostasis** with paintings by Andrei Rublyov. Open 9 am to 5pm, in summer until 6pm. By electric train from the Moscow terminus *Yaroslavsky Vokzal*, *(Metro Komsomolskaya Ploshchad)*.

Suzdal: Although situated 137 mi. / 220 km east of Moscow, this town is one of the most popular tourist destinations because of its **Pokrovsky Convent**, numerous **churches** and the **Open-Air Museum of Wooden Architecture**. It can only be reached by private car or with an organized excursion. Open 9am to 5pm, in summer until 6pm.

Vladimir: In addition to the **Golden Gate,** the **Cathedral of St Demetrius** and the **Cathedral of the Assumption** merit special attention. Of more recent date (1913) is the **Trinity Church**. Open 9am to 5pm, in summer until 6pm. Vladimir is about 100 miles / 160 km from Moscow.

ST. PETERSBURG: THE INNER CITY

ADMIRALTY
MARIINSKY THEATER
ST ISAAC'S CATHEDRAL
PALACE SQUARE / SUMMER GARDEN / RUSSIAN MUSEUM
NEVSKY PROSPEKT
EASTERN ST. PETERSBURG

St. Petersburg

If Kiev is known to Russians as the "Mother of all Russian cities," no such accolade has ever been won by either Moscow or by the "Venice of the North," St. Petersburg. From 1712 until 1917 it was the capital of the Russian Empire (was renamed Petrograd from 1914 to 1924, and then called Leningrad until 1991). Famous for its many rivers, canals and bridges, the fortress city was reclaimed by Peter the Great from the swampy shores of the Gulf of Finland. It has always been Russia's window on the west and a record in stone of the powerful reshaping of Russian society in the 18th century. As André Gide said in 1936: "What I most admire about Leningrad is Saint Petersburg."

ADMIRALTY – DECEMBRISTS' SQUARE – NEW HOLLAND

To see the sights of the historic city center, the best place to begin is in **Palace Square** (*Dvortsovaya Ploshchad*); a return to the same point is quite possible in

Previous pages: St. Petersburg has more bridges than Venice. The General Staff Building on Palace Square. Left: The gilded spire of the Admiralty.

about two hours later. You will pass by the power centers of the former capital of the Russian Empire. Grandeur and magnificence are to be found in abundance but the architecture is coolly elegant – un-Russian in fact.

We begin by turning west and walking along the central avenue, Admiralty Prospekt, which is buried deep in greenery in the summer and deep in snow in the winter. On the right is the massive complex of the **Admiralty** (*Admiralteystvo*), which was originally a shipyard built by Peter the Great in 1704. More than 300 ships were built here over the next century and a half. Fortifications were built around the shipyard as a defense against the Swedes with whom Russia was then at war.

When the dockyard was moved elsewhere, the building was used for purely administrative purposes. It has been altered many times and its present design dates from 1806-23 and was the work of the architect Zakharov. He built the monumental tower, 238 ft (72m) high, crowned by a shiny gilded spire with a weather-vane in the shape of a sailing ship, which is now one of the emblems of the city. The dome and spire were last regilded in 1977. The 28 sculptures on the roof colonnade created by the sculptors Shchedrin, Pimenov and Demut-Mali-

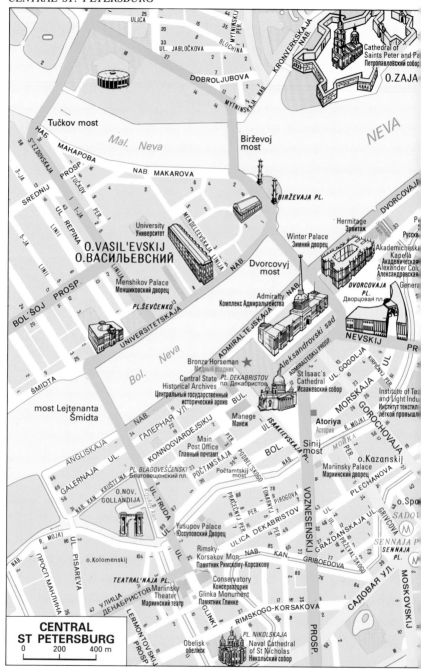

**CENTRAL
ST PETERSBURG**

0   200   400 m

novsky are intended to emphasize the idea of Russia's greatness and strength as a naval power.

Over the past two hundred years, every conceivable kind of naval establishment has occupied the Admiralty: the Ministry of Marine, the Naval General Staff, the College of Shipbuilding and a branch of the Naval Museum. The Naval College is now housed in the complex and unfortunately it is only possible to look at the building from the outside.

The former Gorky Gardens, now the Alexander Gardens, contain a number of busts of famous people: the poets Lermontov and Gogol and the composer Glinka. They are grouped around a fountain which works occasionally in summer. There is also a memorial to the explorer Nikolai Przhevalsky, with a camel lying at his feet. This is a reminder that during his travels in Asia the General discovered a species of camel previously unknown to science and also a wild horse which is named after him.

At the end of the long Admiralty building we turn towards the Neva. On the left is the former Senate Square, now named the **Square of the Decembrists** (*Ploshchad Dekabristov*). The Decembrists were progressively minded army officers who tried in December 1825 to overthrow the Romanovs and establish a more liberal monarchy in Russia under Grand Duke Constantine.

However, the uprising was quickly snuffed out, five of the Decembrists were hanged, many others were exiled to Siberia; and the Romanov czars continued to rule Russia until 1917. The square is dominated by the impressive statue of Peter the Great.

The finest monument in St. Petersburg, and the whole of Russia, to the founder of the city is often called the **Bronze Horseman**, a name which appears in a stirring epic poem by Pushkin dedicated to Peter. The equestrian statue was designed by a Frenchman, E. M. Falconet and Peter's

head was modeled by his pupil, Marie-Anne Collot. The serpent, representing Evil defeated, is the work of the sculptor F. Gordeyev. The statue took ten years to complete – from 1768 until 1778!

The pedestal is a huge piece of natural rock weighing 1600 tons. It was found in the Gulf of Finland and took two whole years to move it the 6 miles (10 km) to its present resting place. A special truck on rails, with 32 giant bronze ball-bearings, was used to transport it. A medallion was later struck to commemorate this extraordinary feat of engineering, which had to be planned down to the last detail.

The monument, which had been commissioned by Catherine the Great, was unveiled on 7th August 1782, to general rejoicing. Its massive base bears the simple inscription in Russian and Latin: "For Peter I from Catherine II." A daughter of the German princely house of

Above: Naval recruits exercising outside the Admiralty. Right: The Bronze Horseman, Peter the Great, in front of the Senate.

Anhalt-Zerbst, Catherine shared Peter's ideals of firm but enlightened rule and became a highly successful – and indeed controversial Empress of Russia.

The two buildings on the other side of Decembrists' Square, joined by a triumphal arch across Galernaya Ulitsa, were formerly the seats of the **Senate** and the **Synod**. The Senate governed Russia in Peter's absence, while the Synod controlled church affairs. Built by the architects Carlo Rossi and A. Staubert between 1829 and 1834, they completed the rigorously classical group of buildings around what was then Senate Square.

The architecture of these buildings is formal; the balconies with their eight Corinthian columns have an elegant harmony and the rounded corner of the Senate with its columns is very effective.

It is with good reason that the two buildings stand side by side. The Senate and the Holy Synod represented temporal and spiritual power.

These buildings suffered heavy damage during the German siege in the Sec-

ond World War and it took a quarter of a century to rebuild them. The sculptures, the decorations on the façade, the interiors and paintings by leading 19th century artists were all restored.

The buildings are now occupied by the St. Petersburg Central State Historical Archives. These contain nearly six and a half million documents from the highest central government organs of the Russian Empire, as well as private documents and many others covering every aspect of St. Petersburg from its foundation onward. Much is still unread and no doubt many secrets will long remain concealed in the dusty files.

This brings us to the corner of Konnogvardeyskiy Boulevard. Right at the top is the **Manege** of the Horse Guards, which used to be called the Drill Hall. This was where officers of the cavalry regiments completed their training and perfected the art of drilling on horseback. The czars used to come here to admire their Guards and show off their own horsemanship. The Manege consisted of one

large enclosed arena covered with sawdust. It was built in the classical style by Giacomo Quarenghi in 1804-07 and there is a broad staircase leading up to its main entrance.

The sculptures at the entrance represent the heavenly twins of Roman mythology Castor and Pollux, and are the work of the Italian sculptor P. Triscorni. The building is now the Central Exhibition Hall. The Manege in Moscow has been put to just the same use.

Like all the other buildings in this area, the Manege is dwarfed by the huge bulk and gilded dome of St. Isaac's Cathedral. For the moment, however, we continue along Konnogvardeyskiy Boulevard. It is bordered on the right hand side by houses which once belonged to the wealthiest people in St. Petersburg. The low yellow buildings opposite were barracks.

After about seven minutes we come to **Blagoveshchenskaya Square** (dedicated to the Annunciation), which under Communist rule was named the Square of Labor (*Ploshchad Truda*). The rose-pink palace on the right hand side belonged to Grand Duke Nikolai Nikolayevich, brother of Czar Alexander II, but in the Soviet period it was occupied by a number of institutions linked to the trade unions, and the building was called the Palace of Labor. It is still the headquarters of various official bodies.

The square will be disfigured for some time by the building of a Metro station This kind of information is not normally mentioned in a travel guide, but because construction projects in Russia now drag on for much longer than used to be the case, these obstacles will be in place for quite a time.

Crossing the square, we come to the Kryukov Canal, which was dug early in the 18th century between the Moyka River and the Admiralty Canal. This created an island which was named **New Holland** (*Gollandiya*). The island is bounded to the north by the Krushteyn Canal.

From early days, that is to say, ever since the Admiralty shipyard was founded, the timber warehouses were located here. The custom of storing the timber to let it season came from Holland and was called simply "Gollandiya."

The gloomy, low-built warehouses of red brick line the Kryukov Canal and a small harbor occupies the center of the island. What lies behind all this is hardly known to few of the citizens of St. Petersburg despite the relatively free reporting since the advent of *glasnost*. Even today New Holland remains one of the most forbidding districts of the city on the Neva. Its first timber-built warehouses were erected here between 1730 and 1740. The brick warehouses which we see today were built on the island in the years 1765-80.

An imposing **arched portal** spans the entrance, but the gate is actually further

Right: Many new talents are forged in the important Vaganova ballet-school.

inside. Over the past few decades, no ordinary mortal has been allowed to enter, because New Holland belonged entirely to the military authorities. It was here that the marine engineer Alexei Krylov set up a test-tank to try out new hull shapes. In 1915 a radio-telegraphy station was installed on New Holland for the Naval Staff and was used in 1917 by the Bolsheviks to issue their decrees and orders. The whole place, although photogenic, is gloomy and mysterious.

We now cross the Moyka by the **Bridge of Kisses** (*Potseluyev Most*). Built in 1768 and restored in 1907, it is a protected historic monument. We follow the Kryukov Canal and straight in front of us is the green north wing of the Mariinsky Theater. On the left is a building in which the composers Stravinsky and Napravnik once lived, as plaques on the wall indicate. It is now in a deplorable condition.

MARIINSKY THEATER

This brings us to Theater Square (*Teatralnaya Ploshchad*), around which we shall walk in an anti-clockwise direction. The famous **Mariinsky Theater** was designed by Albert Cavos and built to replace the St. Petersburg Bolshoi Theater which had burned down in 1859. For many years it was called the Kirov Theater in memory of a Leningrad Bolshevik leader who was murdered on Stalin's orders in 1934.

The theater has been altered and renovated on several occasions, especially after the wartime siege It can now seat 1620 people and nearly always plays to a capacity audience. The first performances of many operas and ballets were given in this theater, especially of works by leading Russian composers such as Borodin, Glinka, Napravnik, Mussorgsky, Dargomyzhsky, Rimsky-Korsakov and Tchaikovsky. In 1836 Mikhail Glinka's opera *A Life for the Czar*, was pre-

miered here under its original title *Ivan Susanin*, which Communist ideologues revived in the 20th century. Others who worked here were the brilliant ballet master Petipa, the incomparable operatic bass, Fyodor Chalyapin and the divine ballerina Anna Pavlova, to whose supremacy was recognized by such artists as Nijinsky, Kzhessinska and the choreographer Fokine. As a backdrop to their unforgettable performances they had sets designed by outstanding artists like K. Korovin and A. Golovin.

The theater was taken over by the state in the 1920s, but the traditions begun by the great masters of the past proved so strong that the *Mariinka* – as the locals continued to call the theater even when it bore the name of Sergei Kirov – has remained one of the leading opera and ballet houses in the world, right up to the present day.

In the Soviet period, the brilliant ballerinas Vaganova, Dudinskaya, Kolpakova, Ulanova and Shelest performed here with their male counterparts Vino-

gradov, Chabukiany, Lopukhov and Sergeyev. From this theater, Natalia Makarova, Rudolf Nureyev and Mikhail Baryshnikov set out to conquer the world. After their "non-return" – as it was officially called at the time – from guest appearances abroad, the Soviet press orchestrated a kind of public execution for them and they were consigned to oblivion as non-persons. Only recently – after the death of Nureyev – have prima ballerina Makarova and "Misha" Baryshnikov been restored to their original audiences, either in person or in films and videos of their legendary performances.

In the opera company, there has been no one to measure up to the great Chaliapin, although the names of Pechkovsky, Irina Bogatshova and Shtokolov are known throughout the country. The ballet-masters and conductors at the theater – Sergeyev, Vinogradov, Jakobson, Temirkanov and Gergiyev, now the chief conductor and artistic director of the theater, have gained world renown in the profession.

Naval Cathedral of St. Nicholas – Marinsky Palace

After passing the Mariinsky Theater, we can see in front of us, down Glinka Street, a blue and white church building crowned by domes with gilded crosses. This is the **Naval Cathedral of St. Nicholas** (*Nikolskiy Sobor*). In Russia St. Nikola Morskoy ("of the sea") has always been the patron saint of sailors. The cathedral dedicated to him was built in 1753-62 by the architect Savva Chevakinsky and has been in continuous use for religious purposes since then. Services are held here in memory of sailors who have lost their lives while serving in the Navy, for example when the Soviet submarine *Komsomolets* sank in the Barents Sea, or of the sailors from the warship *Novorosiysk,* which exploded in the Sevastopol roadstead in 1962.

Above: The gilded domes and spires of the Naval Cathedral of St. Nicholas. Right: St Isaac's Square and the Astoriya Hotel.

In March 1966, a Requiem Mass for the great poetess Anna Akhmatova was held in St. Nicholas. Hundreds of people for whom there was no room in the packed cathedral, crowded into the churchyard or clambered onto the fences, even though attendance at the funeral service of a disgraced writer like Akhmatova was an act of civil disobedience requiring considerable courage.

The groundplan of the cathedral is in the shape of a Greek cross. The projections on the façade are emphasized by clusters of Corinthian columns. Balconies with decorative wrought-iron railings enhance the Baroque splendor of the cathedral. It is completed in the traditional Russian style by five gilded domes, which are periodically regilded at the expense of the parishioners themselves.

The richly-decorated **iconostasis** is the work of the painters M. and F. Kolokolnikov and the woodcarver Ivan Kanayev. Orthodox churches have a special atmosphere of celebration, their space is always richly decorated. A short time spent in a

church such as this one will give you more of a feeling for the soul of the Russian people than any number of books. The solemn atmosphere and the expression of profound religiosity have a great fascination. For a brief period of oblivion you feel you can lay your burdens on the shoulders of the Almighty. And just beyond the entrance are the busy streets and the realities of life.

The four-storey **Bell Tower** tucked away on the banks of the Kryukov Canal is exceptionally beautiful. There is a feeling that the architect intended to juxtapose this dominating structure and the cathedral which stands apart from it, and give them both a dramatic unity.

In the garden of the cathedral there is an **obelisk** in memory of the crew of the cruiser *Imperator Alexander III* who perished in the naval battle of Tsushima in May 1905 during the Russo-Japanese War. Outside the walls of the churchyard is the burial ground of participants in the October Revolution and the Civil War which followed – Communards, as they

were called then. The square was named after them for a time, but then reverted to its old name: *Nikolskaya Ploshchad*.

Returning along the other side of Glinka Street to Theater Square, we pass the Glinka monument, the **Conservatory** and the monument to the composer Rimsky-Korsakov. He was the director of the St. Petersburg Conservatory for many years and taught a number of outstanding composers including Stravinsky and Prokofiev. A little later, Shostakovich studied there under another leading composer, Glazunov.

When we come to the River Moyka, we turn right instead of crossing the bridge with the poetic name of Bridge of Kisses. The composer Utyozov wrote a popular song about it in the 1930s.

The yellow building to the right on the Moyka embankment is the former **Yusupov Palace** which was used for many years as a Palace of Culture for people working in the field of education. It contains one of the most beautiful private theaters in Europe, which was designed

147

by A. Stepanov in 1899 and sumptuously decorated in the neo-Baroque style by E. Liphart.

The palace belonged to one of the wealthiest families in Russia, the princely house of Yusupov. In December 1916 a group of Monarchist conspirators (the owner of the palace, Prince Felix Yusupov, Grand Duke Dimitri Pavlovich, V. Purishkevich, Colonel Sukhotin and Dr. Lazovert) murdered Grigory Rasputin, the mystic and charlatan, who had practically taken over the lives of Nicholas II and his wife Alexandra Fyodorovna. First they tried to poison him, with cakes filled with enough cyanide to kill several normal men, but this did not work. So they shot him, but he managed to get away. They chased him to the railings of the inner courtyard although he was already streaming with blood, and finally dispatched him. Then they threw his body into the Neva. However, this desperate act did nothing to save czarism from the being violently overthrown in the revolution of the following year.

The destination of our walk is now visible on the left – St. Isaac's Cathedral with its gilded dome. This stretch of the former Herzen Street (*Ulitsa Gertsena*) is not particularly imposing, but is lined with some pleasant old houses. They include the home of the Demidovs (No. 43), built by A. de Montferrand in 1840, next door is Princess Gagarina's house (No. 45) built in the 1840's (now the House of Composers), and then the house of Count Nabokov's (No. 47), where the writer Vladimir Nabokov was born in 1899. He emigrated in 1919 and caused quite a stir in 1955 with his novel *Lolita.* The house is now occupied by the Nabokov Foundation and the newspaper *Nevskoye Vremya.* (Neva Times). No. 52 is the House of Architects. This building is designed in the Constructivist style and is

Right: The grand staircase of the Yusupov Palace.

remarkable for the fact that, when it was built in 1940, the German Reformed Church which had stood here since 1862 was incorporated in it. Another point of interest is that the site now occupied by No. 61 was once the estate of the scholar and poet M. Lomonosov – in those days, in the late 18th century, it was right on the outskirts of St. Petersburg.

We now cross the Moyka by a pedestrian suspension bridge, the **Post Office Bridge** (*Pochtamtsky Most*), pass an ugly gray building built in the 1930s' constructivist style, and continue along **Bolshaya Morskaya Ulitsa** (previously *Ulitsa Gertsena*), one of the main streets in the city center, which starts at Palace Square. This is the new face of St. Petersburg where on the one hand there are branches of foreign companies, airlines, shops and banks as the first signs of the new market economy. And there are offices of various institutions and shops, which until the mid 1990's could be recognized from their dusty, shabby windows, and which have now polished up their image to suit the new free market orientation of the nation. The peddlers and nerve-wracking groups of youths, who used to hang about in the proximity of the large hotels selling Soviet army medals to foreign tourists, have now disappeared. For some years now, not only the militsia, but also uniformed security guards have been making sure that the representative shopping street in the midst of the city has an image of law and order.

The street began to take its present shape back in the 18th century. Throughout its history it has been given different names, even in the pre-revolutionary period. The Communists named it after the Russian journalist and democrat Alexander Herzen, who lived in London during his exile and published a magazine there from 1857 to 1867 called *Kolokol* (The Bell), which was banned in Russia. The old name is now back as part

of the general trend of restoring historic street names.

We should digress briefly at this point to explain the present policy on street naming. The intention is only to restore the original historic names and not systematically to erase all ideological, revolutionary or Bolshevik names. As an example, the name Lenin Prospekt remains unchanged for the simple reason that this is its original name – the street did not exist in old St. Petersburg.

On the corner of Kirpichny Pereulok (Lane), No. 18 is a gray building on the left which is easily recognizable as dating from the Soviet period. It is the Institute of Textiles and Light Industry.

A little further on, also on the left, are a jeweler's and a grocery store. The latter used to be a *Beryozka* shop, which sold food and manufactured goods for foreign currency back then. Beryozkas (with their birch-tree symbol) used to be the only place where otherwise unavailable goods could be obtained. Nowadays you can buy the stuff all over for roubles.

At this point Bolshaya Morskaya crosses **Gorokhovaya**, which until recently was named Ulitsa Dzerzhinskovo after the founder of the KGB. No. 15 on the right-hand side, the former Russian Bank of Industry and Commerce (built 1912-14) is again being used for its original purpose, being the headquarters of a large commercial bank. No. 37 and No. 40 used to belong to insurance companies. One of them now houses the head offices of the Northwestern Steamship Company. Next door are the offices of a number of airlines, Telecom and other companies. No. 38, dating from the beginning of the 20th century, used to be the office of the Society for Promotion of the Arts. It now accommodates the House of Artists and an art foundation and gallery.

Crossing St. Isaac Square, we continue along Bolshaya Morskaya. The gloomy red building overlooking the square, with columns made from blocks of granite, was formerly the German Embassy. It was built by Peter Behrens in 1912,

shortly before the start of the First World War, but was only used until 1914.

Not far away we can see the Telephone Exchange for inter-city calls, which was the headquarters of the Azovsko-Donskoy commercial bank until the October Revolution. Like the Astoriya Hotel (No. 39), it is the work of the architect Fyodor Lidval. Long distance calls can be made from the Telephone Exchange, or you can register calls to places in the CIS that are not yet networked for direct dialing. The cost here is considerably lower than from your hotel.

The Main Post Office of St. Petersburg is next door, in Pochtamtskaya Ulitsa. From here, distances were measured by the traditional Russian measure of length, the *verst* (1167 yards or 1067 meters) from St. Petersburg to the cities of the Empire. This was the departure point for the mail coaches which served them.

Above: Dominating the city on the Neva, St. Isaac's Cathedral. Right: The iconostasis in St. Isaac's Cathedral.

Not far from the house where Nabokov was born, we come to another bridge over the Moyka, the **Blue Bridge** (*Siniy Most*), the widest bridge in the city. It is 319 ft (97 m) wide and hardly resembles a bridge at all. Its outer sides are painted blue; there are also Red and Green bridges across the Moyka. Before the abolition of serfdom, there used to be a market here, where serfs were traded like livestock.

Beyond the bridge lies the **Mariinsky Palace** where the City Council now meets, under the democratic Mayor Sobchak, with the Russian tricolor fluttering above the roof. The palace was built in 1839-44 to a design by A. Stakenschneider for the Grand Duchess Maria Nikolayevna, daughter of Czar Nicholas I, whose equestrian statue stands in the middle of the square called **Isaakiyevskaya Ploshchad**.

The palace was bought by the State in 1884 and used by the State Council, whose centenary was celebrated in May 1901 and recorded by the artist Ilya

Repin. The huge canvas now hangs in the nearby Russian Museum.

In April 1902 the Minister of the Interior, Zipyagin, was shot by a Social Revolutionary, F. Balmashev, in the lobby of the palace. In the 1880s the *Narodnaya Volnya* (People's Will) started a wave of terrorism against government officials, and assaults were almost a daily occurrence.

Under Soviet rule, the palace was the home of the Provisional Council of the Russian Republic and the Supreme Soviet of the Economy. When Moscow became the capital, the Industrial Academy and the City Soviet of People's Deputies, popularly known as the "democratic talking shop," met here.

One of the later additions to the square, the **Astoriya Hotel** was built in 1912, designed by the architect F. Lidval. It is by no means unworthy of its location near to the famous St. Isaac's Cathedral. The Astoriya is probably the best hotel in St. Petersburg, especially since its complete refurbishment by a Finnish company during the period 1987-90. The building was extended and upgraded to a five-star-hotel with 800 beds. The former Hotel Angleterre building was also incorporated into the complex. The Angleterre gained tragic notoriety when the poet Sergei Yesenin hanged himself there in December 1925.

ST. ISAAC'S CATHEDRAL

Our walk has now come to its final destination: **St. Isaac's Cathedral**, named in honor of Saint Isaac of Dalmatia whose feast day – 30th May in the old calendar – was also the birthday of Peter the Great.

The first building on the site was a temporary wooden church, followed by one of stone. The first St. Isaac's Cathedral was built between 1768 and 1802. The construction of the present cathedral began not much later in 1818, to a design by A. de Montferrand. The work took 40 years to complete and was personally supervised by Czar Nicholas I. He still looks out onto the cathedral from his bronze horse.

More than 24,000 tarred pine piles were driven into the ground to form the foundations of the cathedral. The building was supported by 112 columns in the interior. Famous painters and sculptors like Bryullov, Bruni, Klodt, Pimenov and Chebuyev worked on its decoration. Until 1917 it was the premier cathedral of the Russian Empire. It is now a museum, but services are still held in it occasionally. The Orthodox community is currently trying to have the cathedral fully restored to their Church.

St. Isaac's Cathedral dominates the skyline of St. Petersburg city center along with the Cathedral of Saints Peter and Paul and the Admiralty. From the viewing platform on the dome, there is a view over Isaac Square and a wonderful panorama of the city, whose beauty touches the heart even now, despite the years of neglect.

PALACE SQUARE

We must now return to the starting point of our tour. A walk across Palace Square to the buildings grouped around it can take between twenty minutes and two hours depending on how much time you devote to the various sights.

Palace Square in the heart of St. Petersburg is the largest enclosed square in Russia. We begin our tour at the foot of the Alexander Column and view the square first from its center. On one side are the lime-green buildings of the Winter Palace and the Hermitage, richly ornamented with sculptures. Opposite them, forming a semicircle, is the yellow **General Staff** building (not open to the public), with its **Chariot of Victory**, the work of the sculptors Pimenov and

Demut-Malinovsky. The huge bronze sculpture crowns the triumphal arch. Also part of the complex is the Guards Headquarters on the banks of the Moyka next to the Singers' Bridge, **Pevchesky Most**. The whole grandiose design of the square is intended as a tribute to Russia's victory over Napoleon in the Patriotic War of 1812.

The red stone column – cut from a single piece of granite – weighs about 650 tons and, with its angel and cross on top, reaches a height of 156 feet (47.5m). It was designed, ironically, by a Frenchman, Auguste de Montferrand and named the **Alexander Column** in honor of the czar. It was erected in 1830-34, after the czar's death. The angel who surmounts it is seen crushing a serpent underfoot – a symbol of the triumph of good over evil. Its sculptor, B. Orlovsky modeled the face of the angel to resemble that of the late czar. But the angel is so high up that it is impossible to see its face. The monument is as tall as a 17storey building!

The stone from which the column was carved came from the Vyborg region and was transported to St. Petersburg on a special barge. To provide a foundation for its plinth, 1250 piles, each 20 ft (6m) long, were driven into the ground. The people of St. Petersburg watched the drama unfold in August 1832, when three thousand soldiers, sailors and laborers hoisted the column using 60 winches and a system of blocks and eased it into the position where it stands today, supported only by its own weight. It is not fixed and might well collapse if there were an earthquake. Fortunately there has never been an earthquake in St. Petersburg. And the vibrations caused by wartime artillery fire had no effect on it.

The pedestal is decorated with bas-reliefs by Svinzov and Leppe. During the war the column only suffered damage from shrapnel, leaving the type of scar which can also be seen on the columns of St. Isaac's Cathedral. It was restored in

Right: The Winter Palace – a wonderful sight at any time of day and in any season.

1963 and clad with green stone in 1977, to mark the 60th anniversary of the October Revolution. At the same time the square was repaved. Even the old street-lamps were replaced, so that now the square looks just as it did in the 1830s.

Winter Palace – Hermitage

The **Winter Palace** was the residence of the czars from the 1760's onwards. Bartolomeo Rastrelli's architecture is so delightful that it would look good in any color. The building is currently painted light green with white columns and ornamentation in dark bronze.

The Winter Palace *(Zimniy Dvorets)* did not, of course, always look the way it does today. Like many other palaces in St. Petersburg, it was rebuilt several times and may well hold the record for the number of different versions it has been through: a total of seven in just fifty years. These included two palaces by Rastrelli, whose third design (1754-62) is the one we see today.

The south façade facing Palace Square has a large triple archway leading into the inner quadrangle, while the long, straight, colonnaded north façade looks on to the river Neva. All the outer walls feature prominent columns and pilasters, the windows are framed in a variety of ways, but are usually decorated with one of Rastrelli's favorite motifs, a mask or a shell. The roof has a balustrade all the way round, with numerous pediments and statues. Above the private chapel is a small gilt dome.

Even if we remember that the palace was designed to be the residence of the large imperial family and its guests, not to mention 1,500 servants, its size may still appear rather exaggerated. It is rectangular in shape with a broad inner courtyard and has 1057 rooms with a total area of more than 11 *acres* (4.6 ha.)! It also has 117 staircases, 1,786 doors and 1,945 windows. One cannot help thinking that both Elizabeth (Yelizaveta Petrovna), daughter of Peter the Great, who ordered the building of the palace,

and Catherine the Great who completed it, foresaw the future and knew that the building would be ideally suited as an art gallery capable of accommodating thousands of visitors at a time. But the royal masters and mistresses of the palace never really thought of this at all. They did what was necessary to the outside of the building and continued to alter it inside.

At the end of the 18th century the architects Giacomo Quarenghi and Ivan Starov remodeled the suite of rooms called the Neva Enfilade, created the **Gala Ballroom** (*Georgiyevskiy Zal*) and linked the palace to the Small Hermitage, where in 1820 Carlo Rossi built a memorial to the heroes of the Patriotic War, the famous portrait gallery of officers of the Russian Army. In 1833 the heliograph tower was erected in the palace, setting up a connection between St. Petersburg

Above: The magnificent staircase of the Winter Palace. Right: In a picture gallery of the Hermitage.

and Warsaw. Using intermittent flashes of sunlight reflected from a mirror, dispatches reached their destination by stages, in three to five hours, an incredibly short time in those days.

In 1837 a fire destroyed the entire interior of the Winter Palace, but it was fully restored in the short space of two years by the architects Stasov, Bryullov, Thon and Staubert. Iron beams and rafters were used for the first time in the restoration.

The palace has also suffered terrorist attacks. Early in 1880, a terrorist named Khalturin, who was a member of the *Narodnaya Volya* (People's Will) was employed at the palace as an unskilled worker. Every day he smuggled a packet of dynamite into the building under his coat and hid it in a chest in the cellar. When the chest was full, he set light to it and ran away. The resulting underground explosion destroyed the ground floor, killed eleven soldiers of the watch and damaged the dining room on the first floor, where by pure chance the czar's family had not yet gathered for a meal.

Following another attack, Nicholas II moved the Imperial residence to Tsarskoye Selo in 1904. When war broke out in 1914, the Winter Palace was converted into a hospital. In February 1917 it was occupied by revolutionary troops and in the summer of that year it became the headquarters of the Provisional Government. This was overthrown in its turn on 25th October 1917 by order of the Revolutionary Committee of the Bolsheviks.

After that the palace was destined for a more peaceful existence. It became a Palace of the Arts, with some of the rooms being used for the Museum of the Revolution. The whole palace became part of the State Hermitage in 1945.

The **Hermitage** is made up of a large complex of buildings including, in addition to the Winter Palace, four other interconnected buildings on *Dvortsovaya Naberezhnaya Nevy*: the Small Hermitage (1764-67, designed by Vallin de la Motte), the Old Hermitage (1771-87, Felten), the Hermitage Theater (1783-87, Quarenghi) and the New Hermitage

(1839-52, Leo von Klenze). Also part of the museum is the Menshikov Palace on Basil's Island, which was built in 1710-27 with the collaboration of many famous architects.

Why the name Hermitage? The word means a place of solitude and this was the name given to several suites of rooms in the Winter Palace. The name was then transferred to the picture gallery set up in the palace, and is now used for the whole museum. In Russian it is spelled *Ermitazh*, and the name should always be pronounced in the French or Russian, rather than the English way.

The first collections in the museum date from the year 1764, when Catherine the Great acquired the Berlin collection of J. E. Gotzkovsky, which consisted of 225 paintings by Dutch and Flemish masters. Subsequent additions, including French, Italian and English works, were made by purchasing other private collections – and not only of paintings.

Valuable antiquities, archaeological finds (e.g. a renowned collection of Scy-

thian gold), weapons and coins, tapestries and prints, jewelry and sculptures – everything found a home in the Hermitage and was housed in a multitude of display rooms and storerooms.

The works of art in the New Hermitage were opened to the public in 1852. For the first time, ordinary citizens were able to cross the threshold of a building that had previously been accessible only to the select few. And after 1917 everything belonged to the "people."

Strange as it may sound, the October Revolution was a blessing in disguise for the museum. The stocks were supplemented within a few years by collections that had been confiscated from their owners. Paintings from the palaces and country houses of the Stroganovs, Yusupovs and Shuvalovs and from the museum of the Academy of Arts and the Museum of Applied Art of Baron Stie-

Above: One of the 2.7 million exhibits in the Hermitage. Right: The Bridge of Whispers. Far Right: Art students.

glitz disappeared (without compensation) into the Hermitage.

Today the museum is one of the great treasure houses of the world. A few statistics will illustrate this. The Hermitage contains 1,720 rooms with an area of 25 acres (10 ha.). It is scarcely an exaggeration to say that every one of the exhibits on show in the 360 display rooms is priceless. And the collections contain nearly three million items!

Administratively, the Hermitage is divided into eight departments: Prehistoric Culture, Antiquity, Oriental Art and Culture, Numismatics, Science and Education, and Restoration. The two remaining departments are the largest. In addition to the interior of the palace, the Department of Russian Culture includes the gallery of the military heroes of 1812, the Peter I exhibition which has been opened in the Hermitage Theater, and the exhibits in the former Menshikov Palace. In 1981 the museum authorities organized an exhibition in the palace on Basil's Island called "Russian culture in the first thirty years of the 18th century" which was considered to be sensational. Paintings, tapestries, prints, bas-reliefs, furniture and tools were assembled from the first years of St. Petersburg when Alexander Menshikov was Governor-General of the city.

The vast **Department of West European Art** contains a large number of Dutch works from the 15th to 18th centuries, German Renaissance, Spanish and Flemish art of the 17th century, masterpieces of Italian art of the 17th and 18th centuries, and French art from the 17th to early 20th centuries.

Three and a half million people visit the Hermitage every year to see these collections. In addition to guided tours, academic conferences and permanent and temporary exhibitions take place here. Catalogues, academic compilations, monographs, albums and travel guides are published.

To name just a few of the most famous of the innumerable masterpieces which are on display: Perugino's *St. Sebastian* (late 15th c.), Leonardo da Vinci's *Madonna Litta* (late 15th c.), Giorgione's *Judith* (1500), Raphael's *The Holy Family* (1505), Titian's *Flight into Egypt*, El Greco's *The Apostles Peter and Paul* (1609), and paintings by Tintoretto, Ribera and Zurbaran, a marvelous collection of works by Rembrandt, including the famous *Danae* (1636), which is still being restored after sulphuric acid was poured over it a few years ago by a mentally disturbed individual.

What a collection of Impressionists and post-Impressionists the Hermitage owns! It would be the envy of any museum in France, no doubt, with a slew of works by Van Gogh and Gauguin, Cézanne, Monet and Manet, Degas, Renoir and Matisse.

The Sculpture Department contains works from antiquity to the present day, including some by Michaelangelo and Rodin.

A few of the exhibits which are an absolute must during your visit to the Hermitage are: the reliquary of Prince Alexander Nevsky, which was produced from Siberian Kolyvan silver in the St. Petersburg Mint in the years 1747-52; fragments of ancient Russian frescoes from the 12th and 13th centuries, the first Russian printed book dating from the 16th century, and the "clothed waxwork" (a lifelike posthumous portrayal of Peter I) created by Rastrelli in 1725.

The expert and highly trained museum guides have an excellent knowledge of art, history and foreign languages. You can rely on them.

We now continue past the Winter Palace and the Hermitage, turn to the right when we reach the **Winter Canal** (*Zimnaya Kanavka*) and walk on to the Moyka. On the opposite bank, the house at No. 12 is where the poet Pushkin died after a duel in February 1837. Crossing the Singers' Bridge – *Pevcheskiy Most* – we continue on the opposite bank of the Moyka to the Kapella building, with its

fine iron gate. The bridge owes its name to its proximity to the **Akademicheskaya Kapella** building, which is the concert hall of the *a capella* choir of the same name. It had its origins in the court male voice choir, the State Choir of Deacons. This was founded by Peter I, a great lover of choral music and himself an enthusiastic chorister. For many years the choir was called the "Court Choir" but now calls itself the "Glinka State Academic Choir." The palace has a small hall with an organ and excellent acoustics.

CHURCH OF THE RESURRECTION – SUMMER GARDEN – RUSSIAN MUSEUM

This pretty walk takes us to the romantic parts of St. Petersburg which have inspired Russian poets from Pushkin to Brodsky, and where lovers like to go in

Above: The Church of the Resurrection, also known as the Bleeding Savior. Right: Two scenes in the Summer Garden.

the "white nights," those northern midsummer nights when the sun only just dips below the horizon.

This tour lasts about 40 minutes, not counting the time you may spend visiting any of the sights, and it takes us to the places where two Czars met violent ends. Like everywhere else in Russia, beauty and terror, love and tragedy, grandeur and misery are closely interwoven.

We start at the **Church of the Resurrection of Christ** (*Khram Voskreseniya Khristova*), west of the Mikhailovsky Sad park, which is popularly known as the Church of the Bleeding Savior (*Spasna Krovy*). It was here that Czar Alexander II – called the " Czar Liberator" because he freed the peasants from serfdom in 1861 – was fatally wounded on 13th March 1881. Nikolai Rysakov, a member of the radical *Narodnaya Volya* (People's Will), blew up the czar's coach with a home-made bomb as he was driving along the Catherine Canal (now the Griboyedov Canal), on his way from the Manege to the Winter Palace.

The czar was not hurt in the attack, but as he climbed out of the wreckage of his coach, it is said that he thanked God for his safety; a second man, named Grinevitsky, shouted "It's too soon to thank God!" and threw a second bomb which blew the czar's legs off. The czar and his assassin both died of their injuries some hours later. The leaders of the conspiracy were publicly hanged in Semyonovsky Square soon afterwards. The assassination was, wrongly, blamed on the Jews, and sparked off the pogroms of 1881-2.

The cathedral took many years to build – from 1883 to 1907. It is based on plans by A. Parland, with assistance from the Archimandrite (or Abbot) Ignatius. The mosaics on the outside and inside were designed by leading artists of the day, such as Vasnetsov, Nesterov and Vrubel.

We now continue along the semi-circle of wrought-iron railings around the Mikhailov Gardens, cross the Moyka and reach the **Mars Field** (*Marsovo Polye*), which is resplendent with greenery during the summer months. The square,

which is more like a park, owes its name to the military parades that used to be held here; it was then completely open, with no trees or shrubs.

Of the buildings lining the square, the former barracks of the Pavlovsk Regiment, built by W. Stasov in 1817-21, are worth a look, as is the gray marble palace on the Neva embankment. It was built in 1768-85 by A. Rinaldi for Prince Orlov, a lover of the Catherine the Great; the Lenin Museum was opened here in 1937.

To the east of it towers the **Monument** to the army commander **Alexander Suvorov**, created by M. Kozlovsky in 1801. The memorial with the Eternal Flame in the middle of the square is dedicated to the soldiers of the Revolution. Until quite recently newly-wed couples used to lay flowers here, but nowadays the young people prefer to visit the monument to Peter the Great. Times change – and customs and habits change with them.

From the Suvorov monument we continue along the Neva embankment and cross a small curving bridge over the Lebyazhy Canal, which was originally dug to form a straight link between the Moyka and the Neva. This brings us to the magnificent iron grillwork screen around the **Summer Gardens** (*Letny Sad*) which were laid out at the end of the 18th century by the architects J. Felten and P. Yegorov. Their refined austerity, beauty and harmony of design are most impressive. No wonder the English wanted to buy the 30 acres (12 ha.) of the garden after the Revolution.

The park, which we enter through an iron gate, was laid out on the orders of Peter I in 1704. D. Trezzini worked for six years here on the Summer Palace for the Czars (which is now a historical and ethnographic museum). The garden ornamentation includes original marble sculptures by 17th and 18th century Italian masters and a memorial to the "Russian Lafontaine," a writer of fables named Krylov. The Summer Gardens are the locals' favorite place to go for a walk – and have been for 280 years. Concerts and ballets are performed here during the traditional festival that begins during the famous "White Nights" in June, and lasts through July.

Walking southwards through the Summer Gardens and rounding the lake with its swans, we find ourselves back at the Moyka. On the opposite bank is the **Engineer's Castle** (*Inzhenerniy Zamok*), also known as Mikhail Castle. It is an imposing red building which is associated with major historical events. It was built in 1797-1800 on the orders of Czar Paul by Vincenzo Brenna; its façade is on the opposite side to the Summer Gardens. In front of it Paul put up a second **equestrian statue** in honor of Peter the Great which bears the laconic inscription: "Great-grandfather, great-grandson" (*pradyed pravnuk*). A short time later Paul, whose behavior was becoming increasingly bi-

zarre, was assassinated in this residence by conspirators. From 1819 the castle was used as a school of engineering, hence its present name. (It was previously Mikhailovsky Dvorets). Among the students at the school was the great writer Fyodor Dostoyevsky. The window of his room was at one corner of the building and looked out on the Fontanka. It has recently been decided to give the building to the Russian Museum, except of the rooms housing the Naval Library.

The St. Petersburg **Circus** building backs onto the square with the statue of Peter I on horseback. It holds 2,350 people and was built in 1877 on the initiative of G. Ciniselli. It passed into state ownership in 1924. Since 1928 there have been continuous performances. There is also a Circus Museum here.

We have now reached Engineer's Street (*Inzhenernaya Ulitsa*). The building opposite the circus, the former Manege (now the Winter Stadium), is only of peripheral interest to us, as we are approaching the **Square of the Arts** (*Ploshchad Iskusstv*). This is one of the finest areas of St. Petersburg.

Before reaching it, we pass the **Ethnographic Museum** on the right-hand side. It was founded in 1901 as a department of the Russian Museum and now has a collection of more than 260,000 objects and 140,000 photographs of the life and culture of the peoples of the Russian Empire and the former Soviet Union. Art exhibitions are also arranged here.

The Square of the Arts used to be called Michael Square after the Michael Palace now occupied by the **Russian Museum**. The square as a whole bears the signature of Carlo Rossi. It contains the Small Opera House (*Maly Teatr Opery i Baleta Imeny Mussorgskovo*), the Grand Philharmonic Hall and the Musical Comedy Theater. But it is the Russian Museum which dominates the square.

It was opened in 1898 as the Alexander III Imperial Museum of Russian Art. In

Right: The Russian Museum shows Russian art and replicas of classical sculptures.

1914-16 Leon Benois built the west wing parallel to the Catherine Canal, near where our tour began.

The Russian Museum has a superb collection of more than 360,000 works of Russian art, from the icons of Andrei Rublyov, wood carvings and paintings by old masters like Borovikovsky, Kiprensky, Bryullov, Ivanov, Levitan and Repin, through to turn-of-the century schools like *Mir Iskusstva* (World of Art) and the "Knave of Diamonds" and on to Filonov, Malevich, Kandinsky and other avant-garde painters.

In the center of the square stands a **statue of Pushkin** erected in 1957, the work of the sculptor M. Anikushin and architect W. Petrov. Pushkin is depicted as a young man, full of creative energy and optimism. Anikushin modeled three statues of Pushkin and they are all to be found in St. Petersburg. The one in the Pushkinskaya Metro station, dating from 1955, shows the writer as a schoolboy and the one at Chornaya Rechka station shows him at the time of the famous duel

on 27th January 1837 in which he was fatally wounded.

If you happen to be staying at the Yevropeyskaya Hotel, the quickest way back is along Mikhailov Street, which until recently was named after the painter Isaak Brodsky – not to be confused with the poet Josif Brodsky. The former painted Lenin and the latter wrote poetry and was condemned by the Communists as "work-shy," sent to a labor camp and exiled. He settled in the USA but continued writing in Russian. He was awarded the Nobel Prize for Literature in 1987.

The centrally-located **Yevropeyskaya Hotel** was built in 1873-75 and decorated in the Art Nouveau style with a Russian bias. In 1910 the Krysha Restaurant (a roof restaurant) was opened with stained glass windows by L. Benois. Over the years, its guests have included Johann Strauss, Claude Debussy, Igor Stravinsky, Maxim Gorky and other famous personalities. It has been altered several times, and is now the elegant, five-star Grand Hotel Europe.

161

NEVSKY PROSPEKT

Nevsky Prospekt – known to the locals just as Nevsky – is the city's main thoroughfare and shopping street. For a long time it has been a part of local history and culture, a favorite meeting place for artists and literati. It has entered the history of literature as a street where Pushkin, Gogol, and Dostoyevsky had their heros stroll. It features in the songs of the bards of today such as Alexander Rosenbaum.

We shall wander along it from Palace Square to Znamenskaya Square, which used to be called Square of the Uprising (*Ploshchad Vosstaniya*). The part that lies beyond this busy square is called *Stary Nevsky* (Old Nevsky) and does not have the splendor and importance to be found in this more spacious section of the boulevard.

In the distant past this whole area was a swampy forest. Then a road was built to link the Admiralty shipyard with the old highway leading to Novgorod. In the 1720s, the section between the Admiralty and the Fontanka was drained, paved and planted with birch trees. It was named Great Perspective Road and formed the main access route into the city. Ten years later it was already known as the Neva Perspective Road, although nowhere does it have any direct views on to the Neva. The Nevsky was not given its present name until the end of the 18th century.

The street is bordered by buildings illustrating three centuries of architectural history. No. 1 Nevsky Prospekt was built in 1910 by the architect Zeidler for a commercial bank. The building next door houses the editorial offices of *Neva*, a literary and arts magazine. The imposing building at No. 7-9 on the corner of Malaya Morskaya Ulitsa (formerly Gogol Street) was also originally designed in 1911-12 as a bank, by the architect Pere-

Left: Nevsky Prospekt – where one goes to see and be seen.

tyatkovich. It now houses the offices of Aeroflot. The well-known biologist and geneticist N. Vavilov lived in the next house, built by Benois in 1908. The science of genetics was frowned upon in Stalin's day and Vavilov was liquidated during the Terror.

Next to Nos. 8 and 10, both monuments of early Classicism, there is another former bank, built by Van der Gjucht in 1910-11. A notice on the school building next door is a reminder of the great siege, which lasted from 1941 to 1944: "Citizens! Under artillery bombardment this is the more dangerous side of the street."

At the junction of Nevsky and Bolshaya Morskaya, there are some bookshops, including one specializing in books on art, and an antiquarian bookshop. The writer Griboyedov and the composer Mussorgsky both lived at No. 13 at different times.

No. 18, which extends from Bolshaya Morskaya to Naberezhnaya Moyky, belongs to the earliest stage of development. After alterations in 1812-16, it accommodated the famous café of Wolf & Beranger. It's main claim to fame is that Pushkin met there with his second on 27th January, 1837, before going to fight the fateful duel during which he lost his life. It is now the **Literature Café**, whose interior still evokes a little of the atmosphere of Pushkin's time.

The building opposite, No. 15, is important in terms of cultural history because the architect Giacomo Quarenghi once lived here; the house was later the headquarters of the Chess Club and the Club of the Nobility.

After the October 1917 Revolution, it was named the House of the Arts and was occupied for a time by the authors Grin, Mandelstam and Zoshchenko, who used to hold literary soirées there. Now it is just a cinema and a café.

We next cross the Moyka by the Narodniy Most (People's Bridge) with its

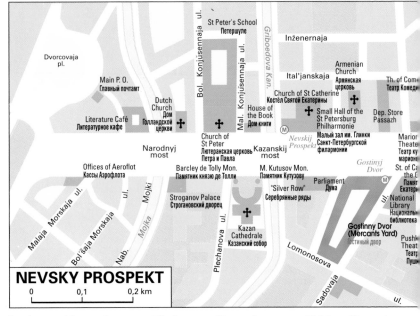

handsome old street lamps, and find ourselves facing Stroganov Palace, built in
1752-54 in the Baroque style, by Bartolomeo Rastrelli. It now belongs to the Hermitage. On the other side of the street,
forming the middle part of the building at
No. 20, is the **Dutch Church**. In the 19th
century this building, dating from 1831-
37, housed the editorial offices of the magazine *Patriotic Notes (Otetshestvennye
Zapisky)*, which was important in Russian literary history. It was closed down
several times, but always came back
under the direction of different editors.
The literary traditions of the building are
maintained today by the Alexander Blok
Library.

Nevsky is now joined on the left by
Bolshaya Konyushennaya Ulitsa, which
until recently bore the name of the terrorist Zhelyabov, who assassinated Alexander II. Since 1997, work has been in progress to develop the street as St. Petersburg's first pedestrian zone, an agreeable
place to stroll about, with cafés and
shops. Between the streets of Bolshaya

Konyushennaya and Malaya Konyushennaya (Great and Little Stable Streets), is
the Lutheran **Church of St. Peter,** which
was designed by A. Bryullov in 1833. In
the Soviet period the church was turned
into a swimming pool, but in 1992 it was
restored to the Lutheran community,
which is in the process of re-establishing
itself with western assistance. Behind it is
St. Peter's School, dating from 1762,
whose former students include the composer Mussorgsky and the Russian-Ita-
lian architect Carlo Rossi.

At Nos. 22 and 24, built in 1837, the
journalist and bookseller Smirdin ran a
lending library which was a meeting
place for the men of letters of Pushkin's
time. No. 28 was built in 1904 for the
American manufacturer of sewing ma-
chines, Singer. Since 1919 it has accommodated the **House of the Book**, (*Dom
Knigy*), the largest bookshop in St. Petersburg, as well as a number of publish-
ers.

Opposite, concealed behind a grandiose semicircular colonnade with 144

Corinthian columns, is the pearl of the Nevsky: the **Kazan Cathedral**. It was built in 1801-11 to plans drawn up by Andrei Voronikhin. Czar Paul I, who has gone down in history as being a little dotty, wanted it to be a copy of the basilica of St. Peter's in Rome. So Voronikhin get about doing his best and succeeded. At the ends of the colonnades are two monuments by the sculptor Boris Orlovsky, one to Prince Barclay de Tolly, who, despite his French-sounding name, was an army commander fighting against Napoleon, and the other to Field Marshal Mikhail Kutuzov, Commander-in-Chief of the army in the same Patriotic War of 1812, who is buried in the Cathedral. Under Soviet rule the church housed the Museum of the History of Religion and Atheism. Nowadays, mass is once again celebrated twice a day, at 11 a.m. and at 6 p.m. At the start of *glasnost* people came along to the cathedral every day and engaged in long and heated debates on the political developments that were taking place in Russia.

Beside the cathedral, the Kazan Bridge (*Kazansky Most*) crosses the Griboyedov Canal formerly known as the Catherine Canal. At the corner of the canal and the Nevsky is the **Small Hall** (*Maly Zal*) of the St. Petersburg Philharmonic, in which Liszt, Hector Berlioz and Anton Rubinstein gave concerts. The entrance to the Nevsky Prospekt Metro station is in the same building. East of it is the Catholic **Church of St. Catherine** (built in 1762-83 by Vallin de la Motte and Rinaldi) in which the last King of Poland is buried.

Nos. 31 and 33, opposite the church (built in 1784-87 by Quarenghi) are an old trading house named "Silver Row" (*Serebryanye Ryady*), so-called because silver goods were traded here. The pentagonal tower with a clock on the top is part of the **parliament** (Duma) building (1799-1804, G. Ferrari) now used by the city administration; in the early 19th century the tower was used for sending messages by heliograph.

One of the churches of many denominations which gave the Nevsky the name

165

"Street of Tolerance" is the **Armenian Church**, built by J. Felten in 1771-80 in the Baroque style but already with touches of early Classicism.

At No. 46, someone opened a night-club, and right next to it stands the Passazh department store. On the south side of the street you can see what is probably the best-known place in the city for shopping, the long building of **Gostinny Dvor** (Merchants Yard, 1785) with its many shops ranged around the inside on two floors, under arcades. It became the model for many other commercial centers in Russia and a number of western companies have now opened up branches here.

A pedestrian tunnel leads to the large delicatessen, the luxurious shop of the Yeliseyev brothers built in 1902 and named after them. During the Soviet era, this shop with splendid Art-Nouveau fur-

Above: Flowers are part of the Nevsky scene.
Right: Belozelsky-Belozyorsky Palace: for-mer stronghold of the Communist Party.

nishings was pragmatically named Gastronom 1. The wares bac in those days were not much different from what you could find in any other store, and the weary consumers could only imagine what unbelievably fine consumer goods had been sold here in the days of the czar. But today, the lamps in the shape of blossoms bathe caviar, smoked salmon, and other delicacies in a warm light. You should not fail to visit this historic building. On the first floor of the building is the popular Comedy Theater.

Another pearl strung along the Nevsky is **Ostrovsky Square** (*Ploshchad Ostrovskovo*), which was designed by Carlo Rossi. The buildings around it include the Russian National Library, the Pushkin Theater with the Chariot of Apollo above the colonnade, cast from a design by Pimenov, and finally the pavilions by Rossi which flank the eastern side of the square. In the center is a statue of Catherine the Great, the pedestal of which is surrounded by bronze figures of contemporaries of the Empress. The area around the monument is a favorite rendezvous for the gay community.

The striking building on the right-hand side of the street is the **Anichkov Palace** (1754) which was built by Elizabeth I for her favorite, Count Razumovsky, and was later lived in by various members of the imperial family. Every occupant had the palace remodeled. In the Soviet era it was used as a recreational center for children and called "Pioneers' Palace."

The palace takes its name from the adjacent **Anichkov Bridge** which was built across the Fontanka in 1785 by an army regiment under Colonel Anchikov. At its four corners are groups of sculptures by Peter Klodt representing the taming of the horse by Man. Czar Nicholas I had copies of the statues cast, and presented them as a gift to his brother-in-law, King Friedrich Wilhelm IV of Prussia. Another set were sent to the King of Naples.

The **Palace** of the Princes **Beloselsky-**

Belozyorsky (No. 41, Nevsky), originally a classical design, was remodeled in the neo-Baroque style by Andreas Stakenschneider in the middle of the 19th century. A cultural center has now been set up in the former palace, which until recently housed the district committee of the Communist Party.

Further on to the east is the first cinema in the country to show talking pictures. It was opened in 1929. It is now called *Znanye* (knowledge). The composer Glinka and the poet Nekrasov used to live opposite at No. 49 – at different times. The building until recently housed a café known unofficially as the Saigon, which for 25 years was a meeting place for the young dissident artists of Leningrad. This corner at the intersection of Vladimir Prospekt has remained something of a scene meeting spot.

No. 86, on the north side of the street, which has a six-columned portico, was built in the late 18th century. It was the home of the composer Balakirev, founder of the group of composers who called themselves "The Mighty Five," and wanted to renew Russian classical music by incorporating elements borrowed from folk-music. Other members were Moussorgsky, Borodin, Cesar Cui and Rimsky-Korsakov. At the end of the 19th century the house belonged to Princess Yusupova. From 1924 it was used as a House of Arts and it is now the Palace of Theatrical Arts.

The crossroads of Nevsky and Ligovsky Prospekt forms **Znamenskaya Square**, which is dominated by a rail terminus, the Moscow Station (built 1845-51).

The Znamenskaya Hotel (now the Oktyabrskaya) was built two years later and was extended in the 1960's. An obelisk was erected in 1985 to commemorate the 40th anniversary of the end of the Great Patriotic War. The center of the square used to contain a statue of Czar Alexander III by the sculptor Pavel Trubetskoy (1906), but this was removed in 1937. It can still be seen standing in the courtyard of the Russian Museum.

167

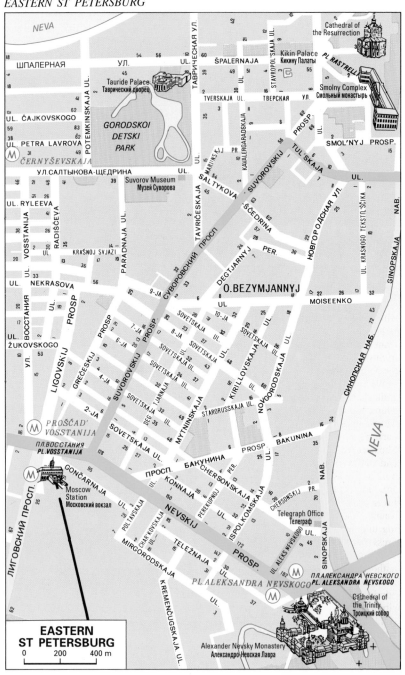

EASTERN
ST PETERSBURG

0   200   400 m

EASTERN ST. PETERSBURG

Tauride Palace

Three historic sites and monuments to the country's history are absolutely essential to visit, but they are some distance apart and quite far from the center. They are the Tauride Palace, the Smolny complex and the area around the Alexander Nevsky monastery, which, together with three other historic Russian monasteries, bears the honorary title of *Lavra*.

A visit to the Tauride Palace can begin at Chernyshevskaya Metro station, which is named after the revolutionary Chernyshevsky, who opposed the czars.

At the exit of the Metro station we turn left into Saltykov-Shchedrin Street and follow it as far as Tavricheskaya Ulitsa. Just before the junction, on the opposite side of the street, we can see the **Suvorov Museum** built in memory of the Russian field marshal. Mosaic frescoes on the front depict episodes from the campaigns of Suvorov, who distinguished himself in the Napoleonic Wars.

We turn left again at the corner and walk along the Tauride Gardens, now the Municipal Children's Park, to the **Tauride Palace**, which backs on to the park. The front of the palace faces Shpalernaya Street, which we reach at the end of Tavricheskaya. The palace was built in 1783-89 by Ivan Starov on the instructions of Catherine the Great, for her lover, Grigory Potemkin, Prince of Tauris, who became legendary for erecting dummy villages to impress the empress on her tours around the country.

The palace is now used by the local authorities, and is not open to the public. However, its classical architecture can be admired from the outside. The exquisite simplicity of its yellow and white façade is in sharp contrast to its once flamboyant interior. The exterior is unchanged: a portico with a double row of six columns in front of the two-storey main building, a low dome above the central section and side wings which end in pavilions. Inside, the domed ceiling in the octagonal hall is richly decorated with moldings. Glittering receptions used to be held in the adjacent Catherine's Hall which is 246 ft (75m) long and opens onto a vast Winter Garden. The gallery, the Chinese Hall, the Tapestry and Divan rooms were decorated with colorful murals.

After Potemkin's death Catherine acquired the palace for the Crown and it became her favorite place for relaxation. After the death of the Empress, her son Paul I, who had hated Potemkin, ordered the palace to be handed over to the Horse Guards and stripped of its contents, which were taken to the Engineer's Palace. But when he was forcibly removed from power, the palace again became an imperial residence. Until the middle of the 19th century the palace looked on to the Neva and was linked to it by a canal, but this was later filled in and the Central Water Works built on it. A more unsuitable place for this hideous edifice could hardly be imagined.

The history of the Tauride Palace in the 20th century is closely associated with the origins of democratic government. The State Duma met here from 1906-17. Briefly, from February 1917 there was dual rule – in addition to the Provisional Committee of the State Duma and the Provisional Government, the Petrograd Soviet of Workers' and Soldiers' Deputies also met here.

After the October Revolution, the first Constituent Assembly gathered here on 5th January 1918, convened to establish the form of government and draft a new constitution. The tragedy of the situation was that although the Legislative Assembly had been democratically elected by universal suffrage and the Social Revolutionary and Social-Democratic parties (later: Mensheviks) constituted a majority, the Bolsheviks were already in power as a result of the Second Soviet

The Kikin Palace

The **Kikin Palace** is reached by continuing along Shpalernaya Street past the Tauride Palace. It is at 9 Stavropol Lane, facing onto Shpalernaya Street. The palace is one of the oldest buildings in St. Petersburg and one of the few remaining landmarks from the earliest days of the city. The architect was probably Andreas Schlueter.

The house was built in 1714 for the Secretary of the Admiralty Kikin, who served under Peter the Great, but he was not privileged to live in it for long. Peter suspected him of being part of a conspiracy organized around his son, the czarevich Alexis, an intelligent but conservative young man, who rejected his father's reforms. Kikin was horribly tortured and then executed in Moscow in 1718.

From 1718-27, on the instructions of the czar, the building was used to house the Chamber of Arts and the Czar's Library, which formed the basis of the present collection of books owned by the Russian Academy of Sciences. Even in Peter's day it was open to the public. The building later became a hospital, a chancellery and the Horse Guards church. It was rebuilt several times and gradually lost its original appearance.

The Kikin Palace was badly damaged by artillery fire and bombs during the War, because the area of the city around the Smolny was a major target. The building was restored to its original condition with the renovations of 1952-57. It is now a school of music.

Smolny Convent – Smolny Institute

At the end of Shpalernaya Street are the premises which until recently were the headquarters of the Party in the metropolis on the Neva. The Soviet name of the square speaks for itself: *Ploshchad Proletarskoy Diktatury*, and it was indeed from here that the proletarian dictatorship

Congress, having previously overthrown the Provisional Government led by Kerensky. The Assembly was forcibly broken up by revolutionary sailors and a pro-democracy demonstration by the people of Petrograd was brutally gunned down by armed troops.

However, the palace continued to serve the causes of politics and politicians indiscriminately. Subsequently, the Third Soviet Congress, and numerous Bolshevik party conferences and congresses of the Communist Internationale were held in it. After the Great Patriotic War of 1941-45, the palace was restored and became the Party College, where loyal officials were trained.

In our time the palace is again dedicated to the ideal of parliamentary government – the Inter-parliamentary Assembly of the Commonwealth of Independent States (CIS) now meets here.

Above: Potemkin's fabled Tauride Palace.
Right: Rastrelli's building style – the Resurrection Cathedral, in the Smolny Monastery.

was exercised by the supreme organs of power in the city. They occupied the magnificent buildings of the **Smolny Convent** (*Smolniy Monastyr*), also called Novodevichy, together with the Cathedral of the Resurrection and the Smolny Institute. The Smolny Convent reflects the styles of two periods of Russian architecture – Baroque and Classicism.

The church and convent were built between 1748 and 1757 by Bartolemeo Rastrelli, who was for all practical purposes the director of all building in St. Petersburg at the time of Elizabeth I, and who also remodeled the Winter Palace. The work was suspended when he fell into disfavor under Catherine the Great. It was not until 1832 that the architect Vasili Stasov was commissioned to restore all the buildings and complete the complex.

From 1764 to 1917, the convent housed the Smolny Institute for the daughters of noblemen, a unique school for the privileged élite where several generations of the top echelons of society completed their studies and were then destined for service at court. At around the same time, in 1765, a department of the Institute was opened for girls from middle class families – the Alexandrovsky Institute. In 1765-66 J. Felten built separate premises for this which are now part of the Smolny complex.

The name Smolny comes from *smola* ("pitch" or "tar"). Under Peter I, tar was produced here for shipbuilding and so this community, far from the center of the city, was called Smolnaya. The people later gave the same name to the Convent and the Institute, however ill-suited it was to their Baroque grandeur. The White Ballroom is a still synonymous with magnificence. Unfortunately, tourists are not admitted.

The **Cathedral of the Resurrection** is a domed Baroque building in the shape of a cross. According to legend, even Giacomo Quarenghi, a champion of Classicism and opponent of Baroque and Rococo, is said to have raised his hat in salute, whenever he walked past the Cathe-

dral and said: "Now that is indeed a temple!"

The projections on the façade of the church are divided by clusters of columns on the lower storey and pilasters on the upper storey. The windows are framed by highly imaginative and attractive panels and the whole magnificent structure is crowned by one main dome and four smaller ones.

Interestingly enough, the splendor of the exterior is in marked contrast to the classical interior of the Cathedral. This is austere, plain and almost modest. The building is now a branch of the Museum of the History of the City; a concert and exhibition complex was opened here in 1990.

The **Smolny Institute**, designed in an austerely classical manner by Giacomo Quarenghi in 1806-08, was for many years the home of the Leningrad District

Above: A relic of the past: Lenin's statue at the Smolny Institute. Right: A national shrine – the Alexander Nevsky monastery.

Committee of the Communist Party, and in those days it was impossible even to get past the gatehouse into the courtyard. The palace is now the seat of the Mayor of St. Petersburg. You can get as far as the front door unchallenged, but a pass is required to enter the building.

The Institute is associated with surely the most dramatic event in Russian history, the Revolution of October 1917. The Pan-Russian Executive Committee of the Soviet and the Petrograd Soviet of Workers' and Soldiers' Deputies moved here from the Tauride Palace in August 1917, having disbanded the Smolny Institute and turned its pupils and teachers out onto the street.

On 25th October 1917 the Second All Russian Soviet Congress began work in the hall of the Smolny. A Bolshevik government was then formed with Lenin at its head – the Council of People's Commissars, putting the seal on its de facto assumption of power. During the night of 25th-26th October the Provisional Government was arrested at the Winter Pa-

lace by armed workers and soldiers. The coup d'état succeeded with hardly a drop of blood spilled on either side, contrary to the myths later disseminated. Stories about an armed uprising and the "Storming of the Winter Palace" belong to the realm of legend.

Lenin left his home and reached the Smolny just in time to announce: "The Revolution which we Bolsheviks have talked of for so long, has at last been achieved!"

Lenin's government worked at the Smolny until March 1918 and then moved out, with all the apparatus of state. Once again Moscow became the capital of the Russian Empire. Over the years Petrograd, which became Leningrad in 1924, lost much that had formed its image as a capital city. But the Bolsheviks did take care of the Smolny complex – in memory of the "Leader of the World Proletariat," whose monument, sculpted by V. Kozlov, and one of the first to be erected – has stood intact at the entrance since 1927.

Alexander Nevsky Monastery

The **Alexander Nevsky Monastery** can be reached by Metro. As we emerge from Ploshchad Alexandra Nevskovo station, we can immediately see the buildings of the Lavra on the opposite side, stretching from Nevsky Prospekt to the Obvodny Canal.

This Orthodox monastery was founded in 1710 by Peter the Great in honor of Alexander Yaroslavovich, Prince of Novgorod, who defeated the Swedes on the banks of the Neva in 1240. After the battle, near Poltava, the Prince was given the title Alexander Nevsky and was hailed as a "Defender of Russian soil" against foreign invaders. He was canonized in 1263. In August 1724 his remains were brought here from Vladimir to the Cathedral of the Annunciation. (*Blagoveshchensky Sobor*). Later they were placed in a silver reliquary which is now in the Hermitage. Peter ranked the Alexander Nevsky Monastery above all other Orthodox monasteries in Russia

and in 1787 it became a *Lavra* – which in the Greek and Russian Orthodox Churches signifies a large and highly commended monastery with many monks.

Here were established the Ecclesiastical Academy – which still exists today –, a library and an archive of ancient manuscripts. The Garden of the Metropolitans was laid out and the City Sculpture Museum was opened in 1932.

The first monastery church was a simple wooden building, but in 1717 Peter commissioned the Church of the Annunciation. It was the first of many stone buildings of the **Lavra**, which were designed by a series of architects of the first rank, including Domenico and A. Trezzini, Theodor Schwertfeger and Rastorguyev, Starov and Petrov, Karpov and Gornostayev. Elements of early and late Baroque are combined with early classical forms. When complete, in 1797, the monastery was given the title "Lavra."

Above: The monument to the composer Alexander Borodin in the Tikhvin cemetery.

Pride of place is given to the **Cathedral of the Trinity** (*Troitsky Sobor*), which was designed by Starov and begun in 1776 on a site chosen by Peter I. It took nearly a quarter of a century to complete.

The plan of the Cathedral forms an elongated cross. The west front has two-storey bell towers and an entrance portal with six columns. The interior is divided into three naves by massive pillars with Corinthian columns arranged in pairs. Its gilded capitals, chancel, gilded bronze altar door, magnificent moldings and paintings on the dome and arches executed to sketches by Quarenghi are well worth a careful look.

The Iconostasis contains copies of works by Peter Paul Rubens and Anthony Van Dyck. The light flooding in through the vast upper windows gives the place a festive atmosphere (but photography during the services is definitely not encouraged!).

Members of the Imperial family, as well as Marshal Suvorov, are buried in the crypt of the **Church of the Annunciation** (*Blagoveshchenskaya Tserkov*). Pushkin's great-grandfather Hannibal and General Sheremetyev are among the famous people buried in the Cathedral of St. Lazarus.

Outside the monastery complex you should visit **the Lazarus** and **Tikhvin Cemeteries** – uniquely rich collections of monumental sculpture of the 17th to 19th centuries. Many famous people from the past three centuries are buried in these cemeteries, including the scientist and poet Lomonosov and the architects and sculptors Rossi, Voronikhin, Zakharov and Starov.

In the necropolis of artists lie the poets and writers Dostoyevsky, Zhukovsky, Karamzin and Krylov, the composers Anton Rubinstein, Glinka, Mussorgsky and Rimsky-Korsakov, and the actors and theatrical directors Asenkova, Komissarzhevskaya, Petipa, Tovstonogov and Cherkasov.

ST. PETERSBURG

Accommodation

The hotels in St Petersburg have been summarized in tabular form in the chapter headed **Travel Information**. See page 243.

Museums

Hermitage (*Winter Palace*), Dvortsovaya Naberezhnaya 34, open daily exc. Mon 10.30am-6pm. Tel: 219 8625. *Branch* in the **Menshikov Palace**: Russian Culture of the 18th C., Universitetskaya Naberezhnaya 15, daily exc. Mon and the last Wed in the month 10.30am-6pm, Sun till 5pm. Tel: 213 1112.

Russian Museum, Inzhenernaya ul. 4, daily except Tuesdays 10am-6pm. Tel: 219 1615.

Musical Instrument Museum, Tel: 314 5394, Izakievskaya Ploshchad 5, daily except Mondays and Tuesdays 12 noon-5pm.

Museum of Theater and Musical Arts, Tel: 315 5243, Ploshchad Ostroskovo 6, daily except Tuesdays 11am-6pm.

Yusupov Palace, Naberezhnaya Moyky 94. Tel: 311 5353, 290 6066.

Kazan Cathedral, Kazanskaya Ploshchad 2, daily except Wednesdays, 11am-6pm Tel: 311 0495.

Museum of Decorative and Applied Arts, Solyanoy Pereulok 13/14, daily 11am-5pm, Saturdays 11am-3pm, closed Sundays, Tel: 273 3258.

Ethnographic Museum, Inzhenernaya ul. 4, daily except Mondays 10am-6pm, Tel: 219 1174.

Suvorov Museum of Military History, Shpalernaya ul. 43, Tel: 279 2628.

Museum of the Arctic and Antarctic, ul. Marata 24, Wed-Sun 10am-6pm. Tel: 311 2549.

Memorial Museums

Anna Akhmatova in the *Fontanny dom*, Naberezhnaya Fontanki 34, daily except Mondays 11am-6pm, Tel: 272 2211. **Alexandr Blok**, ul. Dekabristov 57, daily except Weds 11am-6pm, Tel: 113 8633. **A. S. Pushkin**, Naberezhnaya Moyky 12, daily except Tuesdays 11am-6pm, Tel: 312 1962.

N. A. Rimski-Korsakov, Zagorodny Prospekt 28, Wednesday-Sunday 11am-6.30pm, Tel: 113 3208.

F. M. Dostoyevsky, Kuznechny Pereulok 5/2, daily except Mondays 10.30am-6.30pm, Tel: 311 1804.

Theaters / Concerts / Circus

Mariinsky Opera House, Teatralnaya Ploshchad 1, Tel: 114 4441. **Mussorgsky Opera and Ballet Theater**, Ploshchad Iskusstv 1, Tel: 314 7154. **Shostakovich Philharmonia**, Mikhailovskaya ulitsa 2, Tel: 311 7333; Box-office: 311 2126. **Little Theater**, ul. Rubinshteyna 18, Tel: 113 2095.

Drama and Comedy Theater, Liteyny Prospekt 51, Tel: 273 6152. **Pushkin Theater**, Ploshchad Ostroskovo 2, Tel: 311 6139. **Tovstonogov Theater**, Naberezhnaya Fontanki 65, Tel: 310 0401. **Comedy Theater**, Nevsky Prospekt 56, Tel: 314 2610. **Oktyabrsky**, Ligovsky Prospekt 6, Tel: 275 1286. **Academic Glinka Choir**, Naberezhnaya Moyky 20, Tel: 314 1153 **Glinka Hall**, Nevsky Prospekt 30, Tel: 311 1531. **Big Puppet Theater**, ul. Nekrasova 10, Tel: 272 8215. **Marionette Theater**, Nevsky Prospekt 52, Tel: 311 1900. **Circus**, Naberezhnaya Fontanky 3, Tel: 210 4649.

Restaurants

So long as it is not otherwise defined, all with Russian-European cuisine.

EXPENSIVE: **Wintergarden**, in Hotel Astoria, Bolshaya Morskaya ulitsa 39, Tel: 210 5906. **Europe**, **Brasserie**, **Chopsticks** (Chinese), all in the Grand Hotel, Michailovskaya ulitsa 1, Tel: 392 6000. **Metropol**, Sadovaya ulitsa 22, Tel: 310 1845. **Adament**, Naberezhnaya reki Moiki 72, Tel: 311 5575. Troika (with variety program), Zagorodny Prospekt 27, Tel: 113 5343.

MODERATE: Amdiraliteiski, Bolshaya Morskaya ulitsa 27, Tel: 312 4244. **Ambassador**, Nabereshnaya reki Fontanki 14, Tel: 272 9181. Afrodite (good fish cuisine), Nevsky Prospekt 86, Tel: 275 7620. Literaturnoje Kafe, Nevsky Prospekt 18, Tel: 312 6057. **1001 Nochi** (uzbek cuisine), Millionaya ulitsa 2/6, Tel: 312 2265. **Surpris**, Nevsky Prospekt 113, Tel: 271 1554. Chaika (German cuisine), Nabereshnaya kanala Griboyedova 14, Tel: 312 4631.

FASTFOOD: **Pizza Hut**, Nabershnaya reki Moiki 71/76, Tel: 315 7705. **Bahlsen-LeCafé**, Nevsky Prospekt 142, Tel: 271 2811. **Kafe Drushba**, Nevsky Prospekt 15, Tel: 315 9536.

Post / Telecommunications

Main Post Offices: Pochtamtskaya ul. 9, Tel: 312 8302; Bolshaya Morskaya ul. 3/5, Tel: 312 8915. **Telegraph Office**: Sinopskaya Nab. 14, Tel: 274 2609. Telegrams can also be sent by telephone: 066.

Medical assistance

First Aid is free. Tel: 03.

The **American Medical Center (AMC)** services for payment, doctors perform to Western standards. Nabereshnaya Fontanki 77, Tel: 1196101. **Polyclinic Nr. 2**, Moskovski Prospekt 22, Tel: 316 6272 and 110 1102, also home and hotel visits (Metro Technologicheski Institut).

Police / Authorities

Militsiya, Tel: 02. **Accidents**, Tel: 272 5955. **City Hall**, Liteyny Prospekt 6, Tel: 315 0018.

NORTH OF THE NEVA

**VYBORG SIDE /
PETROGRAD SIDE
PETER AND PAUL FORT
KRONVERK
BASIL ISLAND
NORTHERN ISLANDS
TERMINALS / CEMETERIES**

VYBORG SIDE
PETROGRAD SIDE

The next tour takes us into the northern part of the city, from the Finland Station to what is called the Petrograd Side, on the far side of the Great Nevka. It will take at least two hours.

The **Finland Station** (Metro station, Lenin Square) on the Vyborg Side has become famous through an event in the history of the Revolution in 1917: the legendary return of Lenin from exile in Switzerland. His movements were surrounded at the time by intriguing rumors, which have now apparently been confirmed. In any event, documents have been found which prove that Lenin's journey back to his homeland was paid for by the German imperial authorities. The Russian press, even the papers opposed to the czar, immediately labeled Lenin on his arrival as a "German spy." But this did not prevent him from being given an ecstatic welcome by the people. There and then he gave a speech, standing on an armored car, in which he called for resistance and rebellion.

Later a memorial was erected here to immortalize this historic event. The sta-

Left: An unforgettably dramatic sight: raising the drawbridge over the Neva.

tion forecourt, the Metro, several streets, hospitals, schools and innumerable factories bear the name of Lenin to this day, though the process of renaming them is going ahead. It began in 1991 when Leningrad once again became St. Petersburg.

A slow walk along the embankment will take you to the Hotel St. Petersburg, which is still relatively new. A few years ago, when still called the Hotel Leningrad, it suffered a major fire in which several people died. From this long waterfront a magnificent panorama of the city opens up along the left bank of the Neva.

A little further on, where the river divides into the Great Neva and the Great Nevka, we see the famous battlecruiser **Avrora**, which fired a single shell and entered the pages of history. Since 1948 the warship has been a historic monument and museum. The cruiser was built at the "New Admiralty" dockyard in St. Petersburg and launched in 1900. It was named after a frigate which saw action off Kamchatka in 1853-56.

In 1905 the *Avrora* took part in the Battle of Tsushima, in which the Japanese decimated Russia's Second Pacific Fleet. At the outbreak of the First World War the cruiser was carrying out patrols in the Baltic and in 1916 it went into the Admiralty dockyard for a general refit.

Fraternizing between the sailors and the dockyard workers who were doing the repairs is probably the explanation for the fact that in February 1917 the *Avrora* was one of the first ships in the navy to hoist the red flag.

On 25th October 1917 at 9.40 pm a single shot was fired from one of its big guns, and ushered in "a new era of history," as long-serving Bolsheviks have always maintained. Though aimed at the Winter Palace, the shell missed its target.

The pale blue building next to the *Avrora* is the Admiral Nakhimov Naval College, where young cadets are trained for a career in the service. A short distance further on we come to the oldest house in the city, the so-called **House of Peter the Great**. Behind it rises a tower-block which is popularly known as the "Nest of Gentlefolk" after a novel by Turgenyev. After the war the apartments were let to high-ranking party officials, civil servants and leading artists.

But to return to the house of the city's founder: it was built from birch logs in 1703, the year the city was founded. The outside was painted to look like brickwork, and the inside walls were lined with linen. The czar lived here until his more luxurious and spacious palaces were completed. In 1823 a stone gallery was built right round the house, in 1873 a wrought-iron fence was put up in the front, and the following year a bust of Peter I by P. Sabello was erected.

Since 1930 the house has been a museum. Here you can see many of Peter's personal possessions, and material relating to the Great Northern War and the construction of St. Petersburg.

PETER AND PAUL FORTRESS

We now cross the Kamennoostrovsky Prospekt, which until recently was called Kirov Prospekt and come to the **Peter and Paul Fortress**, which is the historic heart of St. Petersburg. The foundation-

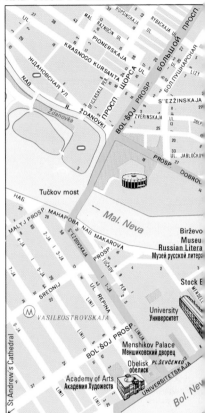

stone was laid by Czar Peter I on 16th May 1703, the day which is reckoned to be the date of the founding of the city. The official designation "Fort St. Petersburg" was retained for about two hundred years, although from the early 18th century the name Peter and Paul Fortress came into common parlance, from the two apostles to whom the fortress's church had been dedicated – first as a wooden building and later as the Peter and Paul Cathedral (*Petropavlovsky Sobor*), whose silhouette still dominates the city skyline.

The fortress stands on Hare Island (*Zayachy Ostrov*), which is mentioned in the 15th century chronicle of Novgorod under the Finnish name of Yänisaari. The

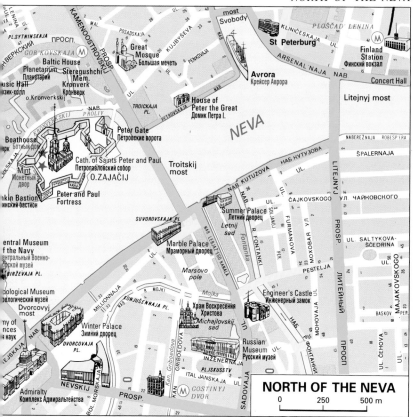

island is about 800 yards (750m) long and 450 yards (400m) wide. For some time after the laying of the foundation-stone was known as Fortress Island (*Krepostnoi Ostrov*).

The original wooden fort was built on the instructions of Peter I, to plans drawn up by a German engineer named Kirchenstein and a French expert, Joseph de Gerenne. Work on the stone fortress was carried out over the period 1706 to 1734 by the Swiss-Italian architect Domenico Trezzini, who also built the **Cathedral of Peter and Paul** (1712-33), which has three naves of equal height. The cathedral became the burial place of all the czars from Peter the Great to Alexander III, with the exception of Peter II and Ivan

IV. The bell tower with its gilded spire surmounted by an angel 10 ft (3.2m) high and a 23 ft (7m) high cross, has become an emblem of St. Petersburg. Between 1896 and 1908 a memorial chapel for the Grand Princes was built. It was used once again in 1992 – for the first time since 1917 – for the funeral of Grand Prince Kiril Vladimirovich. Another of Trezzini's works is the **Peter Gate** (1717-18), which resembles a triumphal arch. Until 1740 the construction of the fortress was in the hands of B. Minikh; he created the Alexeyev and Ivan Ramparts. From the founding of the city, right up until 1954 further work was done on all the gates of the fortress: the Basil, Kronverk, Nikolsky and Nevsky Gates.

179

We enter the fortress across the wooden bridge which connects it with the Petrograd Side. Within the walls there are numerous buildings of different ages and serving a wide variety of purposes; it is a city in itself, albeit uninhabited. The **Commandant's House** (1743-46) is home to an exhibition called "The History of St. Petersburg/Petrograd 1703-1917;" the museum's administration has its offices in the headquarters of the guard; in the **Engineer's House** (1748/49) you will find the exhibition "the Architecture of St. Petersburg from the 18th to the 20th Century." The so-called **Boathouse** (1761/62) was built especially to cover the boat which Peter the Great himself constructed – it can be seen today in the Maritime Museum on Basil Island (*Vasilyevsky Ostrov*). Other buildings of interest are the Senior Officers' House, the Guardhouse, the Treasury and the Mint,

Above: Thirsting for sun on the battlements.
Right: The unmistakable silhouette of the Peter and Paul fortress .

where today, coins, insignia and medals are still struck.

The Fortress of Peter and Paul is both a large museum and a kind of theme park. Until 1917 it was also a cemetery and a prison – it was in the latter capacity that it was best known and most feared by the people. From the beginning of the 18th century the casemates were used to incarcerate those guilty of crimes against the state, that is to say political detainees. At one time the Decembrists, those who took part in the uprising of December 1825, were behind bars here; terrorists, revolutionaries and practically all the *Narodniki* were locked up here before being banished to Siberia or taken to the Schlüsselburg, an even gloomier fortress on Lake Ladoga, near where the Neva flows out of it. Lenin's brother Alexander spent a short time in the Peter and Paul fort before he was hanged for his part in an attempt on the czar's life.

In the Trubetskoy Bastion you can look into cells which are part of an exhibition of prison history and imagine what it was like for the men who were trying to bring about a change in Russian society, and who finally succeeded.

In all its history the fortress only served a military purpose on one occasion, namely in 1917, on the night of the October Revolution. Its guns fired off about 40 shells at the Winter Palace, where the Provisional Government was in session. Militarily, it was a completely pointless action, born no doubt of the wish to put the fear of God into the middle-class democrats.

Every day at noon, the Peter and Paul Fortress reminds the people of the city of its presence. Ever since Peter the Great's time a cannon has been fired from the Naryshkin Bastion at 12.00 precisely.

A recent innovation – and something unusual for Russia – is a memorial to Peter I by M.Shemyakin. The artist now lives abroad, but has made a gift of it to the city of which he was once a citizen.

Outside the walls of the fortress, on the river Neva, are the much-loved city beaches where, even in the first days of spring, sun bathers strip off (almost) to the buff. In summer they are crowded with thousands of Petersburgers in search of relaxation. They attempt to get a tan in the pale northern sun and even swim in the Neva, although for many years the water has not really been fit for bathing.

KRONVERK, ALEXANDER PARK

The arm of the Neva which separates Hare Island from the Petrograd Side, is called Kronverksky. On the opposite bank lies Kronverk – a fortification for the protection of the fort and the mainland. It was built in 1705-08 and renovated in 1752 under the direction of Abram Hannibal, the great-grandfather of Alexander Pushkin.

Hannibal was known as "Peter the Great's Moor." As a boy he came to Russia from Ethiopia and later entered the service of Peter the Great.

In July 1826, Kronverk Square was the place where sentence was publicly passed on the participants in the December revolt, who came mainly from the circles of young aristocratic officers and the soldiers under their command. Nearly all of them were condemned to hard labor in the mines of Siberia. However, five of their number were hanged the same night on the east rampart of Kronverk. No one knows to this day where they were buried; but a memorial marks the place of their execution.

The arsenal of Kronverk was built by P.Tamansky in the years 1849-60. Today it is the home of the **Museum of Military History**. Its own history goes back to 1756, when a collection of weapons, medals and banners was assembled here. But not until 1868 were the rooms of the arsenal put at the disposal of the museum. Today it contains around half a million exhibits: from artillery-pieces and cannon of the 14th century up to contemporary missile systems; weapons for throwing, stabbing and firing, pioneer equip-

ment and communications technology, trophies and decorations, battlefield paintings, uniforms of the army and navy, as well as personal items which were once owned by generals, war heroes and scientists.

The itinerary continues through the Peter and Paul Fortress, across another bridge, and arrives in a broad street which until recently was still named after Gorky, but which once more bears its former name of Kronverksky Prospekt. On one side it is lined with apartment houses, and on the other is a large park, **Alexander Park**.

Opened in the middle of the last century, the park occupies an area of about 54 acres (22 ha.) and enjoys great popularity among the people of the city. Within its boundaries there are several things to visit. Among these are the **Zoo**. This dates back to a menagerie opened in

Above: Artillery Museum in the former arsenal of Kronverk. Right: Some choice entertainment in the Music Hall.

182

1865, which, after the Revolution, was declared to be the property of the people. Today it is run by a committee of scientists. However, the animals seem unhappy in their confined cages.

A little further along our route we reach the Music Hall, the Planetarium and the Baltic House Theater (*Baltisky Dom*), which has appallingly pretentious, yet cold and uninviting interior decor.

The **Music Hall** was the first to be opened in Leningrad, in 1929, and in those days leading personalities such as the popular composer Isaak Dunayevsky were involved in its productions. Even Dmitri Shostakovitch wrote compositions for it. Then this form of entertainment was declared "harmful"by the party officials and the building was turned into a cinema. Not until 1967 was it re-opened as a music hall, and today a mildly erotic flavor is permitted.

The Baltic House theater was built on the foundations of the House of the People, which burned down. Dating from 1932-36, the building is an example of

what is called "Stalinist architecture," in other words, an eclectic combination of many disparate building styles, which most people would call kitsch.

The park also contains the Research Institute of Traumatology and Orthopedics (1902-06), a memorial (by K.Isenberg, 1911) to the crew of the mine-layer *Steregushchi*, who saw action in the Russo-Japanese War, and finally, the pavilion of the Gorkovskaya Metro station.

However, before boarding the Metro and returning to your hotel, you should perhaps take the time to have a look at the mosque, whose minarets can already be seen from quite a distance. At every Islamic festival, the **Great Mosque** (*Bolshoi Mechyet*), presided over by Imam Panchayev, brings together thousands of Moslems from all over the city, mainly Tatars.

The mosque was built between 1910 and 1912 with the help of artists from Central Asia. The design was based on that of the Gur Emir Mausoleum in Samarkand. The inscriptions in glazed ceramic on the façade are quotations from the Koran in the Persian language.

BASIL ISLAND
(Vasilyevsky Ostrov)

One of the special qualities of St. Petersburg is the way its most importamt buildings are inseparably linked to stretches of water. This is true of the group of buildings around Theater Square, the Peter and Paul Fortress and the Field of Mars, but the finest example is probably to be found on Basil Island (*Vasilyevsky Ostrov*). This is the largest island in the city, with an area of over six square miles (16 sq.km), and the build-up of sandbanks is increasing its size all the time.

The spit of land at the eastern end of the island divides the arms of the Great and Little Neva. The complex of buildings on the tip of the island is best seen from a distance – from the former Kirov Bridge, now named Troitsky Most or from the Palace Square. In the middle of

the spit stands the Stock Exchange, and in front of it the gigantic storehouses.

On both embankments there are buildings with towers – the Chamber of Arts on the Great Neva side and the Customs House (now Pushkin House, the Institute of Russian Literature) beside the Little Neva. The two bridges connecting the square in front of the Stock Exchange with the Admiralty and Petrograd Sides, endow the whole ensemble with a unique symmetry. In the first decades after the founding of the city, this was the site of the port, one of the busiest places in the metropolis. Only in the early years of the 19th century did this quarter of the city take on the appearance we see today.

The **Stock Exchange** provides the focal point. It was built in 1805-10 to a design by Thomas de Thomon close to another building, by Giacomo Quarenghi, which remained unfinished and was

eventually pulled down. Thomon's inspiration was the Temple of Poseidon at Paestum in southern Italy. The foundations are of granite, the walls and the 44 Doric columns are of polished brick. The pediment is decorated with a sculpture of "Neptune with two rivers" by Sukhanov. Today the building houses the Central Museum of the Navy.

The so-called **storehouses** of the Stock Exchange were built in 1826-32 by I. F. Lucchini. The south storehouse was originally built for the first Exhibition of Russian Industry in 1829. When that closed the building was given to the Academy of Sciences for use as a zoological museum. In the north storehouse scientific equipment is kept.

In the semicircular forecourt of the Stock Exchange stand two rostral columns (*rostra* means ships' bows). These were once lighthouses marking the harbor entrance. The 16 ft (5m) high allegorical stone figures at their base represent the four great rivers of Russia, the Volga, Neva, Volkhov and Dniepr. In the

Above: The Stock Exchange. Right: The Rostral columns outside the Stock Exchange always surprise people.

shells on top of the columns fires are lit on religious and public holidays.

The **Chamber of Art** on the University Quay was built between 1718 and 1734 to designs by Mattarnovi, Härbel, Chiaveri and Zemtsov. It is one of the few examples of the architecture of Peter the Great's time, which has survived in good condition. Two extended wings with vertical divisions are linked by a magnificent central tower. The building was once intended as a library and as the first museum in Russia. The central part and its tower housed an anatomical theater and Russia's first observatory. In today's Chamber of Art there are collections from the Museum of Anthropology and Ethnology on display. You can also view Peter the Great's own collection of rarities. The Lomonossov Memorial Museum is in the tower of the Chamber of Art.

The main building of the Academy of Sciences is at No. 5 University Quay (*Universitetskaya Naberezhnaya*), and was built in 1783-89 by the master of Classicism, Giacomo Quarenghi. Inside, the main staircase is decorated by Lomonosov's mosaic depicting *The Battle of Poltava*.

The building of the **University** of St. Petersburg, also known as the Twelve Colleges, dates from the years 1720-34 and was originally intended to accommodate the centralized state administrative bodies which Peter I had created. A number of prominent architects took part in a competition for the commission. In the end the work was a co-operative effort by several excellent designers: the lower storey was by Domenico Trezzini, and the upper by Theodor Schwertfeger; overall control of the project was in the hands of Trezzini, and later his kinsman Giuseppe Trezzini – both of Swiss origin.

The building consists of twelve independent parts which nevertheless are linked by a unity of design. The façade overlooks the Mendeleyevskaya Liniya,

along which a canal was originally intended to run. The simple decorative style is typical of the age of Peter the Great: white facings set off the dark red brick, and the windows have white frames. The interior decoration dating from 1700 in the Peter Hall has been preserved. From 1819 the building was used by the university. Its alumni number many scientists of world stature, including Mendeleyev, Pavlov, Popov, Timiryazev, Sechenov and Vernadsky.

The **Menshikov Palace** is one of the oldest historic buildings in St. Petersburg; among its architects were Carlo Fontana and Gottfried Johann Schädel. Originally the palace was surrounded by a formal garden with statues and fountains, and there was a riverside quay in front of the main entrance. Later it was substantially alter-ed, while retaining typical characteristics of the early Baroque period. The interiors of some of the rooms have been preserved exactly as they were in Peter I's time. From 1727 onwards it accommodated the Corps of

Nobles, an educational establishment which was later to become the First Corps of Cadets. Today it is used as an annex of the Hermitage. In the small park nearby stands an obelisk of granite surrounded by iron railings. It commemorates Field-Marshall Rumyantsev.

The building of the **Academy of Arts** (*Universitetskaya Naberezhnaya 17*) is an example of early Classicism with certain Baroque characteristics, and was built in the years 1764-88 by Kokorinov and Vallin de la Motte. Originally there was a passage from the circular inner courtyard through to the river Neva. The suite of rooms on the second floor is decorated with ceiling paintings. The names of many great painters and sculptors are linked with the Academy of Arts.

Running in front of the building is a granite embankment with bronze sconces. Wide steps lead down to the Neva. In

Above: The entrance hall in the Menshikov Palace. Right: The oldest monument in the city, approximately 1400 BC.

place of a balustrade two granite plinths rise up on either side, and on these are an unexpected sight in Russia – two Egyptian sphinxes, dating from the 13th century B.C. They were purchased by the Russian government and brought to St. Petersburg in the 19th century.

On the bank of the Neva (looking downstream towards Lieutenant Schmidt Bridge), you can see many old apartment houses of different period styles. They have all been much altered over the years, but most date back to Peter I's time. The arrangement of the houses is typical – not in a straight line but at different angles, following the bends of the river. Of particular interest are the residence of the Academy of Sciences (1, Lieutenant Schmidt Embankment), the building formerly of the Naval Cadet Corps at No. 17 (now the Naval Academy), the building between the 19th and 20th *linii*), known as the "House of the Grandees," and finally, at the end of our stroll along Lieutenant Schmidt Embankment, the Institute of Mining, at No.

45. Founded in 1773, this was the first technical university in Russia and the second in the world. The two original houses were combined with three more in 1806-08 by the architect A. Voronikhin, who managed to achieve an astonishing unity of style. The doorway of the Institute is graced with twelve Doric columns. The buildings on the other bank form an imaginary gateway through which ships can enter St. Petersburg. The sculpted groups on the façade were executed by Sukhanov after models by Demut-Malinovsky and Pimenov.

St. Andrew's Cathedral on the Bolshoi Prospekt certainly stands out as one of the architectural gems of Basil Island. Designed by A.Wist, it was built on the cusp between Baroque and Classicism, between 1764 and the mid-1780s. Its magnificent wooden altar has been preserved. Beside St. Andrew's (*Sobor Andreya Pervosvannovo*) stand the Church of the Three Holy Bishops (probably built by G. Trezzini, 1740-60) a masterpiece of early St. Petersburg architecture, and the Troyekurov House (1720-30), one of the first stone houses in in the city.

Among the modern buildings on the west side of Basil Island, facing the Baltic, the ship terminal should be noted, as well as the Hotel Pribaltyskaya (*14, ulitsa Korablestroiteley*, or Street of the Shipbuilders). Here you will find several bureaux de change. The façade of the terminal building is clad in metal sheets, which remind one of a billowing sail. The building handles passengers arriving and departing by ship. Nearby is a commercial exhibition center.

At the end of our walk around Basil Island there are two more bridges that really warrant attention: the Castle Bridge and the Lieutenant Schmidt Bridge. Unlike many other bridges (e.g. the small ones over the Fontanka, the Moyka and the canals), neither of the two are especially pretty, but they are interesting feats of engineering – **bascule bridges** which lift to let ships pass. They are a familiar part of the city skyline, when they are opened. Except when the rivers are frozen, the two huge wings of the bridges are raised twice a night to let shipping through – they make an unforgettable impact espec-ially during the long, light midsummer nights. The stately procession of ships, steaming up the Neva makes the scene even more spectacular.

THE NORTHERN ISLANDS

The three islands, Yelagin Ostrov, Kamenny Ostrov and Krestovsky Ostrov, form a separate and quite special part of St. Petersburg. In the early years of the city, they were given by Peter I or Catherine II to noblemen as private estates. On all the islands fine palaces were built with their stables and outhouses, and elegant parks were laid out. Even though great changes in the use of the islands took place in the 19th century, they have retained their character as resorts for relaxation, leisure and sport.

Yelagin Island is named after a courtier of Catherine the Great. The center of architectural interest is the **palace** of the same name (built 1818-22 by C. Rossi). It has two principal façades, one on the side of a landing stage on the river, the other looking over the park. They are decorated with cast-iron lions, baskets of flowers and marble vases. Inside, the palace is lavishly decorated, especially the Oval Hall with Ionic pilasters and caryatids, the Pink Room, the Blue Room, the dining room and the study. After suffering severe damage in World War II, the building was completely restored between 1956 and 1961. The **landscaped park** on Yelagin Island was created in the 1780s, when the owner laid down paths and built dykes to protect the central part from high tides. These works, which were directed by D. Bush, took place at the same time as alterations to the palace, as well as the construction of orangeries, stables and a pavilion. Bush built a series of ponds on the island; and hundreds of oak, ash and maple trees

were planted, which now make it one of the most beautiful parks in the greater St. Petersburg area. It is a favorite place for Petersburgers to come for a day out, and not just in the summer. In winter skating-rinks are laid out, there is a winter sport stadium, and festive winter carnivals are organized.

At the western tip of the island, you can stand beside lions on granite pedestals and gaze out across the Gulf of Finland. On a clear day you can see as far as Kronstadt.

The first owner of **Cross Island** (*Krestovsky Ostrov*) was Alexander Menshikov, a favorite of Peter I. In order to create a park, he had marshland drained, ponds dug and orangeries and hothouses built. In the latter half of the 18th century, the island's new owner, Count Razumovsky, who was President of the Academy of Sciences, built the dead straight Battery Way (today called Morskoi Prospekt), which divides the island in two. Other avenues were laid out, some of which have survived. Razumovsky's own property lay in the south of the island, between Krestovsky Prospekt and the Little Neva. But the island was large enough to provide space for hunting, for several farming villages, and pleasure-gardens for the people of the city.

At the beginning of the 19th century, when the island came into the possession of Count Byeloselsky-Byelozyorsky, further extensions to the palace and the park were carried out. In the second half of the 19th century, numerous wooden houses were built for renting, and at the beginning of this century some stone houses as well. Yet in spite of this extensive residential development, the island continues to be principally a place for sport and recreation. On a city map of 1915 you can see marked: the Imperial River Yacht Club, the St. Petersburg Sailing Club, the Northern Bank Sports Club, the Lawn Tennis Club and the "Arrow" Rowing Club.

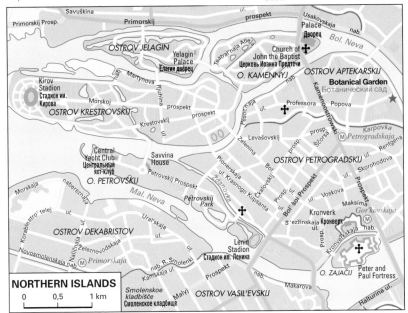

NORTHERN ISLANDS

0   0,5   1 km

After the Revolution, the island played an even more important part in the sporting life of the city: the **sports-grounds** of the various "Dynamo" clubs were laid out here, including three soccer fields, eleven tennis courts with spectator-stands, a rowing-course and a swimming pool. It is the center for Olympic training, the Institute of Physical Culture and many other activities.

The largest sports facility on Cross Island is the **Kirov Stadium,** built in 1950. The arena and stands for 70,000 spectators lie in the bowl of an artificial hill on the western tip of the island. Premier League football matches are played and athletics meetings held here. On the way to the stadium, Victory Park spreads out beside a lake, a wonderful place for walking and jogging.

Stone Island (*Kamenny Ostrov*) is divided in two by the Kamennoostrovsky Prospekt – to the east is the palace, while the much larger western part contains a park. The **palace**, at the beginning of the road, was built in 1776-1784 for Czar Paul I, the son of Catherine the Great, by Felten, Bashenov and Quarenghi. It stands on the site of an earlier country mansion owned by Chancellor Bestushev-Ryumin.

The present palace has two façades and is built in the style of a country house of the later 18th century. In the 19th century it was altered several times, but parts of the interior dating from the turn of the 18th and 19th centuries have been preserved – including the anteroom, and the great hall with its caryatids. The palace garden was laid out in the 18th century but redesigned by Thomon in 1810. At the northern end of Kamennoostrovsky Prospekt stands the church of John the Baptist, built in 1776-78 in the neo-Gothic style by Yuri Felten. It belongs to the pensioners' hospital for the sailors of the Baltic Fleet. The stone orangeries with semicircular columns between the windows, which can be seen on the west side of Kamennoostrovsky Prospekt, are the work of Luigi Rusca, and date from 1814.

189

On the next property, going upstream, stands the wooden **Oldenburgsky Dacha,** built by Shustov in 1831-33, in late Classical style. Other notable buildings from this period include the wooden **theater**. It was built by Shustov in 1827, in just two months, but then demolished in 1884 and rebuilt by A. Cavos, who made some changes to theinterior. At the end of the 19th century it was used as a store for stage scenery and only escaped demolition by a miracle. After further alterations this century it is used as a studio for recording television productions.

Stone Island has a wealth of interesting buildings from the late 19th and early 20th centuries. These include the Becherev House (1914), three wooden dachas in the ethnic Russian style (1865 and 1895), the house of Senator Polovtsev (1911-16) and the house of the architect

Melzer (1901-04). The romantic tower-like wooden house on a stone plinth is called the Fairytale House.

Apothecary Island (*Aptekarsky Ostrov*), separated from Petrograd by the narrow Karpovka river, cannot be regarded as a city district in its own right; it really belongs to the Petrograd Side. There are some particularly pleasant walks to take here; for instance the stretch of Kamennoostrovsky Prospekt from the Karpovka to the Little Neva, lined with appartment houses built at the turn of the century, and another stretch along the bank of the Karpovka, as far as the Botanical Garden.

The forerunner of today's Botanical Garden was the Apothecaries' Garden, which was laid out in 1714 on the orders of Peter I, for the cultivation of medicinal plants. In 1823 this purpose was combined with that of a botanical garden. Today it covers an area of 40 acres (16 ha.) and is a fine park with orangeries, laboratories, a library and a herbarium with over five million exhibits.

Above: At the edge of the huge city a rural idyll still survives. Right: The finest example of Russian neo-Gothic: the Chesma Church.

190

There are several buildings within the park that are worth looking at, such as the "Director's House," dating from 1824.

Petrovsky Ostrov, the island which forms the western part of the Petrograd Side and is separated from it by the river Zhdanovka, fulfills a function similar to that of Yelagin and Krestovsky islands. It contains the 28,000-seat **Lenin Stadium**, the Petrovsky Park, the Central Yacht Club, and a home for retired actors called Savvina House. However, there are also a number of factories on both sides of the Petrovsky Prospekt.

Although this island does not jut as far out into the Gulf of Finland as Basil or Krestovsky islands, the view of the bay from the Yacht Club is excellent at any time of year – in summer, when the distant coast disappears in the mist and the "Meteor" hydrofoils skim past, and in winter, when the glittering snow on the bay is dotted with small black shapes.

RIVER TERMINAL, DOCKS, AIRPORTS

The **river terminal** (*rechnoy voksal*) for passengers on inland waterway journeys, is located on the left bank of the Neva, a little way above Volodarsky Bridge, at 195, Prospekt Obuchovskoy Oborony. From there passenger steamers leave for such destinations as Kizhi on Lake Onega, where there is an open-air museum of traditional Russian wooden architecture, which is on the UNESCO World Heritage list. Ships also go to Valaam, an island in Lake Ladoga which has a historic 19th century monastery. Near the pier is the Hotel Rechnaya.

The **marine docks** are on Basil Island (*Vasiliyevsky Ostrov*), along the Bolshaya Neva. Large passenger liners often have their own courtesy coaches to the city.

The two **airports** of Pulkovo I (domestic) and Pulkovo II (international) are situated south of the city. Remodeling of the international airport (built between 1937 and 1941) 9 miles (15 km) south of the city center, was completed in 1997. The new terminals have bars, cafés, and duty-free shops as well as a car rental agency, Avis (Tel: 235 6444). The ride to the Hotel Pulkovskaya with Bus No. 13, takes only about 15 minutes. The ride to the center of town (Metro station Moskovskaya) takes 45 minutes. Price for a taxi is a question of haggling, but US$2 per kilometer is often demanded by the drivers. The price for the bus or for a ride with the metro is about a US$ 0.50.

Though the number of beds in the city has increased remarkably over the past few years thanks to remodeling or new construction, you should make sure you have reserved a room before embarking on your trip. The biggest hotels (Pribaltiskaya, Pulkovskaya, Oktyabrskaya, Sovietskaya, Moskva, all over 1400 beds), are easily accessed with public transport. The Grand Hotel Europa, the Nevsky Palace Hotel, the Astoriya all stand right in the center of town, and fairly close by is the Oktyabrskaya and the Moskva.

MEMORIAL CEMETERIES

The first memorial cemeteries to mention are those of Piskaryov and Serafimov, where those who died in the siege of 1941-44 are buried. In the Piskaryov Cemetery alone, according to official figures, lie the bodies of 470,000 people who starved to death or were killed by enemy action. Recent research indicates that this figure could well be considerably higher.

There are also some very interesting cemeteries from before the Revolution, where the graves are adorned with the work of many leading sculptors. One such is the **Lazarus Cemetery** (*Lazarevskoye Kladbishche*) in Alexander Nevsky Lavra. It dates back to the days of Peter I. and contains the graves of Lomonosov and the architects Quarenghi and Rossi. Another is the **Tikhvin Cemetery** (*Tikhvinskoye Kladbishche*), where many famous

Above: The Narva Triumphal Arch, designed by Stasov in 1834.

composers, painters and poets are buried, including Karamzin, Krylov, Glinka, Dostoyevsky and Tchaikovsky. Both cemeteries can be reached via the Metro station Ploshchad Alexandra Nevskovo.

In the **Volkov Cemetery** (*Literatorskiye Mostki, Rastannaya ulitsa 30*), lie the authors and poets Goncharov, Lezkov, Saltykov-Shchedrin and Blok. In the **New Maiden Cemetery** (*Novodevichiye Kladbishche*), at Moskovsky Prospekt 100, you can visit the graves of other well-known literati, and in the **Smolensk Cemetery** (*Smolenskoye Kladbishche*) at Kamskaya ulitsa 24, a number of leading poets are buried.

CHESMA CHURCH, TRIUMPHAL GATES, TRAIN STATIONS

Among the buildings of St. Petersburg every imaginable style from Europe, Asia and Africa is represented: Greek and Roman antiquity, echoes of ancient Egypt, Dutch and French Baroque, German Gothic, Italian and Moorish palaces, and the Art Nouveau of northern Europe. One successful experimenter with architectural styles was Yuri Felten. A number of St. Petersburg churches bear his signature: the Lutheran church of St. Anne (*ulitsa Saltykova-Shchedrina 8*) and St. Catherine's church on Basil Island (*Bolshoi Prospekt 1*), the Armenian church (*Nevsky Prospekt 40-42*) and the church of John the Baptist on Stone Island. However, his most original work is the **Chesma church** (1777-80) near the palace of the same name (*ulitsa Lensovyeta*). It is one of the few example of Russian neo-Gothic.

The **Narva Triumphal Gate** (Metro station Narvskaya) was erected to commemorate the Patriotic War of 1812. The first gate, built of wood by Quarenghi, and through which the Russian Guard marched on their return from Europe, was replaced in 1830 by Stasov's brick-built gate clad in copper sheathing. The monument is reminiscent of the triumphal arches of ancient Rome. The quadriga which surmounts it is made from beaten copper, from a model by Klodt. The statue of Victory is the work of Pimenov and those of ancient Russian heroes are by Pimenov and Demut-Malinovsky.

The **Moscow triumphal gate** (completed in 1838; Metro station Moskovskiye Vorota) commemorates Russia's victory over the Turks in the war of 1828. It is made entirely of cast iron, and in its day was the largest construction in the world from this material.

Trains from western Europe terminate at the **Warsaw Station**. To travel on to Moscow, you have to cross to the **Moscow Station**.

The **Finland Station** (*Finlyandsky Voksal*, Metro Ploshchad Lenina) is the starting point for many tourists, holiday-makers, anglers, mushroom hunters and canoeists, heading for Karelia, a natural recreational area north of Lakes Ladoga and Onega, not far from St. Petersburg.

NORTH OF THE NEVA
Accommodation
The hotels have been summarized in the chapter entitled **Travel Information**. See page 243.

Museums
Academy of Arts, Universitetskaya Nab. 17, open 11am-7pm, closed Mon,Tues, Tel: 213 6496. **Museum of Russian Literature** (*Pushkinsky dom*), Naberezhnaya Makarova 4, Tel: 218 05052. **Military History Museum**, Alexander park 7, daily exc.t Tues and Sun, 11am-6pm, Tel: 238 4704. **Central Museum of the Navy**. Birshevaya Ploshchad 4, Tel: 218 2502. **Battleship Avrora**. Petrogradskaya Naberezhnaya, Tel: 230 8440, open daily from 10.30am to 4pm, except Mondas and Fridays. **Peter I's House**, Petrovskaya Naberezhnaya 6, daily except Tues 11am-6pm, Tel: 232 4576. **Museum of Anthropology / Art Chamber**, Universitetskaya Naberezhnaya 1/13, open Sundays-Thursdays, 11am-6pm, Tel: 218 0944. **Botanical Museum**, ulitsa Profesora Popova 2, (*Apothecary Island*), open Wednesdays, Saturdays, Sundays 10am-5pm, Tel: 234 8470. **Zoological Museum**, Universitetskaya Naberezhnaya 1, Sun-Thur, 11am-5pm, Tel: 218 0112. **Fyodor Chalyapin Memorial**, ul. Graftio 2 B, open Wednesdays to Sundays, Tel: 234 1056.

Concert Halls
Concert Hall, Ploshchad Lenina 1, Tel: 542 0944. **Music-Hall**, Alexander park 4, Tel: 232 9201, 233 0243.

Restaurants
LUXURY: **Austeria** (in the Peter and Pauls Fortress), Petropavlov rkaya Krepost, Tel: 238 4262. **Imperial**, Kamennoostrowski Prospekt 53, Tel: 234 3296. **Petrowskij** (ship restaurant), Mytninskaya nabereshnaya 3, Tel: 238 4793. **Schlotburg**, Bolsheokhtinski Prospekt 65, Tel: 222 6385. **Tet-a-Tet**. Bolshoi Prospekt 65, Tel: 232 7548. *MODERATE:* **Antwerpen**, Kronverkskaya ulitsa 13/2, Tel: 233 8482. **Aragwi** (Caucasian cuisine), ulitsa Marschala Tukhatshevskovo 41, Tel: 225 0804. **Forteziya**, ulitsa Kubysheva 7, Tel: 233 9468. **Nevskiye melodii**, Sverdlovskaya nabereshnaya 62, Tel: 227 1596. **Okolitsa**, Primorski Prospekt 15, Tel: 239 6984. **Schwabski Domik** („Swabian house"), Novocherkasskiy Prospekt 28/19, Tel: 528 2211. **Wostok-Orient** (Indian cuisine), Primorski Park Probyedy, Tel: 235 4618.

Tourist Offices / Excursions
Intourist Agency, Pereulok Boizava 7, Tel: 314 6096. **East-West contact service**, ulitsa Mayakowskaya 7, Tel: 327 3416.

Police
Milizija, Tel: 02.

ST. PETERSBURG'S HARBOR

Long after a harbor had been built to serve St. Petersburg, Pushkin dubbed the city "Russia's window on Europe." Oddly enough he did not use the expression "Gateway to the west," which would have been a much better way of summing up the czar's aim of gaining access to the world's oceans.

After the Dutch captain, Jan Hillebrants, had brought the first cargo of goods from western Europe to St. Petersburg in 1703 (for which he gained a handsome financial reward), the harbor was constructed with almost breathtaking speed – in the middle of a deserted landscape of plague-ridden marshes. That the project was completed at all, in the faces of such difficulties, seemed to the Polish author Adam Mickiewicz to be a "work of Satan."

Above: The entrance to the inner harbor of St. Petersburg. Right: Souvenirs for sale by the battle-cruiser "Avrora."

It is a fact that Peter the Great soon made the hitherto landlocked Russia into a seafaring nation. Within a remarkably short space of time he had built a navy from the ground up, and at the same time launched a merchant fleet. Initially both fleets were base at Kotlin Island at the mouth of the Neva, where it enters the Baltic. There were also plans for a strategically secure commercial harbor in the delta of the Neva, but this did not mean that trading activity was separate from military considerations. Even today the civil and naval shipyards, docks and wharfs are in close proximity to each other; merchant ships pass warships and nuclear-powered ice-breakers in the harbor every day.

For decades St. Petersburg has been the port of departure for scientific expeditions into the regions of eternal ice, under the direction of the Arctic and Antarctic Institute. It was from here, in 1928, that the icebreaker *Krassin* set off to rescue the stranded Italian aviator Gen. Nobile. The ship is now a museum.

In czarist times St. Petersburg was the port for exporting Russia's flax, timber, charcoal, pork-fat, wax, honey, ropes, caviare, tar, race horses and wheat. The last of these may sound incredible today, but until 1913 St. Petersburg was famous as a port for the shipment of Russian wheat to the west. Yet half a century later – through one of the ironies of history brought about by extreme mismanagement – the Soviet Union found itself compelled to pay valuable foreign currency for large quantities of imported wheat; meanwhile, the grain silos that had been built for exporting wheat, stood empty. Instead, new docks and handling equipment had to be built to cope with the continually growing volume of imports.

By the end of the Gorbachov era, Leningrad was the second-largest port in the USSR after Vladivostok, and probably holds the same position in today's Russian Republic – but is difficult to tell, because of the much reduced volume of foreign trade and lack of reliable current statistics.

In the early 1970s the Baltic Shipping Company, the only deep-sea fleet operator based in Leningrad, entered the international freight market. Its business policy was directed by the Ministry of Foreign Trade in Moscow, according to purely political criteria. But there were some exceptions: Leningrad exported steam turbines to Argentina and Brazil; electric vehicles and alarm clocks were shipped to Uruguay and Colombia, and during the era of détente, titanium, a strategic military product, was exported to the United States. As a rule, however, the freight carried by the Soviet merchant fleet consisted of raw materials like timber, petroleum or metals.

A characteristic that is peculiar to every Russian port is that it is under the control of a locally based shipping company. That is why, today, the Baltic Shipping Company operates not only the harbor of St. Petersburg, but also those of Vyborg (for trade with Finland), and of Kaliningrad, which, under the name of Königsberg, used to belong to Germany (East Prussia) until 1945. Before very long, even this relic of Soviet state monopolism will be a thing of the past.

All in all, the future of St. Petersburg's port, nearly three centuries after its founding, looks none too rosy: for one thing, work which began on building a dyke to prevent flooding, has thrown up major environmental and technical problems, not least for the shipping itself.

Meanwhile, there are discussions about whether, by infilling part of the Neva estuary, an overland link between the dyke and the city could be created. The culmination of this dubious plan is – in spite of empty city coffers – a campaign being energetically pursued by the Baltic Shipping Company, in favor of building a new harbor on the marshy coast southwest of St. Petersburg. The present commercial docks are on the left (south) bank of the Great Neva, where it enters the Gulf of Finland.

195

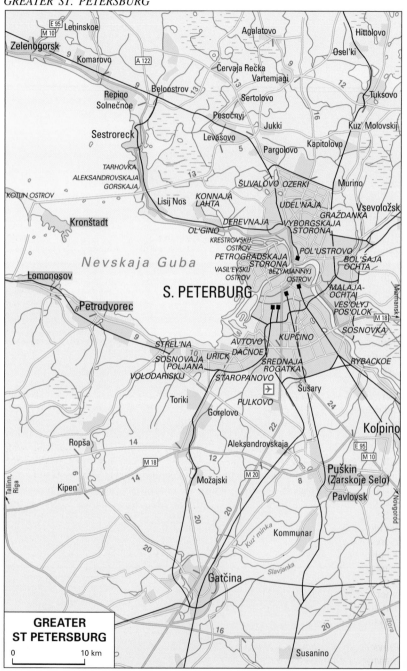

GREATER
ST PETERSBURG

0   10 km

AROUND ST. PETERSBURG

PETRODVORETS
LOMONOSOV
TSARSKOYE SELO
PAVLOVSK
REPINO
LAKES LADOGA AND ONEGA

PETRODVORETS

Petrodvorets (Peter's Palace) was, until the Second World War, known by the German name of Peterhof. It is one of the most famous sights in the St. Petersburg area and well worth a visit. The vast grounds of the palace, 18 miles (29 km) west of the city, are made up of no less than ten parks, each very beautiful in its own way. The first places to visit are the Great Palace and the Lower Park. However, no matter how beautiful the parks and magnificent the palace, it is the **fountains** which give the Peterhof its unique character. In summer, water sparkles from 144 fountains and 3 cascades. You will doubtless be told, rightly, that in their volume and height, these fountains exceed those of Versailles, and in fact are unequaled in the world.

It was Peter the Great himself who had the idea of laying out a park right on the shores of the Gulf of Finland. He drew up the plans incorporating the palace, grotto, fountains, cascades and a canal. His sketches, instructions to the builders and other notes bear witness to this. It is said that he even persuaded foreign ambassadors to lend a hand.

Previous pages: Cascades in front of the Summer Palace at Petrodvorets.

Peterhof is mentioned for the first time in 1705, when St. Petersburg itself was still being built. The Great Northern War against Sweden had not come to an end, but Peter had laid the foundation stone of his new capital on the stretch of Baltic coast that he had recently conquered. In order to give the city reliable protection from the seaward side, the fortress of Kronslot was built on the island of Kotlin, which later became the Kronstadt naval base. Peter devoted a great deal of attention to the construction of the fortress and often visited it. His route there took him along the south shore of the gulf. Facing the offshore island of Kotlin a little "wayside palace" was built, with just two rooms. This was given the name of Peterhof, literally "Peter's Court."

The idea of creating a prestigious summer residence here came to Peter after his victory at Poltava in 1709. But it took another five years before work began on the Great Palace and the Great Grotto with its cascades, and at the same time on the Monplaisir Palace; a harbor was built, linked to the sea by a canal. The fountains were inaugurated just before the end of the Great Northern War. The simple but effective method of feeding the fountains was devised by an engineer named Tuvolkov. Water from the river Kovasha is led through conduits to reservoirs, which,

thanks to the natural slope of the land, provide sufficient pressure for the fountains, without the need for pumps.

The ensemble was completed in 1723, but was extended during the following century. From the end of the 18th to the mid-19th century further parks were created, bordering on the Lower Park. Their design was informal, following the natural landscape, and providing changing vistas, winding avenues, little lakes with secluded islands and romantic pavilions. All this is very different from the precise, geometric layout of the of the older gardens which surround the Great Palace on a natural rise in the land.

The **Great Palace** (*Bolshoi Dvorets*) was built in several stages. At various times the architects engaged on the work were Braunstein, Le Blond and Bartolomeo Rastrelli. It was Rastrelli who added a further storey to the main building, and

Above: The fountain of Petrodvorets: Samson and the lion. Right: The park is an inviting place to sit for a while.

built galleries on each side, which lead into two further buildings – the palace church and the coat-of-arms wing.

Inside he created a series of ceremonial rooms and only left the oak staircase and Peter the Great's study unaltered. Later were added the Baroque splendor of the East and West Chinese Studies, and a number of rooms in the Classical style: The Throne room, the Chesma room and the White Dining room.

On the south side of the Great Palace, on the upper terrace, lies the Upper Garden; while the Lower Park stretches down to the shore of the gulf. Both **parks** are strictly symmetrical in design and ornamented in the Baroque manner – with formal shrubbery, flowerbeds fountains and statues. Of particular interest is the largest fountain in the Upper Garden – the **Neptune Fountain**. It depicts the god of the sea in bronze surrounded by sea horses, tritons, naiads and boys chasing dolphins.

The park is symmetrically divided, first by the central flower bed in the

Upper Garden, then, along the same line, by a canal which runs through the Lower Park to the sea. At the foot of the Great Cascade, on both sides of the canal, there are identical colonnades, built at the beginning of the 19th century to plans by the landscape gardener, Voronikhin, who was also responsible for the Italian fountains. Every large fountain and building on the east side has its exact counterpart on the west side: the Chessboard Cascade is matched by the Cascade of the Golden Mountain, the Monplaisir Palace by the Hermitage, the Fountain of Adam by that of Eve. Avenues radiate from the Adam and Eve fountains to various parts of the park, like the spokes of two wheels. The longest avenue, the Marlynskaya, runs right across the Lower Park. It begins at the Marly Palace and links cascades, lakes and six magnificent fountains into one elegant composition.

The **Great Cascade** consists of 64 fountains, 225 sculptures, reliefs and gargoyles, three waterfalls and two grottoes. It is the largest artificial cascade in the world. Set in a basin at the foot of the cascade, a 10 ft (3m) high figure of Samson stands on a granite plinth, forcing open a lion's mouth, from which a jet of water is thrown 72 ft (22m) in the air. This is the largest of the cascade's fountains and was unveiled in 1734 to commemorate Russia's victory over the Swedes at Poltava, on St. Samson's Day, 1709.

It is impossible to describe every fountain. Let us just stroll through the Lower Park. Some people might like to stop a while at the Sun Fountain or the Pyramid Fountain, others might be more diverted by the "trick" fountains which spray water over them when they least expect it. Other will want to admire the Dutch Garden by the Monplaisir Palace.

You should allow a whole day for this visit, since it is a well-known fact that no one can tear themselves away from this lovely place until the last fountain has been turned off.

LOMONOSOV (ORANIENBAUM)

The group of palaces and pavilions in the park of Oranienbaum, which now bears the name of the poet and polymath, Lomonosov, lies 25 miles (40 km) west of St. Petersburg and dates from the period 1710 to 1777. The land on the south shore of the Gulf of Finland, around Petrodvorets, originally belonged to Alexander Menshikov, the favorite of Peter the Great, but later became the property of the royal family. During the Second World War, Oranienbaum remained outside the area occupied by the German army, so that the buildings and their art treasures have been preserved in excellent condition.

The Great Palace of Oranienbaum was built in 1710-27 by Fontana, Schaedel and Andreas Schlueter. Later alterations were carried out by Rinaldi and Bartolomeo Rastrelli. The spacious palace is at the center of an extensive groups of Baroque buildings. It lies among a chain of small hills near the coast, and comprises

a turreted, two-storeyed central section, which is set forward between two concave curving wings, ending in a church on one side and a Japanese pavilion on the other. From the palace, the ground falls in a series of terraces, down to the Lower Park. On the other side of the palace lies the more formal Upper Park.

The small Palace of Peter III, a two-storeyed stone building, was built by the architect Antonio Rinaldi between 1758 and 1762. The study, bedroom and boudoir are decorated in the finest stucco.

Rinaldi also designed the **Chinese Palace**. Built in 1762-68, most of the 17 rooms have been well preserved; a few of the interiors were inspired by Chinese Rococo and other oriental styles. The Buglework Room still has some of its original glass mosaic floor; and the Great Hall, the lilac-painted guest bedroom, the

Three views of Tsarskoye Selo: Above: The Catherine Palace. Right: Rastrelli's Palace Church. Far right: The Great Hall of the Catherine Palace.

Golden Study of Catherine II and other rooms are elaborately decorated with murals and elegant stucco.

The **Toboggan Pavilion** (*Katalnaya Gorka*) is all that is left of a huge toboggan stretching across the park, which provided amusement for the royal guests in the 18th and 19th centuries. Built by Rinaldi (1762-74) this light, airy, rococo folly houses a porcelain collection.

TSARSKOYE SELO

One of the most beautiful places in easy reach of St. Petersburg is Tsarskoye Selo. Before she became empress, Catherine I had a 16-room house built here (by Johann Braunstein in 1718-24). In the neighborhood there was a village of craftsmen, a brickyard and a factory making ceramic tiles. A garden was laid out in front of the palace and an area of forest fenced in, where wild boar, hares and even elk were kept. In 1724, in the last year of his life, Peter the Great attended a great ball at the palace, and from then on

the place was known as Tsarskoye Selo – the Czar's Village.

The construction of the Great Palace on the site of the small stone house, was begun in 1740, under Peter's daughter Elizabeth I. At the same time the park was enlarged and enhanced with pavilions. At first the palace was relatively small and modestly furnished, but over time it grew larger and more magnificent, in the Baroque manner.

The most celebrated architect of that period was Bartolomeo Rastrelli. From 1752 onward he took charge of the alterations to the Catherine Palace, which Elizabeth had named after her mother. Conditions for the serfs who did the work were harsh, and the enormous cost of the conversion was met by a nationwide increase in the price of salt, which was not accepted without protest. In 1756 the splendid residence was finally completed, and from then on the Great Palace was used for all official receptions outside St. Petersburg. In 1770 work began again; and the Classical style replaced the Baroque. New motifs and new architects came on to the scene, including Felten, Rinaldi, Quarenghi, and the Scotsman, Cameron.

They created superbly landscaped parks and sumptuous interiors. In the following century other names were added to the list of palace architects, including Stasov, a representative of late Classicism, and Menelas, who put up a number of neo-Gothic buildings in the Alexander Park.

The German occupation of 1941-44 caused terrible damage and losses to the whole estate. A large part of the palace and the pavilions were destroyed by artillery fire, and centuries-old trees were felled. The postwar rebuilding and restoration took many years, and in some rooms is still in progress.

The magnificent three-storey Catherine Palace, now a museum, is over 980 ft (300m) long. Enormous columns, pilasters and decorative window frames enliven the façade, and it has many luxurious and attractive interiors. These include the gilded Great Hall, with 130 paintings by west European masters of the 17th and 18th centuries, the Green Dining room, the State Bedroom and State Study of Alexander I.

The north wing is of special interest: a high school was established in it, which was attended by the young Pushkin from 1811 to 1817. The centenary of the poet's death, which was celebrated in 1937, gave the Communist party functionaries an excuse to erase the hated name *Tsarskoye* and rename the place Pushkin.

Apart from the palace, the important buildings of Tsarskoye Selo include:

– the **Cameron Gallery** (built by Charles Cameron in 1780-87), a long, two-storey building which houses an exhibition of sculptures.

– the **Hermitage Pavilion**, by Kvassov, Zemtsov, Chevakinsky and Rastrelli (1744-56), an enchanting piece of garden architecture, which was used by the inner circle of courtiers for small receptions.

– the **Upper Bath Pavilion** (by Neyolov, 1777-79), where the Czar and his family bathed.

– the **Grotto Pavilion** (Rastrelli, 1753-57) dedicated to the sea, it is decorated with woodcarving, stucco and over 200,000 seashells.

In the park you should also look out for the Marble Bridge, the Chesma Columns, the Chinese Arbor and the fountain entitled "Girl with a Jug," (1816).

In the years 1792-96 Quarenghi built the **Alexander Palace** on the northeast edge of the New Garden, which adjoins the Catherine Palace. It is a two-storey building of impeccably classical proportions. After the Revolution of 1905 Nicholas II retreated here.

Before the palace was built, the Alexander Park already contained Rastrelli's Chinese Theater; the "Little Lakes" and the transverse canal had been dug, bridges had been built over the canal, and the earth piled up to create the Hill of Parnassus. At the same time (1782-96) the Chinese Village was built by Cameron and Neyolov.

In the years 1810-20 the former game-park in the forest had been turned into a landscaped park, which, together with the New Garden, formed the Alexander Park. Later, further pavilions were built, such as the White Tower (Menelas, 1825-28) and the Arsenal (1830-35).

PAVLOVSK

Pavlovsk lies a short distance south of Tsarskoye Selo. In 1777 Catherine the Great made a gift of some land to her son, who later became the Czar Paul (*Pavl* in Russian). This is how the estate got its name. From 1780 onward the architect Charles Cameron worked here. He was fascinated by the idea of turning a natural forest into a **parkland setting for architecture**. For the palace he chose as his model the much-copied style of an Italian villa with a low cupola, but the ground plan of the building was that of an old Russian country mansion. The building work continued from 1782 to 1786, after which additions and alterations were carried out by V. Brenna. A fire did considerable damage, and Vorokhinin took charge of the rebuilding in 1803-4. Carlo Rossi made further changes and extensions. An important contribution to the design of the palace and the park was made by the artist and interior designer P. Gonzago. After 1830 hardly any more changes were made to the building.

During the occupation of 1941-44 the Germans looted the furnishings and burned part of the palace down. Fortunately the Russians had removed the museum's valuable collections – paintings, sculpture, bronzes, porcelain and glass – to a safe place beforehand, so that no serious losses were suffered. Restoration

Right: Pavlovsk – this is another place where nature has been tamed.

of the palace took place in stages, up to 1970 and the exhibits, some of them quite unique, were returned.

Among the palace's many rooms, the following should be singled out for mention: the Egyptian Lobby, the Grand Staircase, The Italian Hall, the collection of sculptures from antiquity and the Great Library containing over 20,000 books from the 18th and 19th centuries; the furnished Small Study of Paul I, the Hall of War, a state reception-room which served as a small throne room; and the Grecian Hall, with finely carved and gilded furniture. The story goes that when the furniture was being transported here from St. Petersburg, each piece was put in the arms of a disabled soldier, to prevent it from being damaged.

You should see the Great Hall or **Throne Hall,** a luxurious room with an area of 4,300 sq.ft (400 sq.m). Its dining tables are laid with a 600-piece armorial dinner service. Then there is the Hall of the Knights with its antique sculptures, the tapestry room with Gobelins from France, a gift from Louis XVI, and furniture by Henri Jacob. Finally there is the Dining Hall, where you can see displayed the Guryev Palace Service, one of the largest and most luxurious dinner services ever produced by the St. Petersburg Porcelain Manufactory. It was designed by S. Pimenov in the early 19th century.

The park is artistically laid out with hedges and meadows, pavilions and temples nestling between hills, streams and arched bridges, ponds, statues, staircases, avenues and colonnades. With over thirty monuments, this open-air museum is a jewel of *alfresco* architecture.

REPINO

Until 1939 the little town of Repino went by the Finnish name of Kuokkala and was one of St. Petersburg's local spas. Historically the strip of land around Zelenogorsk, on the north shore of the Gulf of Finland, 30 miles (50 km) to the north-west, had always been inhabited by Finns, though under Russian overlord-

ship. As part of Lenin's 1918 decree establishing Finnish independence, the region was ceded to Finland. Yet even before the Revolution, the area was a popular holiday resort for affluent St. Petersburgers, who built their dachas here.

Repino's importance, as well as its new name, was due to the fact that one of Russia's foremost painters, Ilya Repin, came to live here in 1900 and later built his famous **dacha-studio**, which he named P*e-naty*. Thanks to his hospitality, it became a rendezvous for Petersburg society. Actors, musicians, artists and writers came to Repin's legendary parties, and were frequently painted by their host.

Regular guests at the dacha-studio included the singer Chalyapin, the poets Mayakovsky and Yesenin, the composer Glazunov, the scientists Pavlov and Bekhterev, and the writers Gorky, Kuprin, Andreyev and Korolenko. It was

Above: When free of ice, the 137 mile/ 220km long river Svir is a very important waterway.

customary for them to pose for group photographs, which is how these assemblies of talent came to be recorded.

After the Russo-Finnish War which Stalin provoked in 1939, the territory returned to Russia. Repin was no longer living; and his dacha became a state museum. In 1961 it was restored, since when the rooms and studio have been used for exhibitions. Following tradition, Repino is, even today, a favorite place for the so-called creative intelligentsia to work and relax. In the Soviet era a House of Composers and a House of Film-makers were established here, and in the village of Momarovo there was a House of Writers. In these places artists could live and work, with all their meals provided.

A CRUISE ON LAKE LADOGA AND LAKE ONEGA

It is well worth making an excursion from St. Petersburg, which lasts several days and focuses not on palaces, but on landscape, water and wildlife. This is the

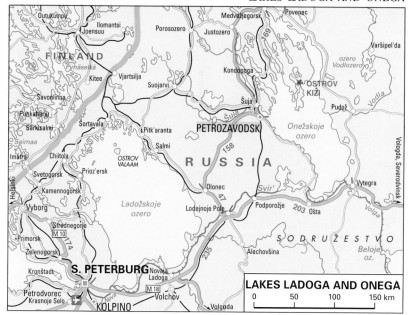

river cruise on the two largest inland seas in Europe. Lake Ladoga (*Ladoshkoye Ozero*), whose waters are 13 ft (4m) above sea-level, is Europe's largest lake. Before and during most of the Soviet era it was the reservoir which provided water for St. Petersburg/Leningrad. But in the past ten years pollution has reached such a level that even the fish stock has been dwindling and could soon die out altogether. The ecological damage here – as well as in Lake Onega and on the Zvir – is incalculable. The lake has an average depth of 167 ft (51m). It is 124 miles (200 km) long and 78 miles (125 km) wide. Lake Ladoga has an outlet via the river Neva to the Gulf of Finland and the Baltic, and is connected to Lake Onega by the 137-mile (220 km) long river Zvir. It has an area (including the islands) of 7,100 sq. miles (18,400 sq. km).

Its most important island is **Valaam**, called Valamo by the Finns which has an area of 10 sq. miles (25 sq.km). Its Orthodox monastery (*Spaso-Preobrazhensky Monastyr*) celebrated the 1000th anniversary of its foundation in 1992. The "Holy Place" is famous for its hermits' cells, where people used to withdraw completely from civilization and dedicate their lives to God. The finest of these is the **Nikolsky Skit**, dedicated to St. Nicholas. The extensive complex was neglected for fifty years and is now in very poor shape. It is only recently that the church has been trying, with the help of local authorities and the Russian Federation, to save some of its valuable heritage.

In 1940, when the Red Army marched into what was then Finnish territory, the superb treasure of the monastery was taken to safety. Since then it has been on display in the modern Museum of the Orthodox church in the Finnish town of Kuipio.

Lake Onega (*Onezhkoye Ozero*) is Europe's second-largest lake: its is 154 miles (248 km) long and has a maximum width of 52 miles (83 km). Its depth is 377 ft (115m). Like Lake Ladoga, it is only free of ice, and navigable, between

April and October. Connected by a network of canals, with many weirs and locks, both lakes form part of the economically important Volga-Baltic Waterway. Not counting its 1,300 or more islands, Lake Onega has an area of 3,687 square miles (9,549 sq. km). By comparison, Hungary's Lake Balaton, the largest lake in Central Europe, has an area of just 228 sq miles (591 sq. km).

The harbor of Petrozavodsk (Peter's Factory), which was founded on the western shore by Peter the Great, was originally an ordnance works for the Great Northern War. The city is now the industrial and cultural center of the Autonomous Republic of Karelia, with a population of about 750,000. It is the home not only of a Finnish theater, but also of the excellent national choral and dance ensemble, *Kantele* – which keeps up the tradition of Karelo-Finnish folklore. An attractive museum of icons presents the culture of this forested and well-watered region, whose undoubted jewel is the little **island of Kizhi**.

Although only 3 3/4 miles (6 km) long and at the most 1100 yards (1 km) wide, the island's importance is documented in an extensive open-air museum, whose chief attraction is a marvelous group of monastery churches. The 120 ft (37m) tall **Church of the Transfiguration**, with its 22 wooden domes on five levels is unique in all Russia. This wooden masterpiece, (*Preobrazhenskaya Tserkov* in Russian) was built in 1714 and has been called the "Wonder of the North." It has been nominated a UNESCO World Heritage site, along with the neighboring *Pokrowskaya Tserkov* (**Church of the Protecting Veil**). Both churches also have valuable iconostases. One's pleasure can often be spoiled, however, by the fact that this gem, which one has traveled hundreds of miles to see, is sometimes closed "for technical reasons." Or the Church of the Transfigura-

Above: This group of wooden buildings in Kizhi are protected as a UNESCO World Heritage site.

tion is "not in service," or "out of order," as the signs laconically put it, and no one can offer any concrete reason.

Several **wooden houses**, which once belonged to wealthy peasants, have been turned into museums furnished in the typical style of the late 19th century, with both secular and religious exhibits. They include: *Dom Butina, Dom Yakovleva, Dom Osheveva* and *Dom Yelizarova*) In the precincts of the Murom monastery, you will scarcely notice the tiny wooden church dating from the second half of the 14th century. The **Tserkov Voskreshcheniya Lazarya** (The Raising of Lazarus) is one of the oldest monuments of wooden construction in Russia.

The inhabitants of the sparsely populated island greet the passengers from the steamer in traditional costume, with old Russian songs and dances. They improve their income by selling hand-made souvenirs at affordable prices as well as standard factory-made souvenirs.

As recently as the turn of the century it took two years and a winter in Rybinsk, to pull barges from St. Petersburg to Moscow, along narrow canals with many locks. Now there is a new waterway capable of accommodating quite large and fast ships, a boon to the economy. In 1993, the route over Lake Ladoga, Lake Onega, the Zvir, the Rybinsk reservoir, the Volga and the Moskva-Volga canal were opened to western tourism for the first time in history.

The comfortable cruise ships, built in East Germany and partly modernized, nowadays hold up to 300 passengers. They take about a week to complete the 900-mile (1400-km) trip to the Russian capital. The cruise includes a visit to the monastery on Valaam, the Karelian capital Petrozavodsk, the museum island of Kizhi, the monastery near Gorizy and the ancient Russian town of Uglich with a kremlin. The mixture of culture, nature, village life, relaxation and on-board recreation make for a fine ride.

TRIPS FROM ST. PETERSBURG

Petrodvorets (*Peter's Palace*): The Czars' residence on the Gulf of Finland is 21 miles / 34 km from the city centre. From May to September the fast and cheap *Meteor* hydrofoils, and other excursion boats leave every 20 minutes for Petrodvorets. (Departures from: Ermitage or Decembrists Square (*Ploshchad Dekabrystov*) Journey time: 30 minutes. By train: Metro to Baltic Station, from there by suburban train and then bus to the palace. Open daily except Mon. 11am-6pm. Closed on last Friday of month. Tel: 427 9527

Oranienbaum (*Lomonosov*): 25 miles / 40 km from the city center, this residence of the Empress Catherine the Great can be reached by electric train from the Baltic Station. Open daily except Tues. 11am-5pm, Tel: 422 4796; the Chinese Palace (*Kitaysky dvorets*) and the Toboggan Pavilion are only open in the high season. Daily except Tues. 11am-6pm. Closed on the last Monday in the month. Tel: 422 3758.

Repino: 27 miles / 44 km from the city center. Repino (*Usadba Penaty*) can be reached by suburban train from the Finland Station (*Finlyandsky Vokzal*) or by the 411 Bus from Manege Square. Open daily exc. Tues 10am-5pm. Closed on the last Friday of the month. Tel: 231 6834.

Tsarskoye Selo (*Pichkin*): To reach the residence of Catherine the Great take the suburban train from Vit-ebsk Station to Tsarskoye Selo, then the bus direct to the Catherine Palace (*Yekaterinsky Dvorets*). Daily exc.Tues. 10am-5pm, in summer until 6pm. Closed on last Mon. in month; Tel: 466 6674. Pushkin Museum: daily exc. Tue 10.30am- 4.30pm. Closed on last Friday in month. Tel: 476 6990.

Pavlovsk: 22 miles / 35 km from city center, reached by electric train from Vitebsk Station. At Pavlovsk take bus from station to palace or walk abt. 30 minutes. Daily exc. Fri. 10am-5pm, in summer until 6pm. Closed on first Monday in month. Tel: 470 2156.

Cruise: Lake Ladoga – Lake Onega – Moscow

A cruise on Europe's largest lakes, **Ladoga** with **Valaam Monastery**, and **Onega** with the UNESCO protected wooden ensemble on **Kizhi** (and optionally on to Moscow) is offered from May to Sept by many European and US operators. All of them make sure that extremely well-trained Russian personnel is on board to guarantee entertainment and the proverbial Russian hospitality.

Brief excursions to Kizhi or Valaamlasting several days can also be booked with Russian travel agents in St. Petersburg.

HEAVEN ON EARTH

The history of the Orthodox Chuch in Russia goes back more than a thousand years. Tradition has it that the beatified Prince Vladimir of Kiev had all his subjects baptized in the river Dniepr in the year 988. He had chosen to adopt Christianity in its (Greek) Orthodox form, after listening to his emissaries, who had visited various neighboring peoples and studied their rites and customs. They returned and reported: " When we came to the Greeks and saw how they serve their God, we knew not if we were in heaven or on earth. For nowhere on earth is such beauty to be found."

Even today, to those not familiar with the Orthodox ritual, it seems like something from another world. Inside, the

Previous pages: Icons in Yaroslavl's Annunciation Church. A typical samovar. Above and right: Russia has regained freedom of worship. Many churches are "working" again, as they say.

churches are admittedly quite small, almost cramped; a cathedral as large as St Isaac's in St Petersburg, is the exception in Russia, rather than the rule. Yet this makes the profusion of paintings, frescoes and icons all the more impressive, the aroma of incense and candle wax all the more intense.

The congregation is separated from the chancel by an iconostasis – a wall of icons which hides the altar, the throne of God, from their sight. Like everything else in the church, the iconostasis has a symbolic meaning. Only at certain moments during the service is its center door, the "Tsar's" or "King's" Door, opened and one can look into the Holy of Holies, where only the priests and deacons may enter.

Two smaller doors to the left and right are used for ceremonial processions, for example the "grand entry," when the clergy come out of the left-hand door and then carry the consecrated bread and wine through the Tsar's Door into the chancel – part of the Communion service and at the dame time a symbolic representation of Jesus' entry into Jerusalem.

Basically, the iconostasis consists of five rows or ranks of icons. In the lowest, or local row, one finds icons which are worshipped in the community served by that church, including – often the second icon to the right of the Tsar's Door – the temple icon, with a representation of the saint or the church festival to which the church is dedicated.

Above it is the so-called "Deesis" or "Intercession row." In the center is Christ in Judgement, with angels to left and right, and saints and fathers of the church, who are bowing down before the Redeemer and interceding for mankind. The third row contains smaller icons representing church festivals. In the two upper rows, we see prophets grouped round the Mother of God, and Patriarchs around a central representation of the Trinity. The iconostasis is often adorned with a crucifixion scene. A number of churches have fewer than five rows, others may have six – with a row of small icons between the local and the intercessional rows, which might portray the Stations of the Cross.

The walls, pillars and inside the dome are also decorated with pictures; the wall facing the iconostasis sometimes has a fresco of the Last Judgement. For all the wealth of paintings and the glint of the gold and silver frames of the icons, you will notice that there are no statues, only two-dimensional art. And furthermore, the rich musical accompaniment to the service is created entirely by the human voice. Musical instruments are never used in the Russian Orthodox Church.

The most beautiful of the services is the one held at Easter, a few days later than in Catholic or Protestant churches, since the Russian Orthodox Church still keeps firmly to the old Julian calendar. At midnight a procession led by priests in colorful vestments, walks round the outside of the church, and ends with the

priest knocking on the closed door of the church – to symbolize a knock at the gate of the Kingdom of Heaven, which has been closed until Christ's Resurrection. Once the priest and congregation have been admitted to the church, the celebration of Easter, the greatest festival in the Orthodox year, begins.

Many Russian churches have in recent years come back into use, following decades of official atheism, and it is well worth getting to know this side of religious life. Every Sunday, and on many other days, you can experience that atmosphere of devotion and worship, which is so deep-rooted in the Russian soul. The Orthodox service is a vehicle for mystic contemplation rather than dogmatic teaching, and is, for all its formality, more drama than ritual. Even if you do not understand a word of the Old Church Slavonic liturgy, you will sense just what the poet Fyodor Tyuchev means, when he says: "One cannot comprehend Russia intellectually; one can only *believe* in Russia."

CHURCHES AND ICONS

In the 14th and 15th centuries, Moscow acted like a magnet, drawing to it the most important artists from all the other Russian principalities, all of whom considered themselves – culturally at least – to be the heir to the kingdom of Kiev, whether it was Vladimir-Suzdal, Novgorod, Pskov or Tver. In all these places, from the 12th to the 16th centuries, there had been an assimilation and development of Byzantine forms. Moscow's artists were among the many who lived off this inheritance but also added their own characteristics to it. It is particularly in church architecture that this process can be traced, since over the centuries the methods of building churches and monasteries in stone remained substantially unchanged. Starting with St. Sophia's Cathedral in Kiev, the basic design of the

Above: The "Mother of God of Tikhin" icon, dating from about 1600. Right: "The Redeemer" icon, painted by Andrei Rublyov.

Russian church remained a cube, on top of which were built four pyramid-like cupolas and a central dome. This is known as the cross-dome church. The flattened Byzantine domed roof was, in Russia before anywhere else, gradually developed into the bulbous onion shape.

After the collapse of the kingdom of Kiev, Vladimir-Suzdal became, for a brief period, the second cradle of Russian culture. The basic plan of the cross-dome church was retained. However, chiefly under north Italian influence, the emphasis switched to rich decorative effects, harmonic proportions and the three-dimensional structure of the porches. Frescoes and icon painting also achieved their first pinnacle of achievement in Vladimir-Suzdal, for example in the huge fresco of *The Last Judgment* in St. Dimitri's Cathedral, or the famous *Vladimir Mother of God*. With the Mongol invasion in the 13th century the cultural flowering of Vladimir-Suzdal came to an abrupt end.

The inheritance passed initially to Novgorod, where, thanks to its protected position, art and culture were able to evolve organically and largely without interruption from the 11th to the 15th century. Novgorod's St. Sophia Cathedral, with its five naves and five domes (1045-50) surpassed it's Kievan model in its unity, massiveness and structural sophistication. The great churches built in Novgorod in the following century were also largely a continuation of the Kievan tradition, particular that of Kiev's Uspensky Cathedral. However, in the 14th century a style of architecture specific to Novgorod did emerge: from now on the central cube-shaped element was surmounted by two crossing saddle-roofs, and the outer walls were topped with clover-leaf arches and decorated with notches and symbols.

The architecture which was evolving simultaneously in Moscow borrowed many structural elements from the church builders of Novgorod, which gave it a dynamic impulse. For example, the supporting pillars were replaced by a supporting construction of tiered arches, reaching over from the outer walls to the central dome. A further characteristic of the "Muscovite style" was the pyramid-shaped tower above the church roof, with *kokoshniks*, round arches resembling the headgear worn by Moscow women. In the course of the 15th century, the synthesis of Byzantine, north Italian and Romanesque elements resulted in the emergence of the specifically Russian style that the builders had been striving for.

However, Russia's most individual and important contribution to the history of world art was undoubtedly its icon painting. Icons are portrayals, painted on wooden panels, of Christ, the Virgin Mary, the Apostles and other saints, as well as biblical scenes or legends associated with saints. The paints used were mineral-based. The icons were covered with a protective coating, and mounted in the iconostasis. Their origins go far back to the Byzantine empire, where, following the Iconoclasm ("Dispute over Images") at the Council of Nicaea in 787 AD, they became objects of veneration, though not of worship, and after 843 were specifically defined and permitted. The painting of icons was deemed a liturgical act and was originally the preserve of monks and clergy. These men were considered to be the tools of God, and the icons were the product of "Archeipoieta," the painting of sacred images by other than human hand. This explains why, even today, icons are venerated in the Russian Orthodox faith.

We know for certain that as early as the Kievan empire, icons were an element in religious practice, though scarcely any examples have survived to prove this. It was not until the cultural zenith of Vladimir-Suzdal that icon-painters broke away from the rigid formality of the Byzantine tradition, and produced identifi-

ably Russian icons, with their realism and portrayal of individual personalities. However, the first great age of icon painting was in Novgorod at the end of the 14th century, when Feofan Grek (Theophanes the Greek) arrived from Byzantium and founded his school of painting. By the use of color, *chiaroscuro*, and dramatic effects, and by integrating elements of folk art into a formal framework, he did much to enrich Russian painting. The most popular motif in 15th century icons was the *umilenye* (emotion) – The Virgin Mary fondling the baby Jesus.

Feofan's most important pupil was Andrei Rublyov, whose artistic career also began in Novgorod, and who followed his master to Moscow. From 1405 the two worked together on the Cathedral of the Annunciation and later the Church of the Savior and the Andronikov Monastery. His last great commission was decorating the Troitse-Sergiyev monastery, for which his masterpiece, the *Holy Trinity* icon, was painted.

FOLK ART AND FOLKLORE

The preference for borrowing from other cultures and for combining things which are incompatible, is a characteristic of the Russians. But this always produces something very unusual, such as the doll inside a doll, the *matryoshka*, which is the archetypal Russian souvenir. The first *matryoshka* was created by the woman painter, Malyavina, for the Paris Exposition at the beginning of the 20th century. And where do you imagine the idea for these dolls first came from? Amazingly enough, from Japan! But they were originally only male.

And what about the *samovar*, in which Russian tea is traditionally brewed? Its home is India. The caravans, which came along the Great Silk Road, brought this efficient water-heating apparatus to Russia. It then became fashionable to drink

Above: A balalaika is a popular souvenir.
Right: These days, Russians will sell anything they can get a price for.

tea all the time. The metal ring on top of the samovar holds the little can of tea-concentrate. One pours some of this into a cup and dilutes it with hot water from the samovar. The variety of shapes, and the festive splendor of these vessels is a feast for the eye. The best ones come from Tula, 160 miles (200km) south of Moscow, and "to take samovars to Tula," is the equivalent of taking "coals to Newcastle" in England. When a Tula samovar begins to boil, they say it is "singing," and that each one has its own individual tune.

In the tourist centers you can buy painted wooden eggs, little icons, carved ladles and painted spoons. There are amber beads from the Baltic, and mirrors with hand-carved wooden frames. You will quite often come across fakes. If you are interested in genuine folk art, you will find examples in the Museum of Decorative and Applied Art in Moscow, at 7 Delegatskaya Ulitsa, and at the Russian Museum in St. Petersburg. Should you wish to buy a genuine piece, then try your luck in the Moscow suburb of Ismailovo. At the weekend flea market there, art and craft items are on sale. You are hardly likely to find a spinning wheel from the time of Tolstoy among the junk there. Nevertheless, the folk art produced under the Communist state monopoly is still highly prized. This can be found in the various art galleries and quality is guaranteed. At the moment, there is a growing interest in old Russian culture, particularly in making and selling cheap, popular imitations. Things are going less well for the official choirs and folk dance ensembles, who were formerly paid by the state and performed before important visitors. The troupes are splitting up, they have to make their own way now, and quite often perform in hotels and variety theaters.

Look out for enamel from Rostov – delicate and colorful painting on porcelain, framed in silver or white gold.

Brooches, rings, earrings or pendants – everything is in soft pastel shades. The textiles from Pavlovski-Posad are printed by hand. The woolen cloth may be white, dark blue, black or raspberry red, and on this background vividly colored patterns or motifs are printed. The dyes are made from secret recipes and are of the highest quality. There is a similarity between these cloths and the trays from Zhostov. However their design, painted on metal and fixed with a special varnish, has only one motif: large, colorful flowers, usually on a black background.

If you like collecting china, you will be very tempted by the faience. The pieces are painted in brilliant white and cobalt blue. Look underneath a cup or statuette, and if you do not find the mark "Gzhel," what you have is an imitation from the "Insulator" factory. There is another type of genuine Gzhel – solid cobalt blue, with gold decoration, usually on tea- or coffee-services.

The lacquer painting from Palekh, Mstyora and Kholui needs no recommen-dation. In these three places jewelry-boxes are made and hand-painted. Palekh ones are always black with delicate gold-painted decoration; those from Mstyora and Kholui have various designs.

The jeweler's craft is also represented by different schools. There is filigree jewelry, delicate silver beads, and silver wire, as well as metal stamp-work from the Caucasus and gorgeous malachite from the Urals. Or perhaps you would rather have a balalaika or a dagger from Central Asia. There is something for every taste.

In Russia, even during the Soviet era, oral folklore has always served as a kind of counterculture. Songs sung to a guitar, which one can certainly class as urban folk culture, and the jokes which poked fun at the regime, were an antidote to the stultifying diet of government propa-ganda. Well-known bards, poets and singers like Galich, Okuzhava and Vy-ssotsky have raised the *chanson* to the level of true art, and the enthusiasm of their fans is almost beyond belief.

THE RUSSIAN MENTALITY

Before the modern word *mentalitet* entered the Russian language, translators had to rack their brains to find a way of conveying the concept of mentality in Russian. The question of the Russian mentality has always troubled foreigners, but in Russia itself, people talk of the "national character" or the "enigmatic Russian soul." It was not until the 1970s that the German word "Mentalität" joined a number of other German words which have made their home in Russian, including *buterbrod* (sandwich) and *pochtamt* (post office).

People who know will assure you that it is precisely because of this accursed mentality that it is impossible to buy a sausage anywhere in Russia. And that all the things which *are* found in Russia – including (until relatively recently) serf-

Above: Straight out of a Tolstoy novel...
Right: Although a museum-piece now, the national costume is still attractive.

dom, as well as theft, drunkenness, laziness, unhealthy collectivism and harmful conservatism – are all due to "mentality."

Russians have difficulty in deciding whether they have a good mentality or a bad one. Foreigners are either enchanted (Their hospitality! Their great literature! The mysterious Russian soul!) or else they think that in order to achieve a normal life within a democracy and a genuine market economy, the Russians must change their mentality swiftly and radically. The Russians have never cherished any illusions about their own mentality. There is a hardly a Russian joke that does not betray a low national self-esteem.

The following example illustrates this: Yeltsin and Clinton are arguing about which of their nations has the greater capacity for suffering. Clinton raises taxes by 2 per cent and prices by 1 per cent; two weeks later he has to resign in the face of massive protests. Yeltsin raises taxes threefold and prices tenfold. Silence from the people. He raises taxes a few more times, takes away people's property and savings, and ceases paying salaries – still not a word. So he decides to go all the way: he gives a speech on television, and announces that on Saturday all Muscovites are to assemble on Red Square, where one in ten will be hanged. Silence, no reaction, no-one phones in. Yeltsin comes on TV again and asks: "Why don't you say something?" Eventually there is just one phone-call from a viewer who asks: "Should we bring our own rope, or will it be provided by the government?"

If, as Winston Churchill once said, Russia is a "riddle wrapped in an enigma," why should this be so? Why does this strange and vast country, with all its weaknesses, still arouse such sympathy and interest throughout the world? Can one find a rational explanation for all the contradictions in Russia's national character, her mentality and her historical destiny? Probably not.

We are brought back again to Tyuchev's aphorism about "simply believing" in Russia.

If you spend no more than a couple of weeks in Russia, you are hardly likely to find answers to these questions. But you will certainly be a little better able to get your bearings, if you keep in mind a few of those things which have helped to shape the Russian national character.

First of all there is the isolation of the country. Experts are of the opinion that the tragic way in which Russia has kept itself apart from the shared experience of the western nations, began, not with the Iron Curtain, but in the fact that the Orthodox faith and the Cyrillic alphabet were adopted a thousand years ago. This is why Russia was never a part of mediaeval western culture, whose common language was Latin.

In recent times these differences and this alienation have only become more profound. Trains from western Europe cannot run on Russian tracks, the plugs on western electrical goods do not fit

Russian sockets, and TV sets bought in the west have to be substantially modified before they can receive Russian broadcasts.

You only have to pick up a Russian envelope and look at the address: it starts with the country, then comes the city and zip code, followed by the street, the number of the building and the apartment in it, then right at the end is the name of the addressee. In other words, it starts with the general, and the personal element only comes very last.

Religious festivals are, to this day, celebrated according to the old Julian calendar, two weeks later than by Christians in the rest of the world. Russia is simply not user-friendly.

What is more serious however, is something that tourists and other visitors will come up against with depressing frequency: the inner division in society. Russia is a country of two cultures. Its intellectual elite has been educated to be pretty much in tune with the values and norms of western culture; and they have

the same cast of mind. But this way of thinking is both incomprehensible and unacceptable to the ordinary people. That is why, in addition to the conflict between classes, there has always been an intense and painful conflict of cultures. In the 19th century even the language of the ruling class was incomprehensible to the masses, since the nobility and the educated classes spoke French or German.

The Russian intelligentsia suffered under this division. Being set apart from the common people gave them a feeling of guilt. This was expressed dramatically in the *Narodnik* (Populist) movement and later in Marxism, the Revolution and the totalitarian regime based on utopian ideals of social unity and equality. There was an attempt – an illusory one – to overcome the isolation from the west with the slogan of "proletarian internationalism." This cultural division has

Above: Some people can only dream of making money. Right: You have to be very musical to play the balalaika.

lasted to the present day, regardless of Communism's attempt to reduce society to one level in an experiment which lasted seventy years. Today, the educated stratum of society is still incredibly remote from the mass of the people. Its lifestyle, its way of thinking and feeling, and its values have almost nothing in common with the interests and lifestyle of the majority of the population. As regards concepts like "democracy," or "free market," despite considerable efforts by the media to instill them into the consciousness of the people, they are still considered by most to be not only utopian but pure fantasy. The third factor, which can explain many social phenomena in Russia, is the culture of the GULAG, of the labor camp, which has pervaded the routine of everyday life. Even before the Revolution, there was a common saying among the people: "There's no way to avoid prison and the begging-bowl." But it was not until the present century that prison and poverty really became part of a common destiny that was shared by almost the entire population, one way or another, under Stalin, and later under Brezhnev. As a result of this, the borderline between imprisonment and society became blurred. At first people disappeared to the Gulags and later the Gulag came to the people. It completely penetrated a society which for so long had been tortured by its own history. Everything took on the character of a prison: the schools, the army, the collective farms, the pioneer camps, and even the nucleus of society, the family. In the seventy years of Soviet power, the private and personal side of people's lives was almost completely destroyed. Anything which was just a little bit better than prison, became acceptable to the Russians. To this day, the registration with the police of every member of the population, is still customary, and designated by the word *propiska* (residence permit). It is only recently that the rule was abolished, whereby each individual was entitled to no more than 54 sq. ft (5 sq. m.) of living space. Nearly half the population still lives in barracks, hostels, mobile homes or communal flats, in conditions of enforced collectivization, promiscuity and alcoholism. Within three generations these people have lost not only the knowledge, but any recollection of the meaning of property. The reforms of Gorbachov and Yeltsin have so far done nothing to change this. That is what is meant by the Gulag culture. Not long ago, official propaganda called this "the evolution of socialism." Black humor is naturally one way of seeing it, as the current riddle shows: "What is communism?" Answer: "The long, painful and bloody road from capitalism to capitalism."

In fact it means that in this century Russia has lived through two world wars, a revolution, collectivization, Stalin's Reign of Terror, the Gulags, the loss of illusions and the collapse of an empire – and now it is stuck between communism and capitalism.

Left-wing politicians in the west are appalled by what they see, and desperately warn Russia to ignore the siren voices of capitalism. Meanwhile, western conservatives impatiently criticize the lack of radicalism and consistency in Russia's attempt to re-introduce capitalism. Within Russian society itself, there is no consensus, other than self-mockery. Jokingly, people say they live in a country with an unpredictable past.

The re-evaluation of their own past continues, and following the revelations of the early years of *glasnost*, there is now a noticeable nostalgia for the certainties of the Soviet era.

Many Russians are unable to bear the painful fate of their country and have chosen to emigrate. Outside the embassies of the USA, Germany, Israel and Australia, people stand for days in lines a mile long, hoping to be able to leave their homeland for ever. Those who stay behind, when asked why they are doing so, reply: " It will be interesting to see how it all ends."

LIFE AFTER SOCIALISM

Who would have thought, a few years ago, that we would be referring to every day life in Russia as "post-socialist"? And who would have thought that in a state where the news broadcasts could be summed up in a single phrase from the famous song, "immeasurably great is my country, my dear country," every imaginable and unimaginable event would now be admitted, and the nation would become a journalist's paradise. But this colossus, the former USSR, was shaking itself and beginning to move – though, admittedly, it is still not clear in what direction. There are people who think it is heading for the abyss; while others say, towards democracy; others again say towards a free market, and in a way, they are all right. In the provinces this new age is only just dawning, while in Moscow

Above: Food is weighed out like gold. Right: As cardboard cutouts, Gorbachov and Yeltsin look friendly, but they were rivals.

the squally winds of change are scattering old and new, good and bad, in confusion, and sprinkling the streets with thousands of kiosks. In the hearts of the Muscovites all this is causing amazement, joy and grief in equal measure. What, they wonder, is new in their everyday lives?

Since the end of the 1980s, the most important member of every family has been the television set. It is switched on when the household is scarcely awake, and will not be switched off again until long after midnight. People have an insatiable appetite for news, especially about politics. They need it like a drug. Many a man goes clean out of his mind from overdosing, sinks into a depression, or else mounts the barricades. If the TV set was once despised by thinking people, it now forces them to take up a position, to love, to hate and to sympathize. TV has become a narcotic, yet no one throws it out – after all, it would never do to miss the latest moves in the Kremlin assembly, or the parliament in the White House, any more than the latest – the 318th – episode of an interminable Mexican (or American, or Brazilian) soap opera.

It is TV, also, that has suddenly brought advertising into Russian homes – a completely new phenomenon in this country. Up to now, consumer goods had never needed advertising: no sooner had someone put about a rumor that something was actually on sale somewhere, than people would be standing in line for it, and within an hour the product and the people would have vanished.

The first western businessmen who tried to talk the GUS inhabitants into buying their stuff nearly went crazy with excitement. They could not believe their eyes. They invested huge sums in advertising and soon enterprising grandmothers and schoolchildren were standing in line all night outside the new shops selling foreign goods, and then in the morning they would sell their places to wealthy playboys.

At the start, people were irritated by TV advertising, because it was so stupid – the nation was starving, and advertisers were trying to persuade them to buy a Mercedes or French perfume. But now people have got used to it, many have money, the shops are well-stocked and the advertising itself has changed. The advertising men had suddenly realized that you get nowhere in Russia by addressing people politely; you have to either frighten them or make them laugh. And it works!

But in addition to this "window on the world," they also have a door on the world, the one they go through into the street. They go outside and find that overnight the street has been given a new name. This hobby of the authorities, that they call the "rebirth of history," is a menace for locals and foreigners alike. There are hardly any new city maps. Yet hundreds of streets, squares and Metro stations have been renamed. Even the old familiar landmarks are disappearing: monuments, cafés and parks are being re-

placed by banks, hotels, restaurants and billboards.

The shops are brimming with foreign goods never seen before, but the salespeople usually know no foreign languages and often have no idea what it is they are selling. So they write a ticket saying "butter" for margarine, call mineral water "fruit juice," and a slimming cocktail is just labeled "drink." There was even a case where a thinner for paint was declared to be an alcoholic drink. It is hard for the average consumer to find their way around, and even harder to figure out what it all costs and whether they can afford it.

Mental nourishment is also needed. Many Muscovites on an income of just a thousand roubles a month, have extremely modest tastes in food, clothing and entertainment, yet they cannot and will not go without the one passion in their life: books and magazines. On bookstalls and in bookshops you will see all the things which, during the years of "stagnation," were secretly read at dead of

225

night, as well as things which had only been heard or dreamt of. You will also see books by authors of the new, free generation and lastly a completely unknown form of literature on every conceivable subject – from Chinese astrology to the Romance of Banking.

And just look at the newspapers and magazines! One gets dizzy when faced with such a variety. However, the public's taste already seems to have calmed down a little. At any rate the porn magazines, which at first excited the imagination of men of all ages, have long since ceased to attract so many buyers. The desperate shopkeepers, who want to make at least something out of them, charge people for the privilege of leafing though magazines of this kind.

The supply of intellectual sustenance would be incomplete without films and theater. From the press one learns that a

continuous flow of new Russian films are being produced. Readers are familiar with the themes, the actors and directors and follow with interest when they receive awards. Yet unfortunately the films never reach an audience. In the provinces, you may see some black-and-white copy that someone has chanced to get hold of, but in Moscow, apart from two or three cinemas, you will never see a Russian film. Most cinemas only show American box-office hits, or some tacky foreign production that the cinema-owner was able to rent cheaply.

The theater, on the other hand, has entered a new Golden Age. Having escaped the clutches of the censor, it is putting on productions of impressive originality, boldness and imagination. There are many good new actors and plays. Admittedly, it is rather depressing to find that one often has to listen to the coarsest and most obscene language on stage: the directors are trying to bring the action as close to reality as possible – a reality that is sadly not very attractive. But perhaps

Above: Uniforms are often seen on the streets. Right: Everywhere there are reminders of the Great Patriotic War.

this is just an adolescent phase. Perhaps the conventions of the theater will once more gain the upper hand. At any rate the theater is keen to involve its audience more than ever.

The new, free market, that is still so imperfect, so wild and unknown, has already stood many cherished values and prejudices on their head. In an incredibly short time it has sucked in thousands of Russians and changed their lives, has turned society completely inside out, and has produced millionaires, beggars and businessmen. It is forcing actors, musicians and painters to take their art into the streets. It has its own harsh laws and has thrown to the bottom of the heap those who previously survived with the support of the state or the family: that is to say, the pensioners and the children.

The whole country is in business, and the city authorities try in vain to restrict the street traders to specified areas. In the center of Moscow you can buy not only books, flowers and vodka, but also medals, dollars and forged documents – all from private individuals. Resourceful kids will jump the line at a restaurant and fetch you a hotdog, or they will wash your car in no time, maybe slipping a hand in your pocket along the way. Here, you can be riding a pony one minute, and the next you are caught in the cross-fire of a gangland shootout. You can be accosted by a currency tout, or by a housewife who wants to sell you macaroni from her own store cupboard.

Yet the official markets continue to exist. It is probably better not to go to the non-food markets, as there is a certain risk involved. But the really expensive food markets are truly magnificent. Be prepared to spend money and time, but go there. The foods you can buy there taste astonishingly good, especially those which really do come from the villages: cottagecheese, sour cream, homemade cheeses, honey, dried apricots, dried meat. And what tomatoes! Another ad-

vantage of shopping at these markets is that you avoid one of the vices of everyday life in Russia: the rudeness of the sales assistants in shops.

One of the important developments in the post-socialist epoch is that city dwellers can now buy plots of land quite cheaply. True, they are extremely small, a long way out of the city and in awkward places to reach, where often no road has been built – but at least it is land. In the springtime, thousands of people stream out of the cities to their gardens, where they grub around in the earth with dedication and regard every little carrot they have grown, as a miracle. City folk can become excellent farmers. The market has proven that. And shown that mathematicians and doctors can make firstclass businessmen, actors can become cooks and engineers jewelers.

The only question remains, which of these professions are more necessary for Russia's confused and rudderless society, and what will this all look like 20 years from now?

RUSSIAN COOKING

To be precise, what we term "genuine Russian cooking," consists in reality of the choicest dishes from the many different nations of the former Soviet Union. For instance, the Ukraine has many dishes made with pork, as well as their own variations on well-known Russian recipes. Vegetable cooking is the specialty of the farming country of Moldavia, on the Romanian border, or the republics of the Caucasus, such as Armenia and Azerbaijan, the traditional suppliers of fruit and vegetables to the Russian empire. The most delicious lamb or mutton dishes – especially shashlik and kebab – have been introduced to Russia from the central Asian republics of Kazakhstan, Turkmenistan or Uzbekistan, where they like to cook with exotic herbs. Chicken is an important element in Georgian

Above: Food is often served on the street. Right: Kvass – a popular non-alcoholic national drink.

cuisine, and, in many different guises, has become popular in Russian national cooking as well. The Baltic republics have contributed, among other things, fish and game dishes, and some delicious desserts. Peas and beans are also popular there, and many solid meals are based on bacon and ham.

"A house is not made beautiful by its walls, but by the hospitality it offers," so runs an old Russian saying. It is true that this cannot deceive us into thinking that Russian cooking is anything but rather monotonous. The Russians have a preference for various kinds of thick soup or porridge, and buckwheat gruel flavored with hot spices. Potatoes are nearly always served, in one form or another, with the main dish, but rice is rarely seen on the table.

Salads are usually very basic, with only vinegar or yogurt as a dressing. Pickled gherkin or sauerkraut (*kapusta*) often takes the place of fresh salad. Marinated herrings are very popular, as are dried fish, fish soup, cabbage soup, and brawn, followed by a wide variety of sweets in all colors and shades.

In earlier times, when long journeys had to be made by wagon or sled, the habit grew up of passing round appetizing little snacks: these hors d'oeuvres are generally known as *zakuska*. No larger meal would be complete without *pirozhka*: these are little pies made of puff-pastry and filled either with finely chopped cabbage, or well spiced minced beef or pork, or stewed mushrooms.

The one example of Russian cuisine that you should definitely try is a *solyanka* – a thick soup of meat or fish, which is nearly always served with rye-bread or whole-wheat bread. A very popular side-dish is *blini,* which are pancakes made of flour, yeast, milk, butter, salt and a pinch of sugar, and fried in hot oil. Traditionally they should be eaten with caviar or smoked salmon, and sour cream, and are just the thing for a romantic dinner for

two, or at a private occasion in someone's home. Your best chance of being invited to eat genuine blinis, is in the spring, during what is known as "Butter Week," when nearly every household prepares their own blini feast. You will often be served these buckwheat crêpes spread with honey or jam.

Blini should not be confused with *pelmeni,* which is the name for a ravioli-like dish, obligatory in every Russian kitchen. In Siberia, pounds and pounds of these little squares of dough are stuffed with minced beef and cooked in readiness for the long, hard winter. The hot broth that goes with them, sprinkled with dill, is very warming on those Siberian nights when the temperature is 40 below.

Another Russian specialty which on no account should be missed is *smetana*, a thick, rich, sour cream. A dollop of *smetana* is always placed on every bowl of the much-loved *borshch* soup, which is made from no less than twenty ingredients including: beef, beet root, white cabbage, carrots, tomatoes, celery, potatoes, onions and various herbs and spices. Russian cooks swear that foreign attempts to produce a *borshch* are always unsuccessful; they apparently do not achieve that particular taste that appeals to the Russian palette.

When it comes to wine, the present economic situation is so dire that the best wine you are likely to find, is whatever happens to be put in front of you... The main wine-growing region of the former USSR is Georgia. However, the most important alcoholic drink – as if you needed to be told – is vodka (the Russian word literally means "little water."), and connoisseurs will tell you that the best vodka comes from the Kuban region.

In summer you should sample *kvass* – an excellent and very refreshing drink made from black bread, yeast, sugar and raisins. This negligibly alcoholic national beverage, is sold by the gallon at every street corner from tank trucks.

Black tea, *chai*, even when not poured from a samovar, is an essential part of every Russian meal.

229

SPORTS

Sport, in the modern sense of the word did not exist in Russia before the middle of the 19th century. Important pioneering work was carried out by the physician P. Lezgaft (1837-1909), a great believer in physical culture, who saw it as his task "to teach people to achieve the highest performance, in the shortest time, with the least expenditure of energy." The term "sport" appeared, according to some sources, for the first time in the Russian vocabulary, when thousands of Muscovites gathered in the Hippodrome to see a race on "spiders," bicycles with a huge front wheel. However, in those days rowing competitions, organized by the yacht-club, were already very popular. Nevertheless, the idea of what was really meant by the word "sport," was still very hazy,

Above: You don't get an Olympic Gold Medal for this. Right: St.Petersburg's largest sports facility, the Kirov Stadium.

even at the turn of the century. According to a Russian encyclopedia, the sort of things which counted as sports in those days included walking on stilts, kite-flying, beekeeping, collecting, autographs, coins and stamps playing dominoes and lotto, shooting pheasant and other game, photography and even embroidery...

The first sporting events in the present-day sense could well be the boxing matches on the frozen Moskva, in which two rows of fighters approached each other – a tradition whose origins are difficult to establish. Then, a kind of race between military transport units were the contests between the "entertainment" regiments, which the hot-blooded young Peter the Great organized with hundreds of his contemporaries.

Under the later czars physical training was included in the curriculum of all civil and military educational establishments in the capital.

Real sport came to the fore in 1908, in London, when Russian athletes took part in the Olympic Games for the first time, and won one Gold and two Silver Medals. The first Russian Olympic champion was Nikolai Papin from St. Petersburg, in figure skating. After that, many sports developed in the city: football, skating, ice hockey, athletics and tennis; and in Moscow there was cycling and motor sport. Both cities quickly adopted each other's sports and became permanent sporting rivals.

This continued into the Soviet era. When the title "Outstanding Champion of Sport of the USSR," was introduced in 1934, the were ten Muscovites and ten Leningraders among the first 22 people to be awarded the title. In 1956 the title of "Outstanding Trainer of the USSR" was introduced and out of the first nine to receive it, four were from Moscow and three from Leningrad. Before the Revolution, St. Petersburg's sportsmen usually beat those from Moscow, but under Soviet rule the position was gradually

reversed. But whatever way the balance of strengths worked out, in many sports there was bitter rivalry between the two cities. If one tries to trace the reasons for their success, one realizes that Moscow had a wider range of first-class sportsmen from whom it could choose, while Leningrad had the benefit of excellent coaches.

The longest tradition of inter-city dueling is in football. This began in 1907, when the Petersburgers beat Moscow at home and away. Between then and 1918, the two opponents met eleven more times. St. Petersburg won seven of the matches and the other four were drawn. In the 1920s and 1930s, when Moscow had some great players (like the four Starostin brothers), the scales tipped in favor of Moscow. Up to 1940, there were 56 matches, of which each team won 22, and twelve were drawn.

Since 1928 Moscow and Leningrad have fielded teams every year in athletics matches, as well as swimming, chess, cycling, motor sport, basketball and volley-ball. In 1934, Shatov of Leningrad lifted, with his left arm, a weight of 78.4 kg. which beat the world record of the day. Other sportsmen used to break world records, but their achievements were not recognized, because the USSR was not yet officially a member of the World Sports Association.

Yet even at their first appearance in international events, Soviet athletes turned in record performances. From 1952, the year of their debut, the USSR was always the winning team at the Olympic Games, and is the most successful team in the international rankings. The first Soviet Olympic champions came from Moscow and Leningrad respectively: Nina Ponomaryeva, in the discus (Helsinki, 1952), and Lyubov Kozyreva in cross-country skiing (Cortina d'Ampezzo, 1956). In a series of ten Winter and Summer Olympiades, athletes from Moscow, individually or in teams, won 400 Gold, 252 Silver and 263 Bronze Medals; athletes from Leningrad won 116 Gold, 96 Silver and 70 Bronze Medals.

THE RUSSIANS AS READERS

Leonid Brezhnev once described the Soviet people as the most voracious readers in the world, and that could have been one of the few times when he came close to the truth.

In Russia it is certainly true that a great deal of reading goes on. Foreigners are always impressed to see so many passengers reading, in the Metro and in buses and streetcars. In the old days western students on exchange programs were first assailed for their books. There are a number of reasons behind this affinity with printed matter: the high esteem once enjoyed by the written word in Russian culture; the ingrained habit, during the Soviet decades, of acquiring from books all the technical (and ideological) knowledge necessary for a successful career; and not least the desire to withdraw from reality, since one had no opportunity for

Above: The Russians are known as a nation of indefatigable readers. •

self-realization. either in politics, business, religion or anything else. This was why reading became something without which life under the Soviet regime would have been unthinkable, intolerable. In the mid-1980s ninety per cent of the adult population read a newspaper regularly, three-quarters read magazines and rather more than half read books.

During the period of *glasnost* (1986-1991) a change came over the Russian reader. At first he was interested in the heavy tomes and journals of opinion, in which for more than a century society has sought answers to social, political, economic and moral questions. Then there came a point when the journals could no longer keep up with the rapid train of events, and newspapers took over. Their number was soon swollen by specialist newspapers covering economics, the stock market and so forth, and pseudo-erotic tabloids of the western kind also began to appear.

Very recently, however, interest in the press has declined: it takes too long to stand in line for newspapers, when one is also trying to find a way of supplementing one's income, the prices of periodicals are rising steeply, and lastly people are just not as interested in politics as they were. That is clearly seen from what they are now reading.

In the 1970s and 1980s bookshops did a roaring trade in epic novels tracing the fortunes of a Soviet family through several generations, stirring tales of the Second World War and political thrillers set in the age of Stalin's Terror. But now the biggest demand is for sex-and-violence novels, the erotic-historic romances of the *Angélique* series, by the French writer Anne Golon, as well as the fantasy and science-fiction genres.

Hundreds of private publishing houses have been started up to publish these types of books, which are then mainly sold from tables out in the streets. These have become a permanent feature of Metro stations, rail termini and the busier streets. The books have lurid jackets, but the authors' names on them are never Russian.

Times are now very hard for home-grown writers – at the moment they can hardly find a publisher for their books. There are at least ten thousand authors living in Moscow alone. There is even an Institute of Literature which awards its graduates the qualification "Prose writer," "Poet," or "Critic" with their diplomas.

Until very recently the literati of Moscow enjoyed a high social standing, thanks to support from the state and the traditional respect accorded to literature in Russia. But during *perestroika*, it was politics and economics which took over the top position, and people realized that no-one really *needed* these writers, who regarded themselves as the prophets and conscience of the nation.

The Writers' Union broke up into several mutually inimical organizations, such as the "Westernizers" (i.e. demo-crats) and the "Patriots" (i.e. fundamentalists), who were only held together by the struggle to get their hands on the financial legacy of the Soviet Writers' Union and the Central House of Men of Letters, the famous villa in Bolshaya Nikitskaya, which Bulgakov describes in his novel *The Master and Margarita* under the name of "The Griboyedov House."

Not only are readers unable to buy books by Russian authors any more – the situation is just as disastrous in the public libraries, where such books used to form the basic stock. This is true, at least, of the general libraries, of which there are more than 500 in Moscow, though not of such famous collections as the Library of the Academy of Sciences, the public State Historical Library, the All-Russian State Library of Foreign Literature, and Moscow's "N.A.Nekrassov" Central City Library. The largest library in Russia and, with 25 million volumes, one of the largest in the world, is the All-Russian State Library, previously called the Lenin Library. It contains priceless items (including a large number of incunabula), which are kept in a book museum that is open to visitors. It also has a manuscript department, an extensive stock of foreign editions and a virtually complete collection of native Russian books and periodicals going back to the invention of printing.

The complex, near the Kremlin, includes a twelve-storey bookstore and a pearl of Moscow architecture, the Pashkov House. The library is now, however, in a critical condition: the buildings and communications system are dilapidated, the books are in danger of fire, leaking water and so forth, but there is no money there for renovation or rebuilding.

In recent years a number of specialized libraries have been created outside the state sphere – religious, ethnic, political and commercial – with the object of making a profit from the Russians' traditional thirst for knowledge.

BALLET AND THEATER

Even in czarist times ballet was considered by the Russians to be a domain in which they could excel; many famous choreographers of the 20th century came originally from Russia, where their ideas had been shaped, or at least strongly influenced, by the ballet schools of Moscow or St. Petersburg. The Bolshoi Theater, with its famous ballet company, has always been in a class of its own, and it is almost impossible for the average Muscovite to get a ticket for it – even if he or she could afford the very high prices.

The dancer Vatslav Nijinsky, a member of that legendary company, Sergei Diaghilev's *Ballet Russe*, thrilled audiences all over Europe and the New World before the First World War.

Above and right: Numerous amateur and professional ballet companies in Moscow and St. Petersburg delight their audiences.

Ever since the first performance of Tchaikovsky's *Swan Lake* in 1877, this ballet has been part of the standard repertoire of all the great ballet theaters. Just before the First World War Igor Stravinsky wrote a number of revolutionary (in an artistic sense) ballets which are still regularly performed all over the world: *The Firebird, Petrushka* and *The Rite of Spring*. While the legendary Bolshoi Theater shone with stars like the prima ballerinas Galina Ulanova or Olga Lepeshinskaya, the Kirov company in Leningrad has, since the 1960s, won the sympathy of audiences in Russia and the whole world with such towering personalities as Rudolph Nureyev, Mikhail Baryshnikov and Natalya Makarova. By an irony of fate, these three dancers – like Nijinski before them, in Paris – achieved their greatest success only after coming to the west.

The people of Russia's great cities have for centuries been very keen on the theater. Companies like the Taganka Theater or the Lenin Komsomol Theater in Moscow were rated so highly in the 1970s and 1980s that fans would stand in line all night for tickets. In the audience, before the start of a performance, there would be an atmosphere of tense anticipation, since one could always reckon to hear some stunning revelation from the stage. At the end there was always long and enthusiastic applause. People went to the theater as if to a temple.

In recent years, however, the situation has changed. During *glasnost*, only a few people really felt the need to go to the theater, so directors tried to put on previously banned plays on sensitive political, religious or erotic themes, but very few of them succeeded.

Numerous studio theaters were established, but none ever lasted for more than a year or two. Currently, interest in the theater seems to be on the increase again, but there will never be a return to the way things used to be.

PREPARATIONS

Moscow in figures

Moscow has an area of 340 sq. miles (879 sq. km) including the suburbs within the so-called *rayon* of the capital. Since 1960 the city boundary has been formed by a motorway ring 68 miles (109 km) in circumference. As Russia's largest city it is the political, economic, cultural and transportation center of the biggest country in the world. Moscow has a population of about 9 million, of whom more than a quarter are either pensioners or children and adolescents. More than half the working population are employed in manufacturing or construction, and one third in the service sector. Metal fabrication and engineering alone account for half of all industrial production. When the Soviet Union was dissolved in 1991, ten per cent of all its industrial capacity was concentrated in Moscow. Statistics from the period before *perestroika* (i.e. before 1985) particularly highlighted the more than 3,000 libraries and the 80 further education colleges; they praised the many sports-grounds and facilities which were provided for the 1980 Olympic Games, the 60 or more museums and numerous theaters. More recent statistics focus not only on the many small and medium-sized private companies that have been set up, but also on the hundreds of thousands of unemployed and homeless.

Location/Climate

Moscow lies on the rivers Moskva and Yauza in the center of the European part of the Russian Federation, between the Smolensk-Moscow highlands in the north, and the mid-Russian lowlands to the south, as well as between the rivers Volga and Oka. The city area measures 25 miles (40km) from north to south and 19 miles (30 km) from east to west.

Moscow has a fairly temperate continental climate. The average temperature in January is -11° C, and in July +19° C. In winter the temperature can sink as low as -30°C, and at the height of summer it can be as hot as 30° C. Ecologists blame heavy industrialization and antiquated heating-systems for the high smog factors. The emissions reach their highest levels in winter.

St. Petersburg in figures

St. Petersburg, Russia's second largest city, has an area of 234 sq. miles (607 sq.km). Including the suburbs this increases to 555 sq. miles (1439 sq.km). The city embraces some 44 islands in the Neva delta, which are connected by more than 550 bridges. Shipping has direct access from the Baltic. The distance from the northern to the southern boundary is 37 miles (60 km) and from east to west, 19 miles (30 km). St. Petersburg has over 5 million inhabitants, of whom over 1 million are pensioners. Roughly half the working population are employed in manufacturing and construction, and the other half in services. Statistics from the 1980s point proudly to the fact that the city had over 200,000 full-time students, and over 1.2 million of the population had some form of higher education.

The latest (1993) statistics indicate that already more than a quarter of a million people are employed in private or cooperative businesses, though the structural problems in the economy cannot be denied.

Location/Climate

St. Petersburg lies on the estuary where the Neva flows into the Gulf of Finnland and is on the same latitude (60° north) as Helsinki and Oslo. On average it rains on 126 days of the year here! The mean January temperature is -7.8°C, and the mean July temperature +17.8°C. Because of its geographical position you have to be prepared for frequent strong winds. One of the contributions of *glasnost* was the publication of an ecological atlas, which graphically presented the growth of smog in different parts of the city. The problem is unlikely to be resolved for decades to come: the need for heating for so much of the year causes enormous pollution, and industry does the rest.

When to go / Festivals

Both Moscow and St. Petersburg should preferably be visited in summer (roughly from May to September). But the two great cities of Russia are world famous for the very many cultural events they offer right through the year. The legendary White Nights (11 June - 2 July) are generally considered the best time to visit St. Petersburg. This is when a cross-section of the city's creative output is presented, and the program is enhanced with guest performances by celebrated artists. Part of the spectacle is the city itself: for a few weeks in June and July the nights hardly get dark, which means that virtually all the city stays awake. Numerous excursion boats run until midnight on the rivers and canals of this "Venice of the North;" young people get together in the parks and, well stocked with vodka or *shampanskoye*, they sing all night to the music of guitars. Both cities are ideal for theater, ballet, gallery, and museum enthusiasts.

There are river trips between Moscow and St. Petersburg, both ways, and to the islands of Valaam and Kizhi, in the two largest lakes in Europe, Onega and Ladoga. But these are only possible between May and September. At other times of year, many of the waterways have a thick layer of ice.

Group and individual tours are offered under the banner of "Russian Winter." The traditional arts festival of the same name takes place in Moscow, usually between 25th December and 5th January. As well as opera and ballet at the Bolshoi and other, smaller venues, there are performances of operetta, folk-music and concerts by famous soloists, choirs and orchestras. Tickets can be obtained,

either from the hall-porter of your hotel, or, if you are lucky, directly from the relevant theater or concert-hall. Either way, you will often have to pay a lot for them. Something very popular with the Russians, and not only the children, is the combined Christmas and New Year's festival, "Little Father Frost." The climax of the celebrations is a sleigh-ride in a *troika*, drawn by three horses. In the towns of the Golden Ring, similar festivities are organized for tourists.

Visas

Nationals of all western countries require a full passport and visa to enter Russia. Obtaining a visa can be a lengthy and fairly complex process, and you are advised to spend a bit extra and use an agency to obtain it for you. Visas are of three types. **Tourist visa**: This has to be for a specific number of days' stay and is limited to 30 days. You must show that you have pre-booked accommodation, unless you are on a package tour, in which case the agency handles all the paperwork, for a fee. **Business visa**: For this you do not have to pre-book a hotel, but you must produce a written invitation from a recognized business or authority in Russia. Again there are agencies which can arrange this for you. **Individual visa**: This is the most difficult, since it requires an authorized invitation from a Russian family, who undertakes to look after you throughout your stay.

To obtain any of these personally, write to the Russian embassy or consulate in your home country for an application-form. Three passport photos are required with the form. It will take about a month to process, unless you pay a heavy fee for a 3-day "express service."

Time zones

Both Moscow and St. Petersburg are three hours ahead of Greenwich Mean Time (GMT), and 8 hours ahead of New York.

Customs and Excise

Personal effects can be brought in duty-free for the duration of your trip. These include (one each per person), a movie-camera, camera with 10 rolls of film, video-recorder, portable radio, tape-recorder, portable TV set, portable typewriter, laptop , or a musical instrument. To avoid any misunderstanding when you leave Russia, it is recommended that you declare all your valuables, including jewelry, expensive musical instruments, as well as currency over US$ 500 in amount, when you enter the country, and hold on to the document you're given by the customs official in the "red channel."

Other things you can bring in with you duty-free include: 250 cigarettes or 250 gram of tobacco; 1 liter of spirits and 2 liters of wine. Larger amounts of wares possible considered commercial (including humanitarian aid), you will have to pay import duties.

You may re-export only the personal items declared on the form completed when you arrived. Exporting antiques, such as icons, or valuable old books, paintings or engravings as well as large amounts of caviar (one jar is generally allowed) is strictly forbidden. If you purchase a work of contemporary art, you should absolutely request a receipt.

Further details about the regulations governing import and export can be obtained either from your Russian embassy or consulate, or from the customs authorities on arrival.

TRAVELING TO AND WITHIN RUSSIA

By air

Moscow can be reached by scheduled flights from all the major airports of the west and the capitals of all the 15 republics of the former USSR, as well as the most important capitals in the rest of the world.The leading airlines of the USA, Asia and western Europe have direct

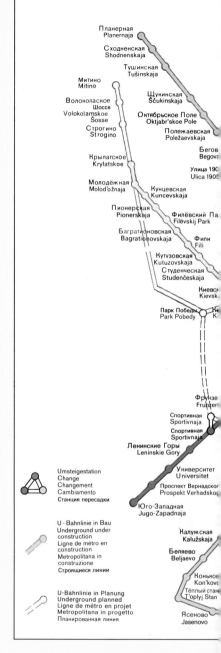

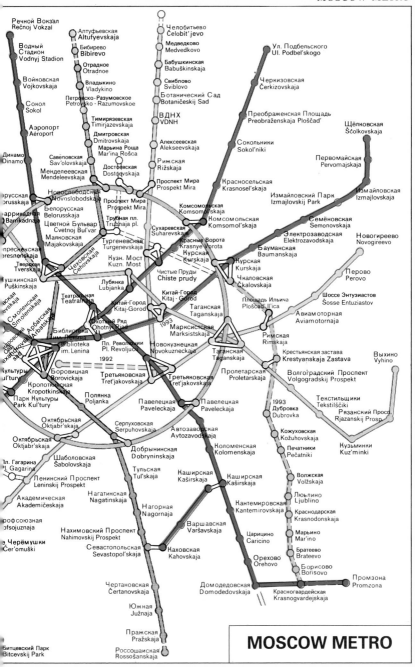

MOSCOW METRO

239

ST. PETERSBURG METRO

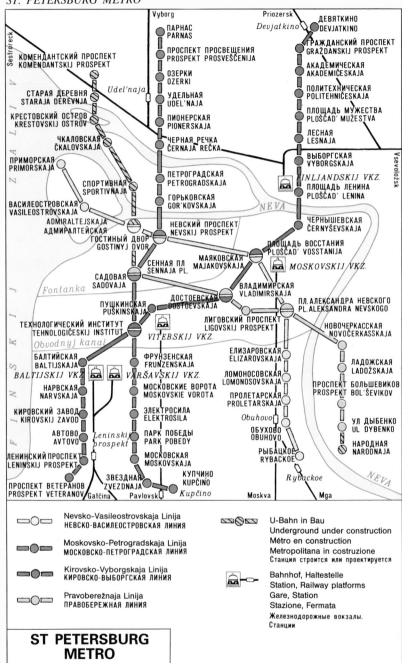

Vyborg
Priozersk

ПАРНАС
PARNAS

ПРОСПЕКТ ПРОСВЕЩЕНИЯ
PROSPEKT PROSVEŠČENIJA

ОЗЕРКИ
OZERKI

УДЕЛЬНАЯ
UDEL'NAJA

ПИОНЕРСКАЯ
PIONERSKAJA

ЧЕРНАЯ РЕЧКА
ČERNAJA REČKA

ДЕВЯТКИНО
Devjatkino DEVJATKINO

ГРАЖДАНСКИЙ ПРОСПЕКТ
GRAŽDANSKIJ PROSPEKT

АКАДЕМИЧЕСКАЯ
AKADEMIČESKAJA

ПОЛИТЕХНИЧЕСКАЯ
POLITEHNIČESKAJA

ПЛОЩАДЬ МУЖЕСТВА
PLOŠČAD' MUŽESTVA

ЛЕСНАЯ
LESNAJA

ВЫБОРГСКАЯ
VYBORGSKAJA

INLJANDSKIJ VKZ.
ПЛОЩАДЬ ЛЕНИНА
PLOŠČAD' LENINA

ЧЕРНЫШЕВСКАЯ
ČERNYŠEVSKAJA

КОМЕНДАНТСКИЙ ПРОСПЕКТ
KOMENDANTSKIJ PROSPEKT

Sestroreck
Udel'naja

СТАРАЯ ДЕРЕВНЯ
STARAJA DEREVNJA

КРЕСТОВСКИЙ ОСТРОВ
KRESTOVSKIJ OSTROV

ЧКАЛОВСКАЯ
ČKALOVSKAJA

ПРИМОРСКАЯ
PRIMORSKAJA

СПОРТИВНАЯ
SPORTIVNAJA

ПЕТРОГРАДСКАЯ
PETROGRADSKAJA

ГОРЬКОВСКАЯ
GOR'KOVSKAJA

НЕВА
NEVA

Vsevoložsk

ВАСИЛЕОСТРОВСКАЯ
VASILEOSTROVSKAJA

АДМИРАЛТЕЙСКАЯ
ADMIRALTEJSKAJA

ГОСТИНЫЙ ДВОР
GOSTINYJ DVOR

НЕВСКИЙ ПРОСПЕКТ
NEVSKIJ PROSPEKT

МАЯКОВСКАЯ
MAJAKOVSKAJA

ПЛОЩАДЬ ВОССТАНИЯ
PLOŠČAD' VOSSTANIJA

MOSKOVSKIJ VKZ.

СЕННАЯ ПЛ.
SENNAJA PL.

САДОВАЯ
SADOVAJA

ПУШКИНСКАЯ
PUŠKINSKAJA

ДОСТОЕВСКАЯ
DOSTOEVSKAJA

ВЛАДИМИРСКАЯ
VLADIMIRSKAJA

ПЛ. АЛЕКСАНДРА НЕВСКОГО
PL. ALEKSANDRA NEVSKOGO

Fontanka

ТЕХНОЛОГИЧЕСКИЙ ИНСТИТУТ
TEHNOLOGIČESKIJ INSTITUT

Obvodnyj kanal

VITEBSKIJ VKZ.

ЛИГОВСКИЙ ПРОСПЕКТ
LIGOVSKIJ PROSPEKT

НОВОЧЕРКАССКАЯ
NOVOČERKASSKAJA

БАЛТИЙСКАЯ
BALTIJSKAJA

BALTIJSKIJ VKZ.

ФРУНЗЕНСКАЯ
FRUNZENSKAJA

VARŠAVSKIJ VKZ.

МОСКОВСКИЕ ВОРОТА
MOSKOVSKIE VOROTA

ЕЛИЗАРОВСКАЯ
ELIZAROVSKAJA

ЛОМОНОСОВСКАЯ
LOMONOSOVSKAJA

ЛАДОЖСКАЯ
LADOŽSKAJA

НАРВСКАЯ
NARVSKAJA

ЭЛЕКТРОСИЛА
ELEKTROSILA

ПРОЛЕТАРСКАЯ
PROLETARSKAJA

ПРОСПЕКТ БОЛЬШЕВИКОВ
PROSPEKT BOL'ŠEVIKOV

КИРОВСКИЙ ЗАВОД
KIROVSKIJ ZAVOD

АВТОВО
AVTOVO

Leninskij prospekt

ПАРК ПОБЕДЫ
PARK POBEDY

Obuhovo

ОБУХОВО
OBUHOVO

УЛ ДЫБЕНКО
UL DYBENKO

ЛЕНИНСКИЙ ПРОСПЕКТ
LENINSKIJ PROSPEKT

МОСКОВСКАЯ
MOSKOVSKAJA

НАРОДНАЯ
NARODNAJA

РЫБАЦКОЕ
RYBACKOE

ПРОСПЕКТ ВЕТЕРАНОВ
PROSPEKT VETERANOV

Gatčina

ЗВЕЗДНАЯ
ZVEZDNAJA

Pavlovsk

КУПЧИНО
KUPČINO

Kupčino

Rybackoe

Moskva

Mga

NEVA

Legend

Nevsko-Vasileostrovskaja Linija
НЕВСКО-ВАСИЛЕОСТРОВСКАЯ ЛИНИЯ

Moskovsko-Petrogradskaja Linija
МОСКОВСКО-ПЕТРОГРАДСКАЯ ЛИНИЯ

Kirovsko-Vyborgskaja Linija
КИРОВСКО-ВЫБОРГСКАЯ ЛИНИЯ

Pravoberežnaja Linija
ПРАВОБЕРЕЖНАЯ ЛИНИЯ

U-Bahn in Bau
Underground under construction
Métro en construction
Metropolitana in costruzione
Станция строится или проектируется

Bahnhof, Haltestelle
Station, Railway platforms
Gare, Station
Stazione, Fermata
Железнодорожные вокзалы.
Станции

ST PETERSBURG METRO

flights to Moscow. However, St. Petersburg has relatively few international connections, and flying there, except from London, often involves changing planes, in Helsinki or Moscow.

Vnukovo is Moscow's oldest airport. It mainly serves the Ukraine and the Black Sea. From *Domodedovo*, Russia's biggest airport, planes leave for Siberia, Central Asia and the Far East. *Sheremetyevo 1* serves internal routes to the northwest, while western Europe and beyond is catered for by *Sheremetyevo 2*, an international airport that seems to have been built for the 21st century.

Pulkovo-II (about 10 miles / 15 km from the city center) is the international airport of **St. Petersburg**. The flight-time from Moscow to St. Petersburg is about one hour.

By train

Trains to Moscow from the west go through Berlin, Warsaw and Belorus (White Russia). There are also connections from other former republics of the USSR. The journey from London takes three days. Trains to St. Petersburg pass through Lithuania and Latvia for which separate visas are required. The express trains between Moscow and St. Petersburg do the journey in 5 hours during the day, and 8 hours at night.

For train information for all Moscow terminals: ring 266-9333 to 9009; for advance booking of tickets to anywhere in Russia ring: 266-8333, or go personally to Komsomolskaya Plochshad 5.

By car

The big Russian border crossings from Finland (Bruznichnoye and Torfyanovka) and Poland (Brest) over Vyborg to St. Petersburg are open round the clock, and from Norway only from 7am to 9pm (mind the time differences).

You can travel with a car, a campmobile or a motorcycle. You will need a national and an international driving permit, the vehicle registration papers, and an insurance card valid for Russia.

Inquire with your insurance company, the automobile club in your home country, or the car rental agency what the current administrative status is. When driving into the country, you must give a written statement that will oblige you to take the car out of the country again. The car will be thoroughly searched on the Russian end. The passengers cross through the border and the customs area separately.

In Russia there is no obligation to carry third-party motor insurance, which can be a big disadvantage if you are involved in an accident with a local driver. Nor is the International Green Insurance Card valid (though you should have one for driving through Poland). Most western insurers will issue you with a special comprehensive cover note You are strongly advised to arrange this. The international car-rental companies have their own insurance policies.

Buying short term third-party insurance is highly advisable, as well as passenger insurance. International rental agencies often have special insurance policies, some even exclude driving to Russia. You can obtain an insurance certificate at the border from the Russian organization INGOSSTRAKH (Head office: 113805 Moscow, Ulitsa Pyatnitskaya 12, Tel: (from abroad) 095/233 2070 or 233 1759, Fax: 095/230 2518).

If you happen to have an accident or break down out in the middle of nowhere, flag down another driver and ask him or her to inform the next police station (GA), since there are no telephones along the roads. I you require help from strangers, remember that a little obolus is expected as a thank you gesture. The same applies to militia members.

Break-down service for Moscow and environs is: Mosgortrans, Tel: 095/231 4787; Angel, Tel: 171 8039; cellular, Tel: 481 0522. For St. Petersburg and envrons: Lenavtoteknika, Tel: 0812 / 978 0000.

Every accident – even with no personal injuries – should be reported to the militia! Never leave the scene of the accident! Make sure the damage to your car is written up and confirmed by the officer at the scene!

Since most major western automobile companies have sales rooms in Moscow and St. Petersburg, finding spare parts is no longer a problem.

Gasoline: You may bring in one full can duty-free – at most enough to fill your tank once. Getting lead-free is no longer a problem in both cities; the bill is to be paid in rubles even if the pump says dollars!

On the main roads out of the cities, private dealers offer fuel direct from tanker-trucks or jerry-cans, but quality is questionable.

By ship

Every year more than 200,000 passengers arrive in St. Petersburg by ship. The city is linked to Moscow via the Baltic-Volga Canal. The sea route from St. Petersburg to Helsinki is 200 miles (320 km), to Stockholm 440 miles (710 km), to London 1,370 miles (2200 km) and New York 5,160 miles (8300 km). In summer there are ferry services from several west European ports, but in winter there are very few regular sailings.

Public transport

The public transport network is quite well laid out in the two big cities, even though comfort is not exactly part of the service. Private car ownership has grown so rapidly, durring the past few years, that even the the huge four-laners are sometimes hopelessly jammed.

The St. Petersburg Metro has four lines, and that of Mocow has eight in all, including the famous Circle Line (*Koltsevaya liniya*). The spacious trains operate daily from 6am until 1am. At peak times the trains run at 90-second intervals The travel tokens (*zheton*) can be bought in the stations or at newspaper kiosks.

Apart from this, you can cover the city and suburbs by a variety of means: suburban trains, streetcars (trams), trolley buses, and buses. Some journeys can be made by river-boat. In a few buses you can buy your ticket from the driver, but every time you change, you have to buy a new ticket.

Smoking is absolutely forbidden on all forms of public transport.

City tours

In both cities trips lasting several hours, by land and water, are offered by various organizations, some now in private ownership. The tour guides are, in general, very well trained and fluent in English and other languages. Hotels can usually book the tour for you.

Many officially licensed taxi-drivers or freelances will also will offer you their services. You can recognize the taxis – usually cars of the Volga brand – from the green light in their windshield and the chechered pattern on their door.

The privateers, on the other hand, have a license with a number posted somewhere. Very few drivers turn their meter on, so you should negotiate a proce before starting the trip. The driver usually regulates his price according to the brand of car he's driving. Never put money down on a trip.

The central number for cabs is: Moscow: 280 3400 and 927 0000; for St. Petersburg: 312 0022.

The cabbies servicing the international airports have haggled out their own pricing system. And they are way above the usual price. Foreign tourists are the favorite prey for the sharks and their inflated prices. The larger hotels with good names have their own taxi service at western prices. You can arrange to be collected at a given time, and no advance payment is required for this.

PRACTICAL TIPS FROM A TO Z

Accommodation

Proof of a reservation at a hotel, motel, camping or at a private person's is the prerequisite for granting a visa. Your travel agent can advise you as to what hotel to choose.

The following list is graded by quality. The nearest Metro station is shown, to help you locate the hotel.

MOSCOW

Luxury: **Aerostar**, Leningradski Prospekt 37 (Metro Dinamo), Tel: 2139000. **Baltshug-Kempinski**, ulitsa Baltshug 1 (near Red Square), Tel: 230 6500. **Danilovskaya**, Bolshoi Starodanilovski pereulok 5, on the monastery grounds (Metro Tulskaya), Tel: 954 0503. **Metropol**, Teatralny projesd 1/4 (Ploshchad Revolyuzii), Tel: 927 6000. **Meshdunarodnaya** (*Sovinzentr*), Krasnopresnenskaya nabereshnaya 12 (Metro Krasnopresnenskaya), Tel: 253 1391, 253 1071. **Nazional**, Ochotny rjad 14/1 (Metro Ochotny rjad), Tel: 258 7000. **Novotel**, airport Sheremetyevo-2, Tel: 926 5900. **Olimpic Penta Renaissance**, Olimpiski Prospekt 18 (Metro Rishskaya), Tel: 931 9000. **Palace**, Tverskaya/Jamskaya 19 (Metro Tverskaya), Tel: 931 9700. **President-otel**, ulitsa Jakimanka 24 (Metro Oktjabrskaya), Tel: 238 7303. **Pullman Iris**, Korovinskoye chaussee 10 (shuttle service), Tel: 488 8000. **Radisson-Slavyanskaya**, Bereshkovskaya nabereshnaya 2 (near the Kiev train station/*Kiyevski voksal*), Tel: 941 8020. **Savoy**, ulitsa Roshdestwenka 3 (Nähe Kreml), Tel: 929 8600.

1. Russian category: **Arbat**, Plotnikov pereulok 12, Tel: 2447635 (Metro Smolenskaya). **Intourist**, Tverskaya ulitsa 3/5, Tel: 956 8304 (near Red Square). **Ismailovo,** Ismailovskoye shosse 71 (Metro Ismailovski park), Tel: 1665272. **Kosmos,** Prospekt Mira 150 (Metro VDNKh), 217 0785, 217 8680. **Lening-**

radskaya, Kalantshevskaya ulitsa 21/40 (Metro Krasnye vorota or Metro Komsomolskaya), Tel: 975 1815. **Moskva**, Ochotny ryad 7 (Metro Ochotny ryad), Tel: 292 1000. **Rossiya**, ulitsa Varvarka 6 (near Red Square), Tel: 232 5000. **Ukraina**, Kutuzovski Prospekt 2/1 (Metro Kievskaya)), Tel: 243 3030, Fax: 956 2078.

Moderate range: **Ismailovo**, Ismailovskoye Chaussee 71 (Metro Ismailovski park), Tel: 166 5040. **Belgrad**, Smolenskaya Ploshchad 8 (Metro Smolenskaya), Tel: 248 2841. **Zentralny Dom Turista,** Leninski Prospekt 146 (Metro Jugo-zapadnaya), Tel. 434 2782.

Economy class: **Zolotoi Kolos**, Jaroslavskaya ulitsa 15/3 (Metro WDNCh), Tel: 286 2703. **Sputnik**, Leninski Prospekt 38 (Metro Leninski Prosp.), Tel: 938 7106. **Varshava**, Leninski Prospekt 2/1 (Metro Oktyabrskaya), Tel: 238 1970.

ST. PETERSBURG

Luxury: **Astoriya**, Bolshaya Morskaya ulitsa 39 (Metro Nevski Prospekt), Tel: 210 5757. **Clarion North Crown Hotel**, Nabereshnaya reki Karpovki 37 (Metro Petrogradska), Tel: 329 7000. **Grandhotel Jewropa**, Michailovskaya ulitsa 1/7 (Metro Nevski Prospekt/Gostiny dvor), Tel: 329 6000. **Nevski Palace**, Nevski Prospekt 57 (Metro Mayakovskaya), Tel: 275 2001.

1. Russian category: **Pribaltiskaya**, ulitsa Korablestroitelei 14 (Metro Primorskaya or Metro Vassilyeostrovskaya, then by tram, bus and/or O-bus, Tel: 356 0001. **Pulkovskaya**, Ploshchad Pobedy 1 (Metro Moskovskaya), Tel: 264 5122, 264 5022.

Middle range: **Morskaya**, (at the harbor), Ploshchad Morskoi slavy 1 (Metro Primorskaya, then with the O-Bus), Tel: 355 1415. **Moskva**, Ploshchad Alexandra Nevskovo 2 (Metro Ploshtshad Aleksandra Nevskovo), Tel: 274 4001. **Okhtinskaya-Victoria**, Bolsheochtinskiy Prospekt 4 (Metro Novotsherkasskaya, followed by the tram), Tel: 227 4438. **Sankt Peter-burg** (formerly the *Leningrad*), Pirogovskaya nabereshnaya 5/2 (Metro station Ploshchad Lenina, then by tram and bus), Tel: 542 9411.

Economy class: **Drushba**, ulitsa Chapygina 4 on the *Apothecary Island* (Metro Petrogradskaya), Tel: 234 1844. **Karelia**, ulitsa Marshala Tuchachevskovo 27/2 (Metro Ploshchad Lenina), Tel: 226 3534. **Oktjabrskaya**, Ligovski Prospekt 10 (Metro Ploshchad Vosstaniya), Tel: 277 6330. **Rossija**, Ploshchad Chernyshevskovo 11 (Metro Park Pobedy), Tel: 2967649. **Olgino** (motel and camping), Primorskoye Chaussee 59, Tel: 238 3009, 238 3550; 11 miles/18 km to the city center. Bus: 110, 411, 416. **Sovietskaya**, Lermontovski Prospekt 43 (Metro Baltiski woksal), Tel: 329 0186. **International Youth Hostel**, Sovietskaya ulitsa 28 (Metro Ploshchad Wosstaniya), Tel: 277 0569.

Business hours

Public authorities work a core period of 8am to 4pm; but their offices are closed on Saturdays. The normal opening hours for banks are 9am to noon and 1 to 6pm, department stores from 8am and may stay open until 9pm. Grocery stores and supermarkets are generally open from 8am to 8pm, and stay open often on Sundays and holidays. Restaurants are usually open from noon to 11pm or midnight, with a break around 4-5pm. Cafés, streetside snackbars, fast-food chains open and close an hour earlier than restaurants. Nightclubs and casinos are open from 10pm to 5 or 6am.

Car rental

In both cities cars can be rented with or without driver. Please note that the miniumum age for drivers is 21. An international driver's permit is required.

Crime

The political and economic changes in Russia have led to a rapid rise in crime.

especially petty larceny. Pickpockets are especially active in crowds. Tourists must be alert and avoid carrying large amounts of cash, passport and other travel documents. Avoid lonely places and underpasses at all times. If you happen to take the night train between Moscow and St. Petersburg, lock your compartment door with the safety lock. Hide any valuables under the bed, on the luggage rack, or wherever you feel they may be safe.

Currency and exchange

1 rouble (rbl.)= 100 kopeks (kop.)

Russia's currency is the rouble. At the beginning of the 190s, huge inflation virtually erased the kopek from the market. Since 1989, the rouble has been devaluated several times, until inflation got completely out of hand in the mid 1990s and eliminated legal savings that the average citizen have tucked away. A currency reform was enacted in January 1998 striking three zeros from the rouble notes and reintroducing the kopek.

During the mean inflation days, the US dollar became the unofficial Russian currency. Nowadays, roubles are the tender all over the place. Credit cards (Visa, MasterCard/Eurocard, American Express, Optima) are accepted in most hotels, restaurants and shops. If you happen to loose one, notify the institution immediately: American Express Moscow, Tel: 956 9000; Visa, Tel: 284 4802; Eurocard/Mastercard, Tel: 216 6871.

Travelers checks are also cashed without trouble, payment of cash on a credit card is also possible. Eurochecks, however, are not accepted all over the place.

The days of blackmarket exchange is over ever since the government legalized possession of a foreign currency. Banks and money-changing offices are in hot and heavy competition for the business. The rates are different, and shopping around a bit is worth it. Changing your roubles back into hard currency is also no longer a problem. Some banks require an ID card or passport for changing money. You don't have to keep your exchange receipts. When leaving the country you must write up the amount of money you are carrying on you in a second customs declaration.

Electric voltages

By and large 220 volts, 110 in mathrooms for razors. Norm plaugs sometimes don't fit in the outlets of older buildings (not in international hotels) You are strongly advised to bring a universal adapter with you.

Emergencies/breakdown

Police (called *militsiya* in Russia)....02 In Moscow, accidents should be reported on 925 5510; and in St. Petersburg on 272 5955.

Media

In international hotels, western daily and weekly newspapers are available though usually a day or two late. Magazines are also on sale. Some of the big hotels in both cities are equipped with satellite TV. Many hotels offer their own video programs in English or German.

Medical help

Accident/rescue (anywhere) . . . . . 03 First aid is free of charge. All other medical services have to be paid for. The **American Medical Center** (AMC) in Moscow is equipped to western standards. Tel: 956 3366; The **AMC** in St. Petersburg, Tel: 119 6101.

Photography

Despite *glasnost,* photographing military or strategically important sites is still forbidden, although if you are caught doing so you are unlikely to be charged with espionage.

Telecommunications

To make a local call from a public booth you will need a token that is available at metro stations. For long-distance calls within the CIS and foreign calls, there are special exchanges (*peregovorny punkt*) with telephone booths with direct dialing.

You can phone abroad from the rooms at better hotels, but the prices are outrageous. The business centers of hotels allow for fax messages to come and go. The cheapest for tourists with knowledge of Russian is to phone from the exchanges for prepayment or with a Russian telephone card. The post offices also have fax service.

In Moscow
Main post-office
Ulitsa Myasnitskaya 26 . . . 928 6311
International post-office, Varshavsoje
Chaussee 37 . . . . 114 4645
Central Telegraph Offices
Ulitsa Tverskaya 19
Ulitsa Vozdvishenka 22 . . . 927 2002

In St. Petersburg
Long-distance calls 07
Main post-offices
Pochtamtskaya Ulitsa 9 . . . 312 8302
Bolshaya Morskaya Ul 3/5 . 312 8915
Central Telegraph office, Sinopskaya
Naberezhnaya 14 . . . . . . 274 2609

Tipping

Whereas in the Soviet Union it was not customary, and in fact was looked down on, to reward service with a tip, it is now part of the normal routine for tourists. As indeed are beggars.

Tourist information

The INTOURIST corporation (with the monopoly on all foreign tourism back in the days of the Soviet Union, now in private hands) is still the largest tourist organization in Russia in spite of a great deal of competition.
In Moscow they are located at: Mokhovaya ulitsa 13, Tel: 292 1278.
St. Petersburg: Pereulok Boizova 7, Tel: 314 6096.

ADDRESSES

Diplomatic representation in Moscow

The following are the addresses of selected foreign embassies in Moscow. When dialling from St. Petersburg, use the prefix 8095:

Australia, Kropotkinskiy Pereulok 13, Tel: 246 5011. **Britain,** Sofiyskaya Naberezhnaya 14, Tel: 231 8511. **Canada**, Starokonyushenniy Pereulok 23, Tel: 241 5882. **Ireland**, Grokholskiy Pereulok 5, Tel: 288 4101. **New Zealand**, Vorovskovo Ulitsa 44. Tel:290 3485. **United States**, Ulitsa Chaykovskovo 19-23, Tel: 252 24 59.

in St. Petersburg

British Consulate, Ploshchad Proletarskiy Diktatury 5, Tel: 312 0072. **United States Consulate**, Furshtadtskaya Ulitsa 15, Tel: 274 8235.

Russian representation abroad

Australia: *Embassy*, 78 Canberra Avenue, Griffith, Canberra ACT 2603, Tel: (062) 95 9474. *Consulate*, 7-9 Fullerton St, Woollahra NSW 2000, Tel: (02) 326 1188. **Britain**: *Embassy*, 5 Kensington Palace Gardens, London W8, Tel: (071) 229 3215. **Canada**: *Embassy,* 52 Range Road, Ottawa, Ontario, K1N 8G5, Tel:(613) 236 7220. *Consulate*, 3655 Avenue du Musée, Montréal, Québec H3G 2E1, Tel: (514) 843 5901. **Ireland**: *Embassy,* 186 Orwell Road, Rathgar, Dublin, Tel:(1) 711 633. **New Zealand**: *Embassy*, 57 Messines Road, Karori, Wellington, Tel: 766 742.**United States**: *Embassy*, 1825 Phelps Place NW, Washington DC 20008 Tel: (202) 332 1483. *Consulate*, 2790 Green St, San Francisco CA 94123, Tel: (415) 922 6642.

Aeroflot offices in Moscow

Korovy val 7; Frunsenskaya nabereshnaya 4; ulitsa Petrovka 20; all three offices share one telephone: 156 80 19.

Aeroflot office in St. Petersburg

Nevsky Prospekt 7/9, Tel: 314 69 43. Telephone information about international flight arrivals and departures at Pulkovo-II can be obtained by dialing 104 3444.

Aeroflot offices abroad

Australia: 17th Floor, Amex Towers, 388 George Street, Sydney N. S. W. 2000. Tel: 61 2 2337911, Fax: 2352821. **Britain**: 70 Piccadilly, London W1, Tel: (071) 355 2233. **Canada**: 615 De Maisonneuve Block west, Montréal, Québec H3A 3C8 Tel: (514) 287 9282. **Ireland**: Sun Alliance, Dawson St, Dublin 2, Tel: (1) 679 1453; and at Shannon airport, Tel: (061) 62 299. **United States**: 630 Fifth Avenue, Suite 1710, New York NY 10111, Tel: (212) 332 1040. California: 9100 Wilshire Blvd. Suite 616, Beverly Hills, Los Angeles CA 90212, Tel: (310) 2815300/01-03, Fax: ((310)-2815304.

Airline offices in Moscow

British Airways: Krasnopresnenskaya Naberezhnaya 12, 19th floor, Tel 253 2492. **Delta:** Krasnopresnenskaya Nab.12, 11th floor, Tel:253 2658/9. **Finnair**: Kemergersky Per. 6, Tel: 292 8788. Japan Airlines, Kuznetsky Most 3, Tel: 921 6448. **KLM**: Krasnopresnenskaya Nb. 12, 13th floor, Tel: 253 2150. **Lufthansa**, Hotel Olympic Penta, Olimpiysky Prospekt 18/1, Tel: 975 2501. **SAS**: Kuznetsky Most 3, Tel: 925 4747. **Swissair**, Hotel Mezhdunarodnaya, Krasnopresnenskaya Naberezhnaya 12, Tel: 253 8988.

In St. Petersburg

British Airways: Bolshaya Morskaya Ulitsa 36, Tel: 311 5820. **Delta**: Bolshaya Morskaya Ul 36, Tel 311 5820. **Finnair**: Malaya Morskaya Ul. 19, Tel: 315 97 36. **KLM:** Pulkovo-II airport, Tel: 104 3437. **Lufthansa**: Prospekt Mayorova 7, Tel 314 4979.

LANGUAGE

Although the Russians arevoracious readers, relatively few speak any foreign language adequately. Except in hotels, museums and up-market shops, or when dealing with pushy street-traders, you are always going to come up against problems of language and mutual comprehension. Foreigners encounter particular difficulties with the pronunciation of certain words, and with the varying stress on syllables. Most signs are in cyrillic script, but occasionally street-names are also reproduced in the Roman alphabet.

А	а	*𝒜 а*	a	a
Б	б	*𝓑 δ*	b	b
В	в	*𝓑 в*	v	v
Г	г	*𝒯 ı*	g	g
Д	д	*𝒟 д q*	d	d
Е	е	*𝓔 е*	e, je	e, ye
Ё	ё	*𝓔 ё*	o, jo	o, yo
Ж	ж	*𝒲 ж*	z	zh
З	з	*𝟥 з*	z	z
И	и	*𝒰 и*	ji, i	i
Й	й	*𝒰 ŭ*	j	y
К	к	*𝒦 к*	k	k
Л	л	*𝓛 л*	l	l
М	м	*𝓜 м*	m	m
Н	н	*𝓝 н*	n	n
О	о	*𝒪 о*	o	o
П	п	*𝒯 п*	p	p
Р	р	*𝒫 ρ*	r	r
С	с	*𝓔 с*	s	s
Т	т	*𝒯 т*	t	t
У	у	*𝒴 у*	u	u
Ф	ф	*𝒻 ф*	f	f
Х	х	*𝒳 х*	ch	kh
Ц	ц	*𝒰 ц*	c	ts
Ч	ч	*𝒰 ı*	c	ch
Ш	ш	*𝒲 ш*	š	sh
Щ	щ	*𝒲 щ*	šc	shch
Ъ	ъ	*– ъ*	–	–
Ы	ы	*– ы*	y	y
Ь	ь	*– ь*	'-	–
Э	э	*𝟫 э*	e	e
Ю	ю	*𝒴𝒪 ю*	'u, ju	yu
Я	я	*𝒜 я*	'a, ja	ya

MINI LANGUAGE GUIDE

Good morning,afternoon . *drávstvuitye*
Good evening . . . . . . *dóbry vécher*
My name is... . . . . . . *minyá zavút...*
This is my husband/wife . . . .
ehta moi múzh / mayá zhená
This is Mr / Mrs... . . . .
ehta gaspadín / gaspazhá
I do not understand Russian . . . . . .
ya nyé panimáyu parússki
I only speak English . . . .
ya gavaryú tólka pa-angléesski
Good-bye. . . . . *dassvidánya*
Excuse me . . . . *izvinéetye, pazhál'sta*
Yes / no . . . . *da / nyet*
Thank you / please *spassíba / pazhál'sta*
You're welcome. . . . . . . *né za shto*
Come in! . . . . *vaidéetye!*
Cheers! . . . . *za váshe zdaróvye!*
Where can I buy foreign
newspapers? . . *gdye ya magú kupéetsh*
inostránniye gazéty?
Can one change money here? . . . . .
mózhna li zdyess abminyátsh valyútu?
Where can one telephone abroad? . . .
gdye mózhna pasvanéetsh zagranítsu?
Help me, please. . . . .
pamagéetye, pazhál'sta
I need medical help. . . . .
mnye nuzhná miditséenskaya pómoshch
Where is . . . . *gdye nakhóditsa?*
...a toilet . . . . *tualyét*
...the cloakroom . . . . . . *garderób*
...a taxi-rank . . . . . . *stayánka taksí*
...the Metro station . . . *stántsiya mitró*
...the train-station . . . . *vakzál*
...a public telephone . . . *tilifón-aftamát*
...a chemist (pharmacy) . . . . *aptyéka*
...a hospital . . . . *balnéetsa*
...a post-office,bank . . . *póchta, bank*
...a car-repair workshop . . . .
aftaremóntnaya mastirskáya
...a police-station . . *atdiléniye miléetsii*
...a restaurant, a café . . *ristarán, kaféh*
...a delicatessen . . . . . . *gastranóm*
...a bakery . . . . *búlochnaya*
..the box-office . . . . *tiatrálnaya kássa*
..a department store . . . . . *univermág*

How does one get (on foot)   *kak praitée*
...to Red Square? . . . .
                        na krássnuyu plóshchad?
..to the Bolshói Theater? . . . .
                        k balshómu tiátru?
How does one get (by transport)... . . .
                        kak prayékhatsh?
...to Sérgiyev Posád? . . . .
                        v syérgiyef pazád?
...to the Arbát? . . . . *na arbát?*
Give me,please . . . .
                        dáitye mnye, pazhál'sta...
...ten tokens (for the Metro) . . . . . .
                        dyéssit zhetónoff
...picture postcards and stamps . . . .
                        atkréetki i márki
...the menu . . . . *minyú*
...a cup of coffee / tea . . . .
                        cháshku kófe / cháyu
...mineral water, beer . . . .
                        minirálnuyu vódu, péeva
..a bottle of wine,champagne . . . . .
                        butylku viná, shampánskava
...cigarettes and matches . . . .
                        sigaréti i spéechki
How much does it cost? . *skólko stóit?*
Write the price down, please! . . . . .
                        napishéetye, pazhál'sta, tsénu
Call a doctor, please . . . .
                        vuizavéetye pazhál'sta vrachá
I have a pain in . . . . .   *u minyá baléet*
...my heart, stomach . *syertze, zhelúdak*
...my head, ear, tooth . *galavá, úkha, zub*
I feel dizzy . . . .
                        u minyá krúzhitsa galavá
Someone stole my money and passport
                        u minyá ukráli dyénggi i pásport
...handbag, briefcase . . . .
                        súmochku, partfyél
...wallet, suitcase . . . .
                        bumázhnik, chimadán
...my camera . . . . *fata-aparát*
0 . . . . *nol*
1 . . . . *adéen*
2 . . . . *dva*
3 . . . . *tri*
4 . . . . *ch'téeri*
5 . . . . *pyat*
6 . . . . *shést*

7 . . . . *syém*
8 . . . . *vóssem*
9 . . . . *dyévit*
10 . . . . *dyéssit*
11 . . . . *adéennatsat*
12 . . . . *dvenátsat*
20 . . . . *dvád'tsat*
30 . . . . *trid'tsat*
40 . . . . *sórok*
50 . . . . *pi'dessyát*
60 . . . . *shest'dessyát*
70 . . . . *syém'dyessat*
80 . . . . *vóssem'dyessat*
90 . . . . *devyanósto*
100 . . . . *sto*
1000 . . . . *téesyacha*
10.000 . . . . *dyéssit téesyacha*
100.000 . . . . *sto téesyacha*

AUTHORS

Niels Brunse is one of Denmark's most respected poets and translators. He has translated such classics as Chekhov, but is also involved with contemporary Russian literature. He contributed the features on *The Metro* and *Heaven on Earth.*

Sergei Burin wrote about the *Hotel Lux.*

Helga Ewert studied German and Russian. She works as a tour guide with Russia as her special area. She has lived in Moscow and St. Petersburg. She updated this *Nelles Guide* in 1998

Mikhail Glinka, who bears a famous name, is an avid essayist and anthologist. For the St. Petersburg section, he has contributed *Basil Island, The Northern Islands, Terminals* and the feature on *Sport.*

Vladimir Ivanitsky has made an intensive study of folklore. A Muscovite, he lives as a freelance writer of poetry and short stories. He is responsible for *Tverskaya, Chekhov Street, Pushkin Square* and the feature on *Folklore.*

Irina Kamenskaya studied in the Economics faculty of Moscow State University. Born in Moscow, she now works at the Institute of Comparative Political Studies in the city. She wrote the chapter on *Moscow's Art and Museums* (except the first tour), *Gorky Park, Andronikov Monastery, Ostankino, The Golden Ring* (except Sergiyev Posad) and the Features on *Moscow circus, Life after Socialism* and *Russian Cooking*.

Georgi Lebedev is a Chief Engineer in the Merchant Navy, and knows St. Petersburg harbor better than just about anyone. He wrote the section about it.

After graduating in history, **Larissa Lissyutkina** spent twenty years at Moscow's Institute of Comparative Political Studies; since 1993 she has been with the BBC Russian Service in London. Hers is the feature on the *Russian Mentality*.

Angela Plöger is the co-editor and translator of all the contributions originally written in Russian. Dr. Plöger studied Finno-Ugrian and Slavonic languages, with Russian her special subject. She also wrote on *Kolomenskoye, Sergiyev Posad*, the feature *New Monuments for Old* and the *Language Guide*.

After studying philosophy, **Abram Reitblat** did research in librarianship at the Central Lenin Library in Moscow. That is why he was chosen to write the feature on *The Russians as Readers*.

Henning Sietz is from Hamburg and studied Slavonic and German literature. He is authored several travel books on the Soviet Union. Hewrote *Moscow's Inner City* and *Novodevichy Convent*.

When still at school in the Slovakian capital, Bratislava, **Hans-Horst Skupy,** the Project Editor, found Russian was one of his favorite subjects. he has been reporting on Russia since the 1960s. For this guide he contributed the articles *A Cruise on Lakes Ladoga and Onega including Kizhi Island.*

Valery Surov made his name with several collections of stories and novels novels. He wrote the article on *Russian History* in collaboration with **Heinz Vestner**. The latter was Managing Editor of Nelles Verlag, and studied English and German literature and history.

Alexander Zhitinsky's literary output is enormous: many of his books of short stories, novels, childrens' books, TV- and film-scripts as well as several volumes of poems have appeared in translation. For this guide hewrote *St. Petersburg's Inner City* and the first three tours *North of the Neva*.

PHOTOGRAPHERS

Archiv für Kunst und Geschichte,
Berlin   12, 14, 15, 16, 17, 19, 20L, 21, 22L, 22R, 24/25, 26, 27, 28, 30, 31L, 31R, 33, 34, 35, 36, 37, 38, 40, 41, 43, 44, 45, 46, 47, 48, 49, 50, 91, 131, 216, 217
Bondzio, Bodo   66
Franke, Peter (Wostok)   100
Gruschwitz, Bernd F.   70, 74, 114
Hartl, Helene und **Skupy**, Hans-Horst cover, 20R, 51, 61, 72, 80, 94, 99, 110, 134/135, 136/137, 138, 156, 157L, 157R, 159L, 159R, 161, 162, 166, 170, 171, 172, 173, 174, 180, 182, 183, 184, 185, 187, 190, 191, 201, 202, 203L, 203R, 205, 206, 208, 212/213, 218, 223, 224, 226, 227, 228, 229, 230, 231, 234, 235
Heimann, Ulrich   194
Heinzelmann, Ingrid (Freelance Press) 196/197
Hinze, Peter   220
Krammisch, Wolfgang   52/53, 116/117, 130
Merlin-Presse, Udo Lauer   85
Plöger, Angela   219, 232
RIA-Nowosti (Wostok)   111
Schmid, Gregor M.   54/55, 68, 69, 71L, 71R, 75, 77, 78, 83, 84, 86, 87, 89, 92, 97, 103, 104, 105, 107, 108, 112, 115, 123, 124, 125, 126, 127, 129, 132, 142, 143, 145, 147, 149, 153, 154, 155, 158, 167, 176, 181, 186, 192, 195, 210/211, 215, 225, backcover
Skupy-Pesek, Jitka   113, 222
Tetzner, Marina   60, 63
Werner, Hans A. 8/9, 10/11, 56, 65, 88, 96, 101, 118, 122, 150, 151, 200, 214, 221.

Explore the World

NELLES MAPS

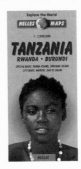

AVAIBLABE TITLES

Afghanistan 1 : 1 500 000
Australia 1 : 4 000 000
Bangkok - *Greater Bangkok, Bangkok City* 1 : 75 000 / 1 : 15 000
Burma → *Myanmar*
Caribbean Islands 1 *Bermuda, Bahamas, Greater Antilles* 1 : 2 500 000
Caribbean Islands 2 *Lesser Antilles* 1 : 2 500 000
Central America 1 : 1 750 000
Colombia - Ecuador 1 : 2 500 000
Crete - *Kreta* 1 : 200 000
China 1 - *Northeastern* 1 : 1 500 000
China 2 - *Northern* 1 : 1 500 000
China 3 - *Central* 1 : 1 500 000
China 4 - *Southern* 1 : 1 500 000
Dominican Republic - Haiti 1 : 600 000
Egypt 1 : 2 500 000 / 1 : 750 000
Hawaiian Islands 1 : 330 000 / 1 : 125 000
Hawaiian Islands 1 *Kauai* 1 : 125 000
Hawaiian Islands 2 *Honolulu - Oahu* 1 : 125 000
Hawaiian Islands 3 *Maui - Molokai - Lanai* 1 : 125 000

Hawaiian Islands 4 *Hawaii, The Big Island* 1 : 330 000 / 1 : 125 000
Himalaya 1 : 1 500 000
Hong Kong 1 : 22 500
Indian Subcontinent 1 : 4 000 000
India 1 - *Northern* 1 : 1 500 000
India 2 - *Western* 1 : 1 500 000
India 3 - *Eastern* 1 : 1 500 000
India 4 - *Southern* 1 : 1 500 000
India 5 - *Northeastern - Bangladesh* 1 : 1 500 000
Indonesia 1 : 4 000 000
Indonesia 1 *Sumatra* 1 : 1 500 000
Indonesia 2 *Java + Nusa Tenggara* 1 : 1 500 000
Indonesia 3 *Bali* 1 : 180 000
Indonesia 4 *Kalimantan* 1 : 1 500 000
Indonesia 5 *Java + Bali* 1 : 650 000
Indonesia 6 *Sulawesi* 1 : 1 500 000
Indonesia 7 *Irian Jaya + Maluku* 1 : 1 500 000
Jakarta 1 : 22 500
Japan 1 : 1 500 000
Kenya 1 : 1 100 000
Korea 1 : 1 500 000
Malaysia 1 : 1 500 000
West Malaysia 1 : 650 000
Manila 1 : 17 500

Mexico 1 : 2 500 000
Myanmar (Burma) 1 : 1 500 000
Nepal 1 : 500 000 / 1 : 1 500 000
Trekking Map *Khumbu Himal / Solu Khumbu* 1 : 75 000
New Zealand 1 : 1 250 000
Pakistan 1 : 1 500 000
Peru - Ecuador 1 : 2 500 000
Philippines 1 : 1 500 000
Singapore 1 : 22 500
Southeast Asia 1 : 4 000 000
Sri Lanka 1 : 450 000
Tanzania - Rwanda, Burundi 1 : 1 500 000
Thailand 1 : 1 500 000
Taiwan 1 : 400 000
Uganda 1 : 700 000
Venezuela - Guyana, Suriname, French Guiana 1 : 2 500 000
Vietnam, Laos, Cambodia 1 : 1 500 000

FORTHCOMING

South Pacific Islands 1 : 13 000 000
Trekking Map *Kathmandu Valley / Helambu, Langtang* 1 : 75 000

Nelles Maps in european top quality!
Relief mapping, kilometer charts and tourist attractions.
Always up-to-date!

Explore the World

AVAILABLE TITLES

Australia
Bali / Lombok
Berlin and Potsdam
Brittany
California
*Las Vegas, Reno,
Baja California*
Cambodia / Laos
Canada
*Ontario, Québec,
Atlantic Provinces*
Canada
*Pacific Coast, the Rockies,
Prairie Provinces, and
the Territories*
Caribbean
*The Greater Antilles,
Bermuda, Bahamas*
Caribbean
The Lesser Antilles
China – Hong Kong
Corsica
Crete
Croatia – *Adriatic Coast*
Cyprus
Egypt
Florida
Greece – *The Mainland*

Hawai'i
Hungary
India
*Northern, Northeastern
and Central India*
India – *Southern India*
Indonesia
*Sumatra, Java, Bali,
Lombok, Sulawesi*
Ireland
Israel - *with Excursions
to Jordan*
Kenya
London, England and
Wales
Malaysia
Mexico
Morocco
Moscow / St Petersburg
Munich
*Excursions to Castels,
Lakes & Mountains*
Nepal
New York – *City and State*
New Zealand
Norway
Paris
Philippines
Portugal
Prague / Czech Republic

Provence
Rome
Scotland
South Africa
South Pacific Islands
Spain – *Pyrenees, Atlantic
Coast, Central Spain*
Spain
*Mediterranean Coast,
Southern Spain,
Balearic Islands*
Sri Lanka
Syria – Lebanon
Tanzania
Thailand
Turkey
Tuscany
U.S.A.
*The East, Midwest and
South*
U.S.A.
*The West, Rockies and
Texas*
Vietnam

FORTHCOMING

Brazil
Myanmar (Burma)

*Nelles Guides – authorative, informed and informative.
Always up-to-date, extensivley illustrated, and with first-rate relief maps.
256 pages, appr. 150 color photos, appr. 25 maps*